D0466314

SCHOLASTIC ENCYCLOPEDIA OF SPORTS IN THE UNITED STATES

KEVIN OSBORN

A Mountain Lion Book

SCHOLASTIC
REFERENCE

New York Toronto London Auckland Sydney

CREDITS
Editor: John J. Monteleone
Photo Research: Ellen Pollak, Joanna Bruno
Production: Steve Stovall, Margaret Trejo of Trejo Productions
Designer: Charles Kreloff

We would like to thank Harvey Frommer, PhD, who has lectured on "Sports and Culture" at Wesleyan and Dartmouth Colleges, for his insightful introduction; Chris Lawlor and Herman L. Masin for their fact-checking; and Carolyn Jackson for her editing and support.

PHOTO CREDITS
All images are from the Library of Congress and the National Archives except for: A/P Wide World Photos: 9, 14 (left), 27, 28, 64 (2), 65 (top left), 93 (left), 94, 95, 105 (2), 107 (2), 108, 114, 123, 124, 125, 132 (top right), 133, 141, 142 (3), 147, 151 (2), 152 (2), 153 (2), 154 (2), 155 (top left & top right), 157 (2), 158, 159 (3), 160 (2), 161 (2), 163 (2), 164 (2), 165 (2), 166 (top left), 167 (2), 168 (3), 169, 170, 172 (2), 173, 174 (2), 175, 176, 177 (2), 178 (3), 179 (2), 180, 181 (2), 182, 183 (2), 184 (2), 185, 186, 187 (2), 188 (2), 189 (2), 190 (2), 191, 192 (3), 197, 198 (4), 199, 200 (3), 201 (2), 202 (2), 203 (2), 204 (3), 205 (2), 206 (2), 207 (2), 208 (2), 209, 210 (2), 211 (2), 212 (2), 213 (2), 214 (2), National Baseball Library & Archive, Cooperstown, NY: 32, 59 (top right), 60, 61 (2), 62 (2), 63, 73 (2), 74, 75 (2), 86 (2), 87, 88, 97 (bottom right), 98 (2); Henning Library at the International Swimming Hall of Fame: 52 (top right), 96 (2), 155 (bottom right), 156 (top left); International Tennis Hall of Fame: 114, 115, 116 (3); World Figure Skating Museum & Hall of Fame: 126, 127 (left); National Handicapped Sports: 156 (2); Sports & Spokes: 166 (top & bottom right); Special Olympics International: 215 (2)
Cover: Focus on Sports (top left); National Baseball Hall of Fame Library Cooperstown, N.Y. (top right); Focus on Sports (bottom left); NBA Photos (bottom right)

Library of Congress Cataloging-in-Publication Data available

ISBN 0-590-69264-X

10 9 8 7 6 5 4 3 2 1

Printed in the U.S.A.
First printing, August 1997

Contents

Names in **bold** denote athletes for whom there is a separate entry.

INTRODUCTION

Sports are spectacle, ritual, a common bond among Americans. They are in many ways the truest reflection of our culture and values. Sports put on display the beauty and joy of play. They provide an arena to watch and enjoy the creative efforts of athletes. Sports are blind to social status and background; they provide a means to move up socially and financially through merit and hard work. Sports represent a unique, ongoing link to the Founding Fathers' belief in the pursuit of happiness and to the American tradition of rewarding excellence.

Who today would ever believe that the colonists who first landed in New England thought that sports were a waste of time and perhaps even evil? It took a long time for athletics to gain acceptance in the United States. Not until after the Civil War did organized teams, like the ones we know today, begin to form.

Native Americans had played sports long before the arrival of Europeans. But unlike the Americans who would follow, competition was not the primary objective of their games.

The first colonial sports took place in the South, where plantation owners had free time to race horses while others did the work. African-American jockeys were popular and often the most successful. Elsewhere, the opportunity to play sports was often a privilege of the well-to-do. Football, for example, first developed in prestigious colleges of the Northeast, and tennis and golf were first played in private clubs. Women in exclusive colleges such as Smith, Vassar, Bryn Mawr, and Wellesley were among the first to experience physical training—and to play baseball and basketball.

But from the beginning, boxing, baseball, and basketball were the sports of ordinary men. Immigrants and their sons—Italians, Jews, Irish, Asians, and Latinos—often sought acceptance on the playing field that they could not find elsewhere in society.

Women were sometimes admitted to athletic events as spectators, but it would take decades before they were given the opportunity to compete in the arena. First they played as amateurs in athletic clubs and in the Olympics. During World War II, women played in a short-lived professional baseball league.

After World War II, women's professional golf and tennis took root and African-American athletes were given their first significant opportunity to play professional sports. In 1947, the Brooklyn Dodgers became the first deliberately integrated baseball team when they signed **Jackie Robinson**. It wasn't until 1961 that all professional baseball, football, and basketball teams had at least one black player.

In the *Scholastic Encyclopedia of Sports in America* you will meet 100 men and women whose achievements brought lasting significance. Often these achievements reached beyond the playing field or the arena into American society. With so many athletes to choose from, naturally, many outstanding ones are left out.

Many of the athletes you will read about here—such as boxer **Jack Johnson**, tennis player **Althea Gibson**, and wheelchair athlete **Sharon Hedrick**—personify courage in the face of discrimination based on race, gender, or disability. Some—such as baseball's **Curt Flood** and golfer **Kathy Whitworth**—played pivotal roles in advancing the opportunities of their fellow players. Others—such as basketball player and future Senator **Bill Bradley** and tennis player **Arthur Ashe**—brought new dignity to sports through their intelligence and personal grace. Still others—baseball's **Ty Cobb** and **Babe Ruth**, for example—were chosen for their sheer dominance of the sports they played.

No matter what sport they played, the athletes featured here strove to be their best. They set records, created standards, re-invented yardsticks, and pushed themselves to the limits of their abilities. From **Jim Abbott** to **Babe Didrikson Zaharias**, they enriched our lives and made the world of sports a very special place.

—Harvey Frommer,
Dartmouth College

CHAPTER 1

FORGING AMERICA

SPORTS IN THE BEGINNING YEARS

1770–1865

Lith & Pub by J. Baillie, 118, Nassau St. N York

RACE BETWEEN PEYTONA & FASHION, FOR $20

On the New York Union Course, May, 13, 1845. Won by Peytona—1st heat 7.39¼ – 2nd heat 7.45¼.

In the nation's early years, Americans held different attitudes and feelings about sports. As a result, the nation produced very few sports heroes. The most famous names in American sports were those of a horse, Eclipse, and a yacht, *America*. Geography and social status played the greatest part in defining these differences. The Puritans who had founded New England believed that idleness was a sin. People who took part in sports were rebuked for abandoning their proper labors, their duty, their families, their community, and their God. New Englanders passed laws forbidding bowling, card playing, dancing, and darts.

Meanwhile, wealthy Southern planters embraced sports. They did not regard labor as a holy duty. They relied on slaves to do the hard work. Sports were status symbols. The amount of time a man could devote to sport—especially horse racing—indicated his standing in the community.

Slavery already had created a division between North and South. Eli Whitney's invention in 1793 of the cotton gin, which separated seeds from cotton, allowed farmers to expand their plantations. Thus, they were more dependent on slave labor. In the North, which had banned slavery by 1804, the economy depended more on trading and shipping than on farming. By 1814, machines made factories much more profitable.

NORTH VS. SOUTH

Until the Civil War, horse racing was the most popular and well-organized sport in North America—especially in the South. Harness racing, or trotting, also became popular in the early 1800s.

In 1823, a series of three horse races pitted Sir Henry, the Southern champion, against Eclipse, the best in the North. Nearly 100,000 people turned out. Though Sir Henry won the first race, Eclipse came back to win the final two—and a $20,000 wager for its owner.

The wealthy enjoyed races between rowing crews, lawn bowling, and fox hunting (a favorite pastime of George Washington). In Southern and mid-Atlantic states, brutal "blood sports," though cruel to animals, were very popular among both the wealthy and the poor. These sports included cock fighting (two roosters trying to slash each other to death) and bull or bear baiting (chaining the animal and then having a team of dogs attack).

Some blood sports involved humans. These included bare-knuckle boxing, wrestling, and gouging. In both 1810 and 1811, former American slave Tom Molineaux twice fought for the boxing championship of England. Few Americans even knew about these bouts. But prizefighting, though illegal, became increasingly popular.

Sports were a man's world throughout the 19th century. Women could not play although they were welcome to attend events such as horse racing. A group of pioneering feminists held a convention in Seneca Falls, New York, in 1848, kicking off the women's rights movement. Not until 1877 would women form a Ladies Club for Outdoor Sports (tennis, archery, rowing).

IMPORTED SPORTS

By the mid-1800s in the Mid-Atlantic states from New York to Maryland, horse racing, bowling, ice skating, cricket, town ball (a softball-like game), and archery were popular urban activities. Some religious groups passed laws to restrict the enjoyment of sports. But growing numbers of these new immigrants earned wealth in the trading and shipping industries. They brought with them traditional English, German, and Dutch leisure activities. Urban pubs sponsored games to attract crowds. These events led to organized sports.

The nation continued to expand westward. In the 1840s, settlers traveled the Oregon Trail from Independence, Missouri, to the Pacific coast. After the Mexican War (1846–48), the United States forced Mexico to accept $15 million for the New Mexico and California territories. The California Gold Rush of 1849 attracted 80,000 Americans to that new territory. In the 1850s, workers laid down 21,000 miles of track throughout the continent. By 1853, the present borders of the continental United States had been established.

The growth of industry in the cities of the North created a great demand for labor. Three million immigrants—most from Ireland or Germany—came between 1844 and 1854. They often banded together in the cities. Workers increasingly turned to sports to fill in their leisure time.

BASEBALL SPREADS

Baseball developed from a community pastime to a spectator sport. Alexander Cartwright wrote down the rules in 1845. In 1860, the Brooklyn Excelsiors, the nation's first touring baseball team, spread the game to upstate New York, Philadelphia, Wilmington, and Baltimore. New baseball clubs sprang up in their wake. Some baseball clubs then turned semiprofessional, paying one or two players to join their teams.

A few athletes earned large sums of money. Foot racers called "pedestrians"—such as John Gildersleeve and William Howett—toured the country. They challenged locals to race them for a healthy wager. These events sometimes drew as many as 25,000 spectators. In 1861, Edward Weston bet that he could walk the 478 miles from Boston to Washington in ten straight days. He did, arriving in time to dance at the inaugural ball of President Abraham Lincoln.

Wealthy steamship heir and sports promoter John Cox Stevens, who had arranged the

Eclipse-Sir Henry horse races in 1823, founded the New York Yacht Club in 1844. Seven years later, his yacht, *America*, defeated an English yacht in the first America's Cup race.

But not many Americans made a living at sports. There were no play-for-pay associations that sponsored competition. Most Americans viewed sports and athletics simply as a way to get some exercise and have fun.

After Abraham Lincoln won the 1860 presidential election, 11 Southern states broke away from the union to form the Confederate States of America. The divided nation soon went to war.

The Civil War broke up the sporting clubs that had formed in the North. Union soldiers, however, soon organized themselves into teams. Between drills and battles, soldiers would play baseball or football or take part in shooting contests, running races, boxing, or gymnastics.

By the time the Confederacy surrendered in 1865, both sides had suffered tremendous losses. Of the 2,300,000 soldiers from the North and the South, more than 600,000 died and 500,000 were wounded.

After the Civil War, football rooted itself in colleges, and cities began professional baseball teams. A new era would emerge.

All for One and One for All:

Sports Native Americans Played

The Iroquois played lacrosse. They used sticks with a small net at one end to carry or throw a hard ball. The goal was the opponent's six-foot-square net. The Iroquois also played a winter game called snow snake, which they believed could help cure illness. After digging a trench and icing it down, players would compete to see who could slide a spear or miniature canoe the farthest. Wagering on these contests was common.

The Shawnee pitted men against women in a game that resembled soccer and football. Although the female players could carry the ball, the males could move the ball only with their feet.

The Oklahoma, Seminole, and Creek tribes played a similar game but moved the ball with sticks. They also played the single pole game. The object was to score points by hitting a target (a cow skull or figure of a fish) placed at the top of a tall pole. The women could use their hands, but the men had to use two "ballsticks" to carry or throw the ball.

Chapter 2

America Expands

Athletics as a New Business

1866–1900

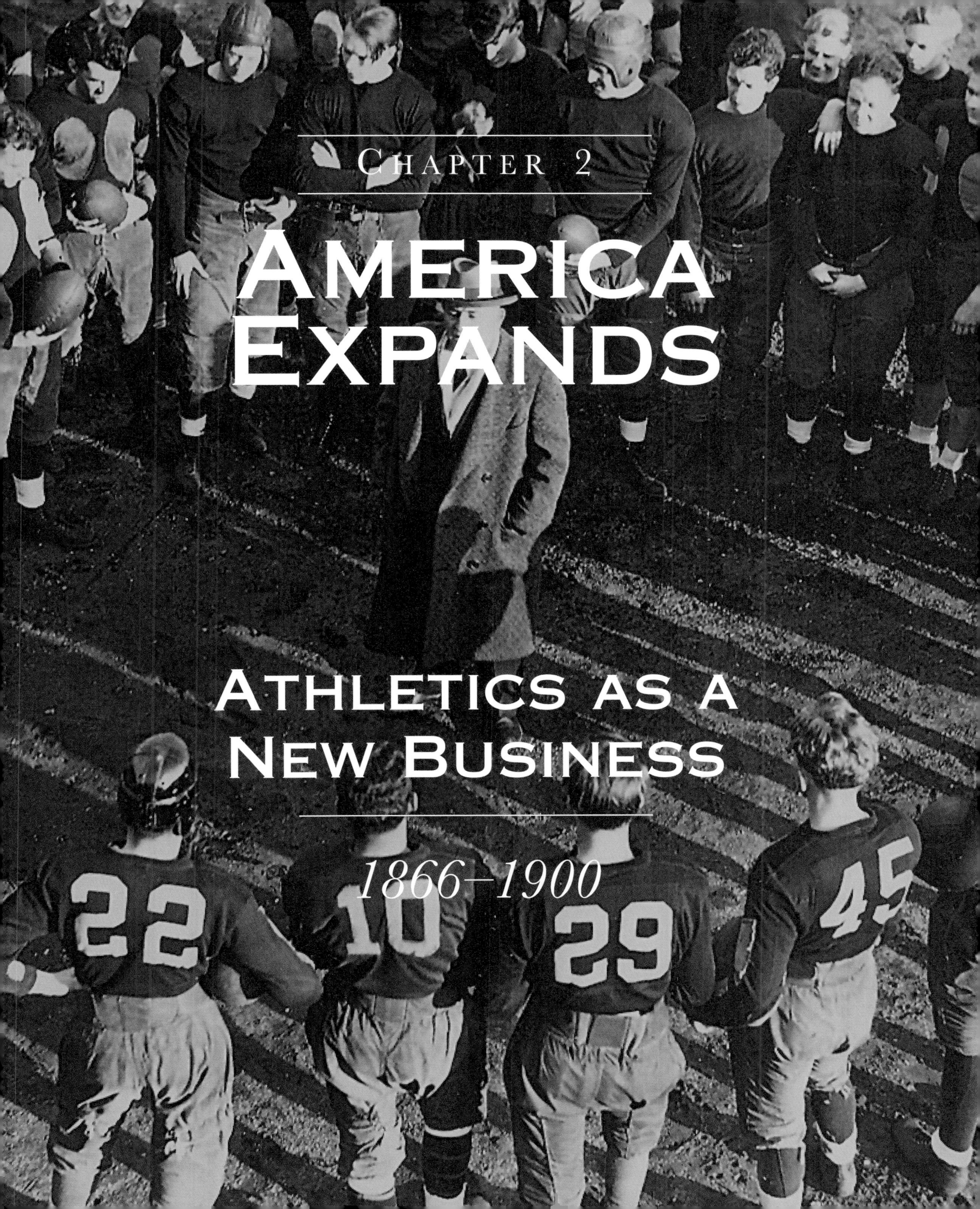

Southerners who were taught baseball by Northern prisoners during the Civil War took up the game. The war had destroyed many of their homes, farms, and businesses. Four million freed slaves struggled to find jobs and a place to live. For more than a dozen years, federal troops controlled government and life in the South. When Congress finally ended this Reconstruction in 1877, most Southern states had already enacted Jim Crow laws. These laws kept blacks from participating with whites in professional sports for nearly a century.

In the North, factories had increased production to keep up with the wartime demand for guns, equipment, and clothing. After the war, these factories kept humming. The population of American cities more than tripled between 1865 and 1895. By the century's end, nearly half of all Americans lived in cities rather than farming towns. Many of these new urban dwellers were immigrants drawn to the United States by the promise of work.

Employees worked ten hours a day, six days a week for low wages. Factories were dark, poorly ventilated, and dangerous. Social reformers focused on the dirty, crowded, and unhealthy living conditions of workers. The Chicago fire of 1871 left 90,000 people homeless. By the last two decades of the century, the labor movement had begun to organize workers into unions.

Sports Gain Status

At the war's end, American sports changed in different ways, attracted new followers, and prospered. Baseball became organized, boxing ended bare-knuckle events and established weight classes, and horse racing staged events that paid large sums to the winner.

Baseball quickly became the national game. It produced the nation's first sports stars, Harry and George Wright. In 1869, Harry founded the Cincinnati (Ohio) Red Stockings, the first all-professional baseball team. His brother, George, who played shortstop on the team, was the earliest player enshrined in the Baseball Hall of Fame. The team toured the nation, winning 79 straight games before losing their first in 1870. Six years later, the National League was formed. By the end of the century, three other major baseball leagues, including one organized by the players in their own labor movement in 1890, had come and gone.

In 1888, "Casey at the Bat" was first performed on an American stage. Baseball information and talk developed a unifying bond among people everywhere. Americans recognized the names of baseball heroes and talked about their achievements.

As all sports grew more acceptable, they became a way for immigrants to learn and adopt American values. Baseball emerged as the most popular and influential of the new professional sports. By setting standards of individual ability, skill, and determination, baseball taught all Americans to honor a winner without regard to background or race. Unfortunately, this would soon change.

Sports distracted people from social ills.

Horse racing continued to be a major spectator sport. Tracks opened in Chicago, Cincinnati, Springfield, Baltimore, Boston, Memphis, New Orleans, and Louisville. The Churchill Downs track in Louisville sponsored the first Kentucky Derby in 1875. Horse racing was given a big boost near the end of the Civil War by John Morrissey, a former prize- fighter who started racing horses at Saratoga Springs, New York. Morrissey named America's first race offering a large money prize the "Travers." It is the oldest contest of its kind in the United States. By 1870, harness and dog racing also drew large crowds.

Promoters recognized the profitability of bringing new sporting events to the nation's rapidly growing cities. Boxing, though still illegal in most states in 1866, attracted thousands of new fans. The *Police Gazette* published the first full account of a heavyweight boxing match in 1880. The issue sold 400,000 copies and convinced newspapers to add coverage of boxing to their own sports pages. In 1892, bare-knuckle boxing ended as **James J. Corbett** knocked out champion **John L. Sullivan** in the first title bout fought with gloves.

AMATEURS THRIVE

Most sports remained at the amateur level. The 1868 founding of the New York Athletic Club, which built the nation's first cinder track, made amateur track and field popular. The club still provides money and training for aspiring Olympic athletes.

James Naismith

In 1869, the first intercollegiate football game was played between Rutgers and Princeton, though the game still resembled rugby and soccer more than today's American football. By the end of the century, Yale University's **Walter Camp** and others had standardized the rules of the modern game, and colleges sponsored organized competition in rowing. The YMCA, which operated just three gymnasiums in 1869, had built nearly 300 by 1900. YMCA physical education instructor James Naismith invented basketball in 1891. The first modern Olympic Games took place in Athens, Greece, in 1896. The first Boston Marathon was held a year later. Among the wealthy, tennis became increasingly popular in the 1880s, and the United States Tennis Association was formed in 1881. Golf was the rage in the 1890s, and the first U.S. Open was held in 1895.

Few Women and Blacks

Women were considered too delicate for most sports. Those wealthy enough to attend the elite women's colleges in the Northeast could take part in physical education programs (exercising and gymnastics). In 1893, young women at Smith College played basketball, which was introduced by Senda Berenson. Her rules were used until the 1960s. Shinnecock Hills Golf Club on Long Island, New York, home of the U.S. Open Championship, opened its doors to women in 1891. In 1900, U.S. golfer Margaret Abbott won the first gold medal at the Olympics in Paris.

Professional sports excluded blacks. Sullivan refused to face black boxers. Baseball barred African Americans in the 1890s. Though **Isaac Murphy** and other black jockeys had dominated horse racing, new jockey clubs refused to grant licenses to blacks in the 1890s.

With the completion of the Transcontinental Railroad in 1869, more people moved west. Between 1876 and 1894, Alexander Graham Bell introduced the telephone, and Thomas Edison invented the electric lightbulb, the phonograph, and the motion-picture camera. Sports fans ate the first hot dog in 1880, enjoyed the first Ladies Day (when women were allowed into baseball parks free or at a reduced fee) in 1883, and sipped the first Coca Cola in 1886.

Sandlots and Playgrounds

The Young Men's Christian Association (YMCA) rapidly spread across the nation. YMCA gymnasiums in the country leaped from three in 1869 to 261 in the mid-1890s. Most YMCAs offered programs in team sports such as basketball, baseball, and football, as well as individual sports such as swimming, bowling, and weight lifting.

Social reformers began focusing on ways to improve living conditions. Jane Addams founded Hull House in Chicago in 1889. The nation's first "settlement house" helped immigrants and others settle into productive, urban lives.

One of the ways settlement-house workers attempted to improve city life was through city playgrounds and organized sports programs. Sports offered children an escape from the hardships of poverty, helped Americanize immigrants, and kept kids out of trouble.

The playground movement reached its peak in the years leading up to America's involvement in World War I. From 1911 to 1917, the number of playgrounds in cities jumped from 1,543 to 3,940. After the war, public schools took over the role of playground organizers. By 1930, when 36 of the 48 states required physical education programs, the playground movement had ended.

WALTER CAMP

April 7, 1859–March 14, 1925

NO ONE CONTRIBUTED MORE to the development of the game of football than Walter Camp. The Father of Football, Camp devised or fine-tuned most of the rules by which the gridiron game is played today. His innovations helped transform football from a mere clash of brute strength into a physical battle that emphasized tactics and strategy, intelligence and skill.

Walter Chauncey Camp grew up in New Haven, Connecticut, home of Yale University. As a freshman at Yale, Camp helped organize the school's first football team in 1876. This team won the first championship of the American Intercollegiate Football Association (AIFA). No rules yet limited the number of years a player could remain on a team, so Camp played halfback for Yale for more than six seasons. (After getting his bachelor's degree, he enrolled at Yale Medical School.) With Camp as halfback, Yale lost only one game, while winning 25 and tying six. He served as captain of the team—essentially performing a head coach's duties—in 1878, 1879, and 1881. He later coached the Yale football team to a 67–2 record over five years (1888–92).

In 1880, Camp redefined American football at the AIFA rules conference. He proposed that football have a "scrimmage line" that would allow the team with the ball to stop play, retain possession, and begin the next play where the previous play had ended. This rule put an end to the kind of continuous action commonly seen in the British game rugby. Camp suggested that each play begin with the "snapback" (now called the center) kicking the football back with his foot to another player, the "quarterback." This rule established the quarterback as the most important offensive player. Camp also supported the idea that teams consist of just eleven men on the field.

At the 1882 rules conference, Camp came up with the idea of yards-in-downs: The team with the ball would have to gain a certain amount of yards within a certain amount of plays (or downs). If the team failed to get this yardage, the ball would go to the other team. The original rule required the offensive team to gain at least five yards in three downs. (The yardage was increased to 10 in 1906 and the number of downs to four in 1912.)

In 1883, Camp assigned point values to each scoring play. The early game emphasized kicking, as Camp's point values show: Field goals were worth five points, while touchdowns were only two. A successful kick after a touchdown added four points, and a safety scored one. (The present-day values for touchdowns, 6; points after, 1; field goals, 3; and safeties, 2, were established by 1912.)

Camp was a halfback at Yale for six seasons.

In 1889, Camp selected the first All-American team, identifying the nation's best college players at each position. This tradition would continue even after Camp's death in 1925.

Camp headed the American Football Rules Committee in 1906. In addition to increasing the yardage needed for a first down, this committee approved the use of the forward pass and reduced game time from 70 to 60 minutes. It also adopted the "neutral zone" that separates the offensive and defensive linemen by the length of the football (an idea first proposed by Camp in 1885). Camp died of a heart attack in a New York hotel room. He had come there to do what he had done all his life: to meet with the football rules committee and try to improve the game.

Career Capsule

Played for Yale in its first game against Harvard on Nov. 17, 1876. Proposed rules such as: 11 men per side, scrimmage line, center snap, yards, and downs. Founded the All-America selections in 1889.

Jim Corbett

September 1, 1866–February 18, 1933

"Gentleman Jim" Corbett brought boxing into the modern era. Corbett was boxing's first heavyweight champion to wear boxing gloves. He also moved boxing away from sheer brawn and brawling to a science of hitting and evasion, jabbing, and dancing away.

Corbett first gained a national reputation in 1890, when he crushed bare-knuckle heavyweight contender Jake Kilrain in six rounds. The following year, Corbett fought Australian Peter Jackson, a bigger and more experienced boxer, to a 61-round draw! A four-round exhibition bout with heavyweight champion **John L. Sullivan** convinced Corbett that he could sidestep the champ's powerful blows while landing his own innovative punches: hooks and jabs. The 1892 match between Corbett and Sullivan was the first heavyweight title fight in which both boxers wore gloves. Corbett enraged Sullivan—and the crowd—by dancing away from the champion's sweeping punches. In the 21st round, Corbett became the only boxer ever to knock out Sullivan. The victory—and the use of gloves—brought new respectability to the sport of boxing.

Corbett trained for fighting Jim Jeffries by working out with a heavy punching bag.

Though he had few bouts, the new champ held the title for five years. In 1897, Bob Fitzsimmons took the title away by knocking out Corbett with a shot to the stomach in the 14th round. Corbett attempted to regain the title in a fight against former sparring partner **Jim Jeffries** in 1900. Though Corbett outfought the champion for 16 rounds, Jeffries—nearly eight years younger—outlasted him and finally knocked him out in the 23rd round. After Jeffries knocked Corbett out in the 10th round of their 1903 rematch, Corbett retired from the ring.

CAREER CAPSULE

Won heavyweight title in 1892 in first heavyweight title fight using boxing gloves. Career record of 19 fights: 11 wins—7 by knockout—4 losses, and 4 draws.

JOHN J. McDERMOTT

September 23, 1871–August 3, 1915

ON A COLD AND RAINY DAY in September 1896, John J. McDermott won the first marathon ever staged in the United States. Just five months after the first modern Olympic marathon in Athens, Greece, New York's Knickerbocker Athletic Club sponsored the first U.S. marathon.

A field of 30 runners rode the train to Stamford, Connecticut, and then ran 25 miles back to the Columbia Oval track in New York City. The course—rough cobblestone streets and numerous hills—would have been challenging under the best of conditions. But the rain, mud, and slush made it nearly impossible. Only 10 of the 30 runners slogged their way to the finish. Eventually, McDermott entered the oval to wild applause from the crowd, which was gathered to watch other track events. He had completed the race in three hours, 25 minutes, and 55 seconds—nearly 30 minutes slower than that year's first Olympic marathon champion, but fast enough to win the first U.S. marathon by more than two minutes.

The winner of the first marathon held in the United States.

In April 1897, McDermott entered the first Boston Marathon, sponsored by the Boston Athletic Association. Fifteen runners started the race; only eight would finish it. Despite a leg cramp, McDermott completed the 24.7-mile course from suburban Ashland to downtown Boston in just under three hours (2:55:10). This set a new record for the marathon. McDermott cut 3½ minutes from the time of the Olympic marathon champion, Spiridon Louis of Greece. By winning the first two marathon races held on American soil, McDermott was a pioneer of distance running in the United States.

CAREER CAPSULE

Won the first two marathons held in the United States, the first in 1896, when he won a marathon which started in Connecticut and finished in New York City. The next year he won the first Boston Marathon during which he broke the Olympic marathon record.

ISAAC MURPHY

April 16, 1861–February 12, 1896

THE KING OF HORSE RACING in the latter part of the nineteenth century, Isaac Murphy was one of the great African-American jockeys.

Isaac Burns was born just four days after the U.S. Civil War began. Though born on a farm in Kentucky (a slave-holding state), Isaac was the son of free blacks. His father, a Union soldier, died in a Confederate prison camp. Isaac learned about riding horses from a black trainer in the area.

In the second half of the nineteenth century, horse racing was the biggest spectator sport in the nation. And black jockeys dominated the sport. Fourteen of the 15 jockeys who rode in the first

Kentucky Derby in 1875 were black. Half of the Derby winners before the turn of the century were jockeyed by African Americans.

At age 15, Isaac rode his first winner in a horse race in Lexington, Kentucky. At his mother's request, he adopted her maiden name—Murphy—in 1877. By 1883, before winning a single Derby, he was already earning the enormous sum of $10,000 a year. He collected a bonus of $15 for every horse he rode and $25 if he won the race. In 1884, aboard Buchanan, he won the Kentucky Derby, the most famous horse race in the country. Six years later, on Riley, he became the first jockey to win the Derby twice. Then in 1891, Murphy rode Kingman to his third straight win at the run for the roses. No other jockey would match his three Derby wins until 1930—and no one would surpass it until Eddie Arcaro rode his fourth winner in 1948.

In 1894, the Jockey Club was formed to regulate the profession. Blacks who applied for jockeying licenses were routinely denied. Murphy died of pneumonia at age 35 in 1896. The remaining black jockeys were phased out of horse racing over the next 15 years. No black jockey has ridden in the Kentucky Derby since 1911.

CAREER CAPSULE

Amassed 628 wins in 1,412 career horse races for an incredible winning percentage of .445. Three came in the Kentucky Derby.

AMOS ALONZO STAGG 

August 16, 1862–March 17, 1965

OFTEN CALLED THE GRAND old man of college football, Amos Alonzo Stagg—who never drank, smoked, or swore—served as a head coach for an incredible 54 years! Five times he led his team to undefeated seasons. Overall, Stagg's teams won 314 games, lost 199, and finished in 35 ties. (Only two other college coaches—Grambling's Eddie Robinson and Alabama's Paul "Bear" Bryant—led their teams to more victories.) One of the first coaches to use a T-formation, Stagg also pioneered the forward pass. He also helped develop such mainstays of football as the huddle, the shift play, and the use of tackling dummies in practice. Stagg, who also played in the first basketball game ever staged, is the only person ever elected to both the college football and basketball halls of fame.

Stagg was named college football's coach of the year at age 81.

The son of a shoemaker, "Lon" was born the fifth of eight children in West Orange, New Jersey. Since the first college football game was not played until 1869, when he was seven years old, Lon was older than the game itself. An excellent baseball player, he was offered a full scholarship to Dartmouth College. Instead, he chose to attend Yale, where he planned to study for the ministry. In college, Lon was so poor that he ate little more than crackers. Once, he was hospitalized for malnutrition. Yet he pitched the Yale baseball team to five cham-

Stagg coached at the University of Chicago for 41 years. Over his lifetime, he coached for 71 years before finally retiring at age 98.

pionships. He even beat the major league's Boston Braves, 2–1, in an exhibition game in 1888. Stagg also starred as an end on the Yale football team during those five years. In 1889, **Walter Camp** named Stagg to the first All-American football team.

After leaving Yale, Stagg taught at the International Young Men's Christian Association Training School in Springfield, Massachusetts. There, Stagg played in the first game of basketball, invented by his colleague James Naismith in 1891. He also coached the YMCA college's football team.

In 1892, the new University of Chicago hired Stagg to coach its football team. He would remain there until 1932. In his 41 years at Chicago, Stagg's teams won the national championship once and five other Western Conference (Big Ten) titles. In 1896, Stagg coached Chicago's basketball team to a victory over Iowa in a historic first: the first college basketball game played with just five players on each side.

The university asked Stagg to retire in 1932. The 70-year-old turned down an honorary position because he still wanted to work. So he accepted a coaching job at the University of the Pacific in Stockton, California. In 1943, at age 81, he led the small school to a 7–2 record. Stagg was named college football's Coach of the Year and Football Man

Stagg coached at the University of Chicago for 41 years, winning five Western Conference titles and one national championship.

of the Year. Three years later, Pacific too asked him to retire and accept an advisory position. Instead, Stagg joined his son Amos Jr., the head coach at Susquehanna College in Pennsylvania. At Susquehanna, Stagg served as offensive coordinator and coaching advisor. There, he remained on the field as a coach until he was 90.

In 1953, Stagg's wife became unable to travel between their home in Stockton and his job in Pennsylvania, so Stagg finally accepted an advisory position at Stockton Junior College. In 1960, Stagg sent the following letter to Stockton's head coach: "For the past 70 years I have been a coach. At 98 years of age it seems like a good time to stop." After 71 years on college football coaching staffs, Stagg retired. He lived for five more years.

CAREER CAPSULE

A college football head coach for 54 years, he led his University of Chicago team to a national championship in 1905. During his reign, Chicago won the Big Ten title in 1899, 1905, 1907, 1908, 1913, and 1924—and tied for the conference championship in 1922. Coach of the year at age 81 and elected to both college football and basketball Halls of Fame. Career record 314–199–35.

JOHN L. SULLIVAN

October 15, 1858–February 2, 1918

THE LAST OF THE bare-knuckled boxing champions, John L. Sullivan popularized boxing in the United States. The heavyweight champion for ten years, Sullivan lost only one fight in his career. Sullivan was the most popular athlete in the nineteenth century. He became the first mythic American sports hero.

The son of Irish immigrants, Sullivan was born in Roxbury, Massachusetts. Although his mother wanted him to pursue the priesthood, John preferred hard drinking, high living, and barroom brawling. As a young man, he developed a local reputation for great strength. He reportedly could juggle beer kegs, lift a piano by himself, and knock a horse down with a single punch. In his first professional fight in 1878, Sullivan—5 feet, 10½ inches tall and 190 pounds—knocked out local Boston brawler Cockey Woods. He then went on a boxing tour, staging four-round exhibition fights. Sullivan soundly beat such fighters as the Massachusetts heavyweight champion Dan Dwyer, world middleweight champion Mike Donovan, and onetime world heavyweight champion Joe Goss.

In the 1880s, New York City was the center of the boxing world. Since boxing was still illegal in most places, Sullivan's first New York fight took place in 1881 on a barge anchored in the Hudson River. Five hundred spectators paid $10 each—a large sum in those days—to see the fight. Under the London Prize Rules that governed boxing, each round lasted until one fighter was knocked off his feet. Sullivan knocked John Flood down to end every round. Sullivan earned $750 and a shot at the world heavyweight title with the eight-round victory.

Sullivan met the champion, Paddy Ryan, in Mississippi City, Mississippi, in 1882. Each side put up a $2,500 bet on the outcome of the bare-knuckled bout. Sullivan pounded Ryan for eight rounds, then scored a knockout in the ninth. It was the first time the term "knockout," coined by Sullivan's trainer Billy Madden, was used in boxing.

Sullivan, the new heavyweight champion, held the title for ten years. He fought almost all challengers, although he refused to fight black boxers. Sullivan toured the country, offering anyone $1,000 if they could last four rounds with him. Only one boxer managed to fight to a draw. In a rematch with Ryan in 1886, Sullivan knocked out the former champion in just three rounds.

Five years after knocking Charley Mitchell, England's best boxer, out of the ring, Sullivan traveled to France in 1888 for a rematch. In an epic bare-fisted battle staged in a muddy outdoor ring under a light rain, Sullivan and Mitchell fought 39 rounds. The fight ended in a draw.

Sullivan (left), the last of the bare-knuckled champions fighting Jake Kilrain. Sullivan won in the 75th round. Today, boxing matches rarely last even 15 rounds.

In 1889, Sullivan met Jake Kilrain in the last championship bout fought with bare knuckles under London Prize Rules. Sullivan outlasted Kilrain, finally knocking him out in the 75th round!

In 1892, Sullivan fought "Gentleman" **Jim Corbett** for the heavyweight title in New Orleans, Louisiana. Sullivan was overweight and out of shape. "I'd have rather fought 12 dozen times," he once explained, "than train once." His idea of exercise was hoisting kegs of nails over his head. He trained for fights by washing with a secret brew of white wine, rock salt, and other ingredients that he claimed hardened his hands and face.

For the first time in a championship bout, both boxers wore gloves. Corbett used boxing skill against Sullivan's brawn. When Sullivan attacked, Corbett danced away. A worn-down Sullivan was finally knocked out by Corbett in the 21st round.

After retiring from the ring, Sullivan had a successful 25-year career on stage. People paid to see Sullivan act and, in later years, to hear him lecture on the evils of alcohol. (Sullivan had stopped drinking in 1905.) Long after his death in 1918, he was still considered the Champion of Champions.

Despite never training for a fight, Sullivan lost just one time in 42 bouts. He was considered the "Champion of Champions" during his era.

Career Capsule

In 14 years—the last of the bare-knuckled champions—collected 38 wins (33 by knockout), 3 draws, and just 1 loss. Was the heavyweight title holder 1882–92.

Chapter 3

Play On

At War and in School

1901–1920

uring the early 1900s, American sports got a great boost from the "rough 'n' ready" President Theodore Roosevelt. The president loved horseback riding, hiking, swimming, hunting big game, boxing, and wrestling. Named the honorary president of the Playground Association of America in 1907, Roosevelt endorsed sports as a character builder and helped spur the growing movement to make athletics accessible to everyone.

He challenged Americans to get involved in sports with these inspirational words: "Far better it is to dare mighty things, to win glorious triumphs, even though checkered by failure, than to take rank with those poor spirits who neither enjoy much nor suffer much because they live in the twilight that knows not victory nor defeat."

In 1905, the president urged the three colleges that had dominated football for three decades—Harvard, Yale, and Princeton—to rid the game of brutality. These colleges helped form the National Collegiate Athletic Association that year, and the American Football Rules Committee a year later. This committee opened up the game by increasing the yardage needed for a first down from five to ten. The committee also legalized the forward pass, though it would remain little used until Notre Dame's Gus Dorais and **Knute Rockne** mastered the tactic in 1913. Michigan and Stanford met in the first major bowl game, the Rose Bowl, in 1902. (The second would not be played until 1916, when it became an annual event.)

Magnificent Machines Race

In 1903, Orville and Wilbur Wright made the first successful powered flight. Five years later, automaker Henry Ford introduced his first Model T. Americans would buy 15 million of the cars over the next two decades. American auto racing had already begun in 1904, when the Vanderbilt Cup races drew crowds as large as 500,000. The Indianapolis 500, which quickly became a showcase for new ways to engineer faster and more powerful cars, was first held in 1911. Ray Harroun won that first race at the wheel of a six-cylinder Marmon Wasp in 6 hours, 42 minutes, and 8 seconds, for an average speed of 74.59 miles per hour. The Indy 500 auto race is held each Memorial Day weekend. It would become America's single greatest auto-racing event and eventually attract more fans than any other sport in the United States.

THE NATION'S PASTIME

But in the early 1900s, baseball became the most popular sport in the nation, thanks to such heroes as **Cy Young**, **Honus Wagner**, and **Ty Cobb**. Cobb's legend is so complete that in 1995, nearly 70 years after playing his last game, a movie was made about his life. The American League was founded in 1901. In 1903, the champions of both American and National leagues met in the first World Series. When President William Howard Taft opened the 1909 season by throwing out the first ball, this became a baseball—and presidential—tradition. No further proof seemed needed that baseball was the national pastime.

Among the wealthy, tennis, polo, and golf remained favorite recreations. In 1895, the U.S. Golf Association (USGA) sponsored the first U.S. Open Championship among five clubs from New York, Massachusetts, Rhode Island, and Illinois. The first USGA Women's Amateur Championship was held a year later at the Meadow Brook Club of New York. The number of U.S. golf clubs increased from 50 in 1895 to more than 1,000 in 1900. By the 1920s, more than two million Americans played golf. Though still primarily an amateur game, the U.S. Professional Golfers' Association organized and sponsored its first championship in 1916. In tennis, Harvard's Dwight Davis established the Davis Cup in 1900, the first international team competition, and helped the United States defeat the British, five games to none.

OUTSIDE HEROES

Most organized sports continued to exclude blacks. But a black man, **Jack Johnson**, became boxing's heavyweight champion in 1908. Johnson's success sparked so much racial hatred that promoters searched for "The Great White Hope," a white boxer to regain the title. Former champion **Jim Jeffries**, who came out of retirement after five years, was one of those defeated by Johnson. Another African American, Joe Gans, was lightweight champion. He was so good that to get fights he sometimes had to agree to lose or take the smaller share of the money put up for the fight.

Jim Thorpe, one of the greatest all-around athletes of all time, dazzled the world at the 1912 Olympics in Stockholm when he won the five-event pentathlon and ten-event decathlon. Thorpe was a Native American and America's first super athlete.

Though welcomed in the stands, women still had few opportunities to compete in sports. They were confined to playing tennis, croquet, archery, and golf. In 1920, women won the right to vote.

In 1917, the United States entered World War I on the side of Great Britain, France, and their allies against Germany and its allies. During the next two years, one million Americans would fight in this terrible European war. Few prominent professional athletes were called to serve. However, baseball Hall-of-Fame pitcher Christy Mathewson entered the army and was sent to Germany to fight. He inhaled poison gas and as a result, he died seven years later.

The war had one indirect but important effect on sports. Army Major Branch Rickey, who served in France in 1918, never forgot the service of black soldiers who served their segregated nation bravely in segregated units. He reminded Americans about this in 1947 when he brought a black professional baseball player to the major leagues.

"Say It Ain't So":

The Black Sox Scandal

In 1919, a cheating scandal tarnished baseball's biggest event, the World Series. Players on the Chicago White Sox conspired to lose the World Series to the Cincinnati Reds. Gamblers who bet heavily on the Reds had bribed the White Sox players to "throw" the games.

As the 1919 World Series approached, the White Sox were heavily favored due to their superior talent. Yet they lost the series, five games to three. The scandal began leaking out a year later. Two players admitted taking part in the fix. Despite a close pennant race, White Sox owner Charles Comiskey immediately suspended all eight players for the final three games of the 1920 season. The scandal led to the creation of the position of Commissioner of Baseball. The commissioner was expected to maintain the honesty and integrity of the game of baseball.

In August 1921, the eight players were tried in criminal court. Those on trial were first baseman Chuck Gandil, shortstop Swede Risberg, third basemen Buck Weaver and Fred McMullin, outfielders Happy Felsch and Shoeless Joe Jackson, and starting pitchers Lefty Williams and Eddie Cicotte. (Weaver knew about the fix, but never agreed to help throw the series.) The jury acquitted all eight. Despite this verdict, the new commissioner, Kenesaw Mountain Landis, banned all eight from baseball for the rest of their lives.

Joe Jackson

TY COBB

December 18, 1886–July 17, 1961

NO QUESTION ABOUT IT, Ty Cobb could play baseball. Owner of a .367 career batting average—the best of all time—Cobb scored a record 2,245 runs. Yet Cobb—a fierce and often nasty competitor—also earned a reputation as one of the meanest men ever to play the game.

Tyrus Raymond Cobb was born in Narrows, Georgia, and began playing baseball at age nine. His father, a schoolteacher, was an extremely demanding man. When Ty left home at age 17 to play professional ball, his father told him not to come home if he failed.

During the next year, Grantland Rice, the famed sports columnist for *The Atlanta Journal*, began getting letters from all over the South, urging him to go see this young outfielder play. The letters aroused Rice's curiosity and he soon wrote a story about Cobb, then playing centerfield in Anniston, Alabama. (Rice later gave Cobb his famous nickname, the Georgia Peach.) Only years later did the sportswriter find out that Cobb himself had written all of the letters. "I wanted to get my name in his column," Cobb later explained. "My father read it regularly, and he would think I was making good."

In 1905, while Ty was playing in Augusta, Georgia, he learned that his mother, apparently mistaking her husband for a burglar, had shot and killed his father. Although his father had been tough on him, Ty never forgave his mother. He remained bitter for the rest of his life.

Several weeks after the tragedy, the Detroit Tigers bought Cobb's contract for $700. Cobb batted just .240 that year—the only season in his 24-year career that he failed to hit at least .320. The next year, he hit .320, but suffered a mental breakdown in midseason and was hospitalized for a month.

When he returned, Cobb turned up the heat on opposing pitchers. From 1907 to 1915, he won a record nine straight American League batting titles, his average ranging from .324 to an incredible .420! He also led the league in runs batted in (RBIs) for three straight years (1907–09) and in slugging average six times in a row (1907–12). In 1909, Cobb won the league's Triple Crown, leading the league in hitting (.377), RBIs (115), and home runs (9).

The Tigers reached the World Series three straight years from 1907 to 1909. In 1909, he stole home against the Pittsburgh Pirates to spark a rally that tied the series at one game apiece. Yet Cobb batted only .262 in 17 post-season games as the

In Griffith Stadium, Cobb played against the Washington Senators.

Tigers lost all three series. Cobb would play 19 more years, but never again reached the World Series.

Despite his success, Cobb was feared and hated around the league. He played to win—and he played very hard. Tough and aggressive, he got into fist fights with opponents, teammates, fans, and even an umpire. "They gave it to me as hard as I gave it to them," Cobb later argued. "The only difference was I never gave them the satisfaction of hearing me squawk. I'd sooner let them cut out my tongue than let them know I was hurt."

Cobb helped his teammates with batting advice.

Jack O'Connor, manager of the St. Louis Browns, hated Cobb too much—so much that he tried to cheat Cobb out of a batting title. In the final games of the 1910 season, O'Connor ordered his third baseman to play deep against the Indians. He wanted to give Cleveland's Nap Lajoie every opportunity to bunt for the base hits he needed to beat Cobb for the batting title. Lajoie still fell one point short, hitting .384 to Cobb's .385. O'Connor, however, was soon found out and banned from baseball for life.

The following year, the game's greatest hitter had his greatest season. Cobb led the league in everything but home runs (he hit eight to finish second). He batted .420 with a slugging average of .621. He set a major-league record with 248 hits (later broken). He had 47 doubles and 24 triples. He scored 147 runs and knocked in another 144. All of these figures were career highs for Cobb. He led both major leagues in all of these categories except triples. He also set a major-league record with 83 stolen bases. Cobb was recognized as the American League's Most Valuable Player.

Cobb batted .410 in 1912 to become the first player in this century to hit over .400 in two straight seasons. He even received a rare show of support from his teammates after he was suspended for attacking a New York fan who had been taunting him from the stands. The team protested the suspension by refusing to take the field. The Tigers put up a woeful team of replacement players who lost to the Philadelphia Athletics, 24–2. Cobb himself then urged his teammates to end their strike. The grateful league president, Ban Johnson, immediately lifted Cobb's suspension.

In 1915, Cobb broke his own record with 96 steals (topped in 1962 by Maury Wills). Cobb batted .371 in 1916, but failed to win the batting crown for the first time in ten years. However, he then came back to win three more batting titles in the next three years.

While continuing to play, Cobb managed the Tigers to five winning seasons in six years from 1921 to 1927. He hit over .400 (.401) for the third time in 1922, but lost the batting title to George Sisler, who hit .420.

Cut from the Tigers after the 1926 season, Cobb played two more years with the Athletics. When he retired in 1928, he held almost every career record in baseball. In the first election for the new Baseball Hall of Fame in 1936, Cobb got more votes than anyone else—even Babe Ruth.

Career Capsule

In 24 seasons, Cobb was the all-time leader in runs scored (2,245) and batting average (.367), second most hits (4,191), and fourth most stolen bases (892). Led the American League in hitting a record 12 times. Won MVP and Triple Crown (leader in batting average, home runs, and runs batted in) in 1911. Led the league in hits seven times, steals six times, and runs scored five times. Career span 1905–28.

JIM JEFFRIES

April 15, 1875–March 3, 1953

THE FIRST HEAVYWEIGHT champion ever to retire undefeated, Jim Jeffries lacked style and boxing skill. But he had incredible endurance. Jeffries withstood terrific punishment in the ring, yet he was almost never knocked down—and never knocked out.

The son of a Los Angeles, California, street-corner preacher, Jeffries stood six feet, two inches and weighed 220 pounds. Jeffries had already won several bouts by knockouts when heavyweight champion **Jim Corbett** hired him as his sparring partner in 1897. Two years later, Jeffries met new champion Bob Fitzsimmons in his first title defense since taking the crown from Corbett. Jeffries, considered slow and ungainly, was given little chance of winning the fight. Fitzsimmons pounded him for nine rounds. In the 11th round, however, Jeffries knocked the champion down three times. The third—a knockout blow—gave Jeffries the upset victory.

Five months later, Jeffries' first title defense lasted 25 rounds before he beat Tom Sharkey in a brutal fight. In 1900, Corbett led Jeffries on points after 22 rounds, but Jeffries knocked the former champion out in the 23rd. Jeffries took another beating in a 1902 rematch against Fitzsimmons. Yet he knocked out Fitzsimmons in the eighth round. He knocked out Corbett in the 10th round of their 1903 rematch. Jeffries retired in 1905.

Jeffries struck a fighter's familiar pose in 1909 while training for the last fight of his career against Jack Johnson.

Five years later, Jeffries unwisely attempted a comeback against the first black heavyweight champion, **Jack Johnson**. Most white boxing promoters, fighters, and fans wanted a white man to recapture the heavyweight crown. Johnson, however, had crushed all white challengers, leaving an aging Jeffries as the last "Great White Hope." Yet Johnson pummeled the former champion for 15 rounds, and Jeffries suffered his only loss in 23 career fights. Feeling that he had let down the entire white race, the embittered Jeffries retired to a cattle ranch in Burbank, California.

CAREER CAPSULE

Undefeated as heavyweight boxing champion, Jeffries lost just one fight: a comeback attempt five years after first retiring. He finished with a record of 18 wins, 1 loss, and 2 draws.

JACK JOHNSON

March 31, 1878–June 10, 1946

THE FIRST BLACK heavyweight champion, Jack Johnson was an outstanding fighter. His success, however, made him a target of racism. Boxing promoters searched desperately for seven years to find the "Great White Hope," a white boxer who could wrest the heavyweight title from him.

The son of former slaves, John Arthur Johnson was born in Galveston, Texas, where he picked cotton and worked as a stable boy. He established himself as a contender for the heavyweight crown by losing just three bouts between 1902 and 1908. But Tommy Burns, the heavyweight champion, did not want to fight Johnson. Johnson followed him to

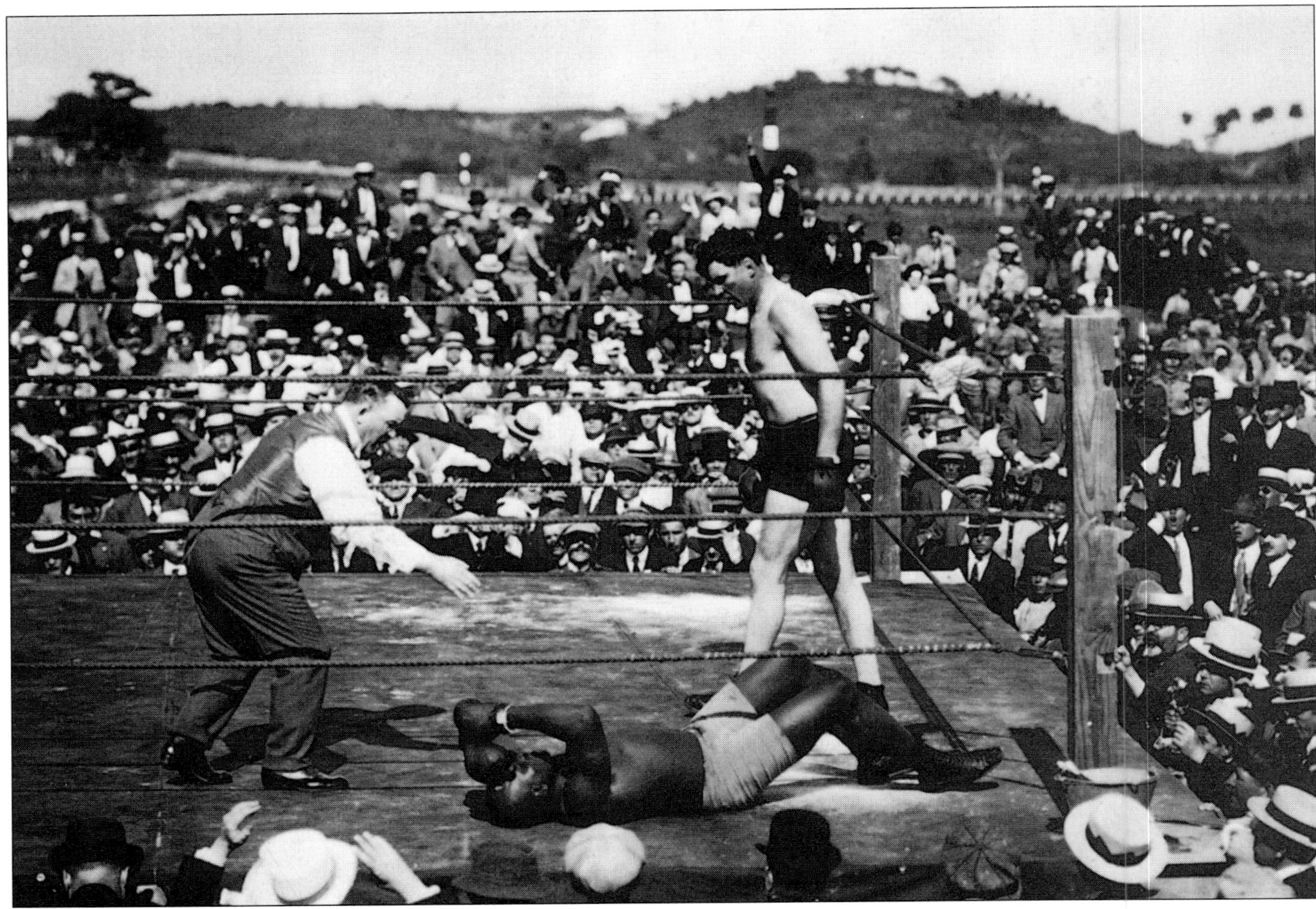

In the 1915 fight with Willard, Johnson went down in the 26th round. The event was scheduled to go 45 rounds, but the sun and heat took its toll on Johnson.

England and then Australia in 1908, challenging him to a bout. When Burns reluctantly agreed, Johnson pounded the champion for 14 rounds. Police in Sydney, Australia, stopped the fight. In his 68th career fight, Johnson had finally won the heavyweight title.

Johnson was hated by most white boxing fans. Not only had he become the first black champion but he had been married twice, each time to a white woman. When Johnson defeated every possible white contender, promoters convinced **Jim Jeffries**, who had retired undefeated five years earlier, to return to the ring in 1910. Johnson knocked out Jeffries to collect $120,000—a record purse until the 1920s.

In 1912, Johnson fled the country. He had been sentenced to one year in jail for violating the Mann Act (crossing state lines with an underage woman, his future wife). For the next three years, he defended his title in fights in Europe and South America. In his absence, "Gunboat" Smith was declared the "White Heavyweight Champion."

In an outdoor ring in Havana, Cuba, in 1915, Johnson met Jess Willard in the last scheduled 45-round fight in boxing history. Johnson led through 20 rounds, but the hot sun wore him down. Willard took the title with a 26th-round knockout. Johnson later claimed he had "thrown" the fight, but few people believed him. He had fought too hard.

After fighting for five more years in Europe, Johnson turned himself over to U.S. marshals in 1920. After serving his time, Johnson remained an active boxer until 1928. Having squandered his boxing purses, Johnson then eked out a living through lectures and personal appearances at museums and in carnival sideshows.

Career Capsule

The first black heavyweight boxing champion (1908–15), Johnson amassed a career record of 78 wins (45 of them by knockout), 8 losses, and 12 draws.

Knute Rockne

March 4, 1888–March 31, 1931

THE LEGENDARY college football coach Knute Rockne turned the Fighting Irish of the University of Notre Dame into a football powerhouse. Rockne was a brilliant strategist. He established an enduring pattern of excellence for the Indiana school's football teams. Rockne's teams won nearly eight out of every nine games played. His career winning percentage of .881 is the highest of any football coach in history. During what has been called the Golden Age of Sports, Rockne led the Notre Dame team to the national championship three times.

Knute was born in Voss, Norway. His family immigrated to the United States when he was five, and settled in Chicago. After graduating from high school, Knute worked as a mail clerk and a railroad braker. In six years, he saved the $1,000 he needed to pay for college. He had planned to go to the University of Illinois. Instead, because he thought living in South Bend might be cheaper, he joined two friends who enrolled at Notre Dame in 1910.

Already 22 years old, Rockne had no plans to become a star athlete. He played the flute in the school band, was active in the theater, and worked on the yearbook. He later admitted that, "College players were supermen to whose heights I could never aspire." Yet he excelled as a half-miler and pole vaulter on the track team and played end on the football team. By 1913, Rockne was captain. Over the summer, he and quarterback Charles "Gus" Dorais practiced passing and receiving every day. The forward pass was a little-used offensive weapon in those days. So Dorais and Rockne surprised everyone when they used it to help Notre Dame defeat Army for the first time ever, 35 to 13. Dorais completed 13 of 17 passes at West Point, many of them to Rockne. Their success helped transform football from a ground game into one that combined passing and rushing. Army asked Dorais and Rockne to remain at West Point for several days after the game. They wanted the Notre Dame players to show them exactly how they had managed to win.

Rockne graduated magna cum laude with a degree in chemistry in 1914. He stayed at Notre Dame, however, as a part-time chemistry instructor and as the assistant football coach. Four years later, he was named head coach. Rockne's success as a coach came quickly. From 1918 to 1921, the Fighting Irish went undefeated in 22 straight games (though one game ended in a tie). The team won all nine of their games in both 1919 and 1920.

As he had during his playing days, coach Rockne increased the use of the forward pass. An innovator, Rockne helped perfect the shift play on offense: Just before the center would snap the ball to the quarterback to begin a play, some players would shift position. This strategy baffled defenses everywhere. As opposing players attempted to adjust, they often found themselves out of position. Notre Dame would then exploit this confusion by breaking through the hole in the coverage or passing to the man left open.

After its two undefeated seasons, Notre Dame lost just one game a year from 1921 to 1923. Rockne fielded perhaps the greatest backfield in college history from 1922 to 1924. The fabled Four Horsemen (Harry Stuhldreher, Jimmy Crowley, Don Miller, and Elmer Layden) carried the Irish to a 10–0 record in 1924—and recognition as national champions. Notre Dame rewarded Rockne by signing him to a surprising ten-year coaching contract.

The following year, Columbia University offered Rockne a raise from $10,000 to $25,000 if he could get Notre Dame to release him from his contract. The deal was called off when the press got word of

In Rockne's day, college teams traveled across country by train, not plane.

the story before the details had been settled. In 1928, the Irish went 5–4, the only time in Rockne's career that the team lost more than two games. Rockne responded by stressing the importance of hard work, blocking, and practice. "A lot of people seem to think there is some sort of magic in making a winning football team," he later remarked. "There isn't, but there's plenty of work." Rockne's players, who regarded him almost as a god, did everything he asked of them. He spent hour after hour coaching the players in blocking. Rockne believed that his team could score on any play from any point on the field. But every player on the team had to do his job properly to achieve this goal. A team did not need trick plays to win, he insisted. All it needed to do was to carry out simple plays flawlessly.

The use of these "perfect plays" propelled the Irish to a 9–0 record and another national championship in 1929. In the off-season, the football rules committee muzzled one of Rockne's favorite weapons. The committee ruled that at least one second must pass between the end of a shift and the snap that begins a play. Rockne compared this restriction on last-second shifts to banning a boxer's right to feint. It diminished strategy and reduced the sport to a mere slugging contest. Despite the new rule, the Irish won all ten games in 1930 to keep their national championship.

The following spring, Rockne died when his plane crashed in a Kansas cow pasture. Yet Rockne's influence on college football outlasted him. He carried football to a new level of excellence, made Notre Dame the most popular football team in the country, and created a tradition unmatched by any other school. Further, nearly two dozen of the men who played for him went on to become head coaches themselves.

Career Capsule

Won national championship three times (1924, consecutively 1929–30). All-time highest winning percentage (.881). Career record 106–12–5, including five undefeated seasons. Coached Notre Dame from 1918 to 1930.

Jim Thorpe

May 28, 1888–March 28, 1953

Perhaps the century's greatest all-around athlete, Jim Thorpe was a marvelous runner, jumper, and thrower. Thorpe won Olympic medals in both the decathlon and the pentathlon. He also played an important role in organizing and popularizing professional football in its early days.

James Francis Thorpe was born on a farm near Prague, in the Indian Territory, now part of Oklahoma. His father, from the Sac and Fox tribe, was a rancher. Jim's mother, from the Potawatome tribe, named him Wa-Tho-Huck, or Bright Path. Jim's twin brother died of pneumonia at age nine, but two other brothers and two sisters survived childhood. Jim showed athletic skill from an early age. He was riding horses at three and swimming by five.

When Thorpe played, football players didn't even wear helmets.

By the time Jim was 15, both his parents had died. He was placed in Pennsylvania's Carlisle School, a work-study school for Native Americans run by the U.S. government. Under legendary football coach Pop Warner, Jim began playing halfback in 1907. In his first start in 1908, Jim ran 65 and 85 yards for two touchdowns. The following year, he left Carlisle and went to the University of North Carolina for the school's work program. While there, he played some semipro baseball for $60 a month—a move that would later come to haunt him.

Thorpe returned to Carlisle, majoring in business administration, in 1911. On the Carlisle football team, he kicked four field goals and ran for a touchdown to score all of the team's 18 points in an 18-15 upset victory over previously unbeaten Harvard. **Walter Camp** chose Thorpe for that year's All-America Team. He again made All-American the following year, when he ran for 25 touchdowns and scored 198 points. Thorpe earned varsity letters in ten sports, including baseball, basketball, hockey, track, tennis, and boxing. He also won the 1912 intercollegiate ballroom dancing title.

At the 1912 Olympic Games in Stockholm, Sweden, Thorpe won gold medals in both the pentathlon and the decathlon—an achievement no one else has ever matched. In the pentathlon, Thorpe finished first in four events (the long jump, the 200-meter dash, the discus throw, and the 1,500-meter race) and third in the fifth event (the javelin throw). In the decathlon, he won four events (the 110-meter hurdles, the shotput, the high jump, and the discus). He finished second in two others (the 100-meter dash and the 1,500-meter race) and third in the other four (the long jump, the 400-meter race, pole vaulting, and the javelin throw). His 8,412.96 points beat the silver medalist by almost 700 points and would remain a world record for the next 15 years. "Sir, you are the greatest athlete in the world," King Gustaf V of Sweden told Thorpe as he presented him with a medal. "Thanks, King," Thorpe humbly replied.

Thorpe returned home to a hero's welcome. President Theodore Roosevelt sent a telegram of congratulations. New York held a ticker-tape parade. "I heard people yelling my name," Thorpe later recalled, "and I couldn't realize how one fellow could have so many friends." In 1913, however, the Amateur Athletic Union (AAU) revoked his amateur status. The AAU ruled that because Thorpe had accepted money to play baseball in 1909 and 1910, he could not be considered an amateur. "I did not play for the money," Thorpe insisted. "I played because I liked baseball." But the AAU stripped him of his Olympic medals. (Both the pentathlon silver medalist, Norwegian Ferdinand Bie, and the decathlon runner-up, Swede Hugo Wieslander, refused to accept the gold medals.)

After graduating from Carlisle in 1913, Thorpe signed a contract with baseball's New York Giants. He played parts of six seasons as an outfielder with the Giants, Cincinnati Reds, and Boston Braves. Thorpe had trouble hitting a curveball, however, and wound up his career with a .252 average.

In 1915, Thorpe organized the Canton (Ohio) Bulldogs, a professional football team. The first big-name athlete to play football professionally, Thorpe played halfback with the Bulldogs for three seasons.

Against Harvard, Thorpe kicked four field goals in a winning effort.

In 1920, he helped found the American Professional Football Association (APFA) in Canton, Ohio. APFA, which changed its name to the National Football League (NFL) in 1922, elected Thorpe as its first president. He continued to play professional football until 1928.

After retiring from football, Thorpe took bit parts in movies, mostly Westerns. In 1937, he led a movement to get the Sac-Fox tribe to reject a new constitution. Thorpe felt that the tribe was giving up the power to govern itself and conceding too much to the U.S. government.

In 1950, an Associated Press poll of sports writers selected Thorpe as both the greatest male athlete and the greatest football player of the half century. In the first category, Thorpe received 875 points—outdistancing by far **Babe Ruth**'s 539, Jack Dempsey's 246, and **Ty Cobb**'s 148.

Despite appeals by the Oklahoma legislature in 1943 and the U.S. Congress in 1952, the AAU had still refused to restore Thorpe's Olympic medals before he died in 1953. Thorpe was buried in Mauch Chunk, Pennsylvania. The town agreed to change its name to Jim Thorpe, to honor his final resting place. In 1983, 30 years after his death, the AAU restored Thorpe's medals to his children.

Thorpe earned membership in more athletic halls of fame than any other athlete. He was elected to the Professional Football Hall of Fame, the National Football Hall of Fame, the American Indian Athletic Hall of Fame, the National Track and Field Hall of Fame, and the United States Track and Field Hall of Fame.

Career Capsule

Gold medalist in decathlon and pentathlon at 1912 Olympics. Played pro baseball with New York (NL) and Cincinnati from 1913 to 1919 and pro football with several teams from 1919 to 1926. Also All America two times with Carlisle.

Thorpe, with his family, was a member of five sports halls of fame.

HONUS WAGNER

February 24, 1874–December 6, 1955

BASEBALL'S GREATEST shortstop, Honus Wagner, played 21 years in the major leagues. Nicknamed the "Flying Dutchman," Wagner was a solid fielder and a great hitter. His good humor made him even more popular.

Wagner played during baseball's "dead ball" era: a period in which the ball did not travel well off the bat because the twine inside the ball was not tightly wrapped. While the National League (NL) batting average was typically around .250 during the first two decades of this century, Wagner hit a lifetime .328. Also a sensational base runner, Wagner made the most of his speed both on the base lines and in the field.

John Peter Wagner was born in the coal country of Carnegie, Pennsylvania, the son of German immigrants. As a teenager, John—also known as Honus or Hans—worked loading coal cars. When Honus was 18, he left home to become a barber. His play in local sandlot games won him a tryout with a club in Steubenville, Ohio, in 1895. The club actually wanted his older brother Albert, but Albert refused to sign a contract unless the club signed Honus, too. After a season in Steubenville, Wagner played a year for the Paterson (New Jersey) team of the Atlantic League.

By 1897, Wagner had proved he belonged in the majors. The Louisville Colonels, a National League team, made Wagner an outfielder. In half a season as a rookie, he hit .344—the first of a record 17 straight seasons in which he hit over .300. In 1898, splitting his time between first and third base, Wagner hit .305 and drove in 105 runs. The next year, Wagner hit .345 with 102 runs and 113 RBIs.

After Louisville and three other National League teams disbanded in 1900, Barney Dreyfuss, the Colonels president, bought the Pittsburgh Pirates. The loyal Wagner went with him and batted a league-leading .381 with a .572 slugging average, both career highs.

Wagner played shortstop for 16 seasons.

In 1901, Wagner moved to shortstop, a position he would play for the next 16 seasons. That year, he led the league in stolen bases (49) and RBIs (126). In 1902, he again led the league in steals (42), RBIs

Wagner's career batting average was a lofty .328, which led to his becoming the first professional baseball player to endorse a bat.

(91), and runs scored (105). Wagner covered a lot of ground at shortstop and led the league in double plays five times. Though he made at least 49 errors in each of his first eight full seasons at shortstop, he never led the league in miscues.

Wagner led the league in hitting with a .355 average in 1903, but in the first World Series ever held, he batted just .222. He also committed six errors as the Pirates blew a three-games-to-one series lead and lost to the Boston Red Sox, three games to five. Two years later, Wagner hit .363—his highest batting average between 1903 and 1909. Ironically, it was the only time in that seven-year period that he failed to win the batting crown.

That same year, the sporting goods company Hillerich & Bradsby thought its sales of bats might increase if it got the endorsements of professional players. Wagner became the first American sports hero to endorse a piece of sports equipment—an autographed bat.

Wagner stole a career-high 61 bases in 1907 to lead the league for the fourth time. The following year, he hit .354, stole 53 bases, and drove in 109 runs—topping the National League in each category. In 1909, he hit .339 to lead the league for the fourth straight season. The player of the decade, Wagner had led the league in hitting and doubles seven times since 1900. He had also led the league in slugging six times, steals five times, and RBIs four times. The Pirates went 110–42 in 1909 to win the NL pennant. In the World Series against **Ty Cobb** and the Detroit Tigers, Wagner starred in the third game with three hits, three steals, and three RBIs. In the seventh and deciding game, Wagner drove in two runs to give the Pirates their first World Series triumph.

The star of the National League, Wagner had an even temperament that contrasted sharply with the American League's best player, the mean-spirited Cobb. In the era before **Babe Ruth**, Wagner was the best-loved player in the game. Wagner was cheerful and good-natured, a gentleman on and off the field. He seldom argued with umpires and had no salary disputes. (He reportedly often signed blank contracts, trusting the Pirate management to add in a fair salary.) A hard worker and team player, Wagner served as role model and advisor for Pirate rookies.

Wagner was an early opponent of the use of tobacco. In 1910, a brand called Piedmont cigarettes printed a baseball card with his picture on it. When Wagner threatened a lawsuit, the card was immediately pulled out of circulation. His firm stand—and Piedmont's quick withdrawal—made the card one of the rarest in collecting history. (In 1990, hockey star Wayne Gretzky paid a record $451,000 for a mint-condition Piedmont card of Honus Wagner.)

In 1911, Wagner hit .334 to win his eighth career batting title—still the NL record. Although his hitting began to fade after 1911, his fielding had become exemplary. He led the league's shortstops in fielding average three times between 1912 and 1915.

Wagner retired at age 43 in 1917, but he played semipro ball for another decade. When he went bankrupt in the 1930s, the Pirates offered him a job as coach. He remained with the team until 1951. Wagner was one of the first stars elected to the Baseball Hall of Fame in 1936.

Career Capsule

A lifetime .328 hitter, Wagner had 3,415 career hits and hit over .300 for 15 consecutive seasons. He led the league in doubles eight times, stolen bases five times, RBI four times, and won the batting title eight times. He hit 252 triples and stole 703 bases during his career (1897–1917) with Pittsburgh.

Cy Young

March 29, 1867–November 4, 1955

Baseball's first great pitcher, Cy Young pitched and won and lost more major-league games than anyone before or since. Young won 30 or more games in a season five different times. He won 20 or more games in 16 different seasons—including 14 in a row.

Denton True Young was born on a farm in Gilmore, Ohio, just after the Civil War. The gawky country boy—six feet, two inches tall and 210 pounds—first attracted attention while pitching with the Canton, Ohio, team in the Tri-State League. His performance with Canton led to a tryout with the National League's Cleveland Spiders. "I thought I had to show all my stuff and I almost tore the boards off the grandstand with my fast ball," Young later recalled. "One of the fellows called me 'Cyclone,' but finally shortened it to 'Cy,' and it's been that ever since."

Young had pinpoint control from the very beginning. As a rookie with the Spiders in 1890, he led the league in fewest walks per nine innings (1.8). He would go on to have the league's best control seven more times—including five straight from 1896 to 1900. In 1891, his first full season in the majors, he won 27 games and lost 20. This was the first of 14 straight seasons in which he won 20 or more games. Young had his best season in the National League in 1892. He won 36 games and lost only 11. He had an Earned Run Average (ERA) of just 1.93 and tossed nine shutouts. The following year, he went 32–16 and in 1895, he was 35–10. A good hitter, too, Young batted .289 with 3 home runs in 1896. A year later, he fired his first no-hitter to beat Cincinnati, 6–0.

In 1901, Young began pitching for the Boston Red Sox in the new American League. Young christened the new league by winning the "triple crown" of pitching: He led the league in wins (33), ERA (1.62), and strikeouts (158). He won 30 games for the last time in 1902, going 32–10 with a 2.15 ERA.

Young is the all-time leading pitcher with 511 wins and he had over 200 wins in both the American and National Leagues.

Again, he was the best control pitcher in the league—giving up the fewest walks per nine innings in five of his first six seasons in the American League. In 1903, he went 28–10 with a league-leading seven shutouts. Young then threw the first pitch of the very first World Series as the starter for the home-team Red Sox. Though he gave up four runs in the first inning to lose the first game, he came back to win games five and seven to help the Red Sox win the first World Series, five games to three, over the Pittsburgh Pirates.

In 1904, Young pitched 23 consecutive innings over three games without giving up a single hit. The middle game, against the Philadelphia Athletics on May 5, was the first perfect game—no runs, no hits, no base runners—in the American League. This also made him the first pitcher ever to toss no-hitters in each league. He went 26–16 that year and again led the league in shutouts with 10. In 1908, against the New York Highlanders, he pitched his third no-hitter—a record that would last until 1965, when Sandy Koufax pitched his fourth.

Young retired at age 44 after the 1911 season. He was elected to the Baseball Hall of Fame in 1937, the second year of voting. In 1956, when baseball established an annual award to honor its best pitchers, it was named for the man who set the standard: Cy Young.

Career Capsule

The only pitcher to win at least 200 games in both the National and American Leagues. All-time leader in wins (511), losses (313), innings pitched (7,354.2), and complete games (749). Had career ERA of 2.63 and pitched three no-hitters including a perfect game. Pitching award named in his honor. Career span 1890–1911 with Cleveland and Boston.

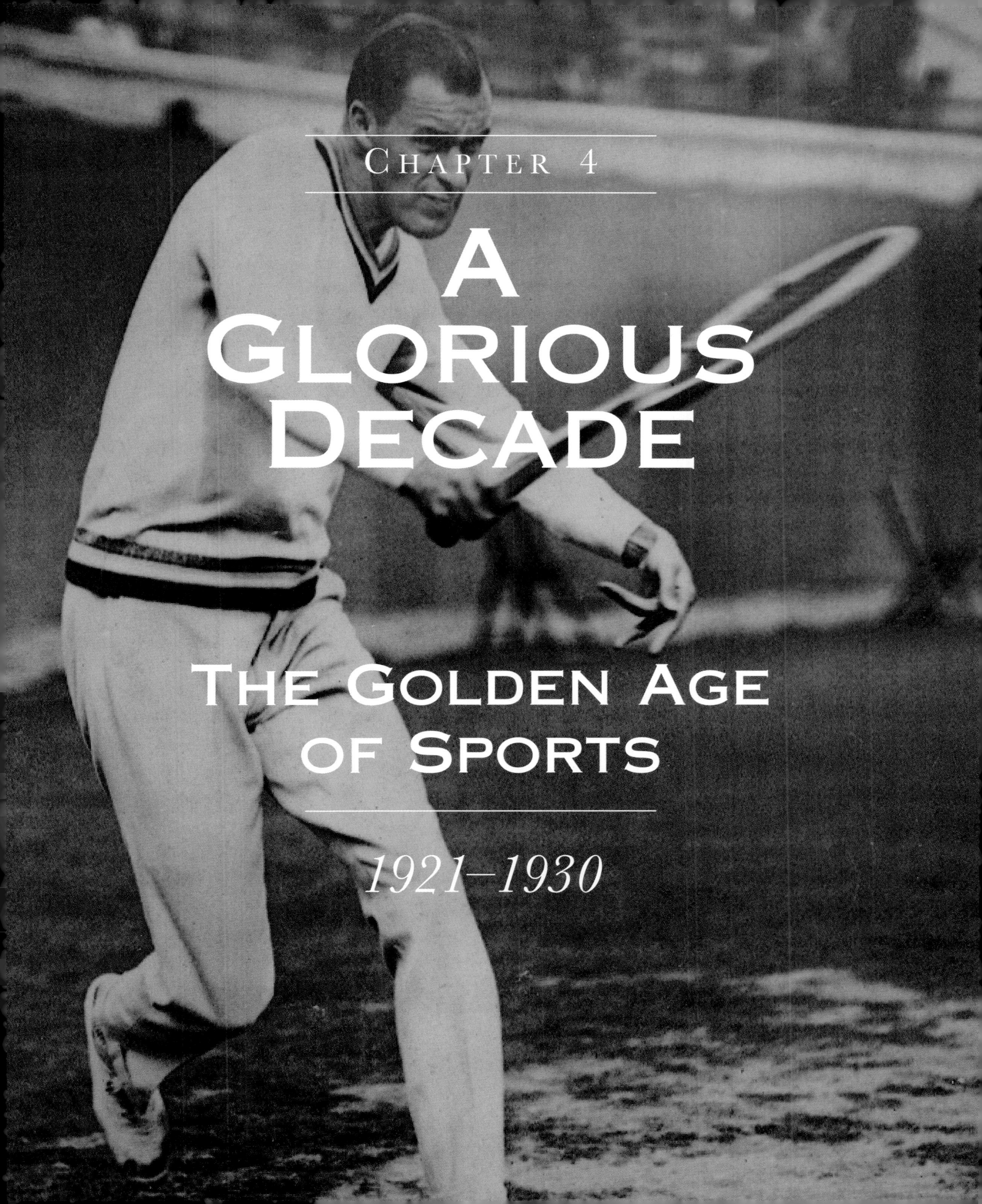

Chapter 4

A Glorious Decade

The Golden Age of Sports

1921–1930

The "Roaring Twenties" was an exciting time in the United States, and the people were enthusiastic and often extravagant. World War I was over. The economy slowed down for a short time after the war, but it soon picked up again. The new prosperity brought new audiences to organized sports. People had more money and time to spend watching sports. The 1920s became known as the Golden Age of Sports. It was an age of champions, of extraordinary events and superb performances. Never before nor since has there been such a concentration of athletic genius in so many fields of sports. The athletes of the Twenties were more than record breakers. They had color, that intangible quality that put them above the great ones of every other age. Call it crowd appeal, class, or personality—whatever you will—they had it. Fans can argue that there are just as many stars today and that most of the records of the old-timers have long since been surpassed. True enough. The games have changed. The rules are different. Equipment is improved, and today's athletes train and eat better. But it cannot be disputed that the great performers of the Twenties stood out from their teammates and competitors to a greater degree than did those of any other period.

The Golden Age started off with a bang. The 1921 fight between Jack Dempsey and French boxer Georges Carpentier was the first bout ever to sell more than $1 million in tickets. In fact, ticket sales reached $1,789,238. And boxing was not the only game in town. People everywhere turned out for all types of sporting events in record numbers.

LEGENDARY CHAMPIONS

Sports rewarded their fans' new devotion with a host of legendary champions. It seemed as though every popular sport featured one or two athletes who stood head and shoulders above the rest. **Babe Ruth** shattered records in professional baseball, and Lou Gehrig, the "Iron Horse," began his incredible streak of playing in 2,130 consecutive games, a record which stood until 1995, when it was broken by the Baltimore Orioles' Cal Ripken. Cool Papa Bell, the fastest man ever to play in the Negro Leagues, helped them build a huge following in African-American communities. Running back **Red Grange** thrilled football fans who flocked to stadiums to see him lead the University of Illinois and later the Chicago Bears. Dempsey brought new fans to boxing. Golfers **Bobby Jones** and **Glenna Collett Vare** outplayed all opponents on the links. Swimmers **Johnny Weissmuller** and **Gertrude Ederle** set new records. **Bill Tilden** and **Helen Wills Moody** excelled on the tennis courts. Man O'War, the champion thoroughbred, broke either a track record or world record in eight of his eleven races in 1920. Nat Holman, America's first great basketball player, led the original Celtics, a professional team from New York City, to an incredible 1922–23 record of 102 victories, six losses.

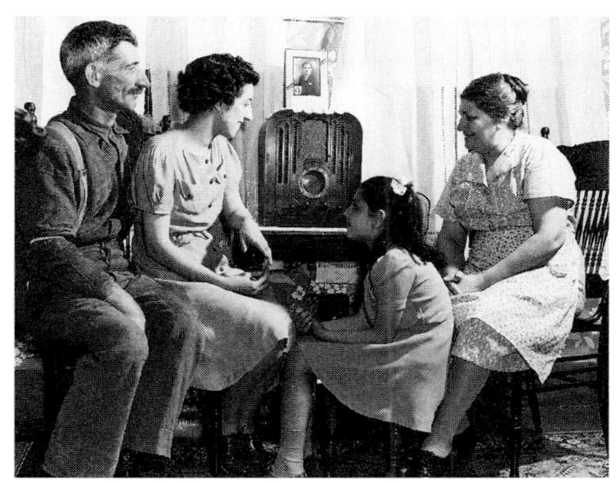

Sports paid great sums of money to the reigning stars. By 1930, the salary of Yankees' slugger Babe Ruth ($80,000) was greater than that of President Herbert Hoover. But more than any other factor, it was the mass media—the new medium of radio and the long-established national newspapers and magazines—that made sports stars so popular in this golden age. Between 1922 and 1923, the number of radio stations broadcasting jumped from 30 to more than 500. Live coverage of sports was in reach of everyone with a radio. By 1927, a second bout between Dempsey and Gene Tunney attracted a radio audience of 50 million people. The "Golden Age of Sports" was reported by some of America's most gifted writers. They included Damon Runyon, Heywood Broun, and Ring Lardner, who wrote dramatically about the great sports events and personalities.

Johnny Weissmuller

With the upsurge of mass media came a new kind of American hero, the celebrity. The fame of earlier champions had often been limited to a specific region. But radio, newspapers, and magazines gave the champions of the 1920s national stature. Most of the stars became folk heroes: personable, often colorful, and seemingly larger than life. These images were often created by promoters and press agents hired by team owners and, in some cases, individual players. Ruth was the first athlete to have his own press agent. Grange hired one too. Weissmuller went on to a movie career playing Tarzan.

THE NEGRO LEAGUE

African Americans and women kept searching for opportunities to break into the sports world. Giving up hope that major-league baseball would ever allow African Americans to play, black entrepreneurs formed the Negro National League in 1920. Other Negro leagues formed, but they were not very successful because the strongest teams, such as the Homestead Grays (Pittsburgh, PA), remained independent. The Grays, and teams like them, could make more money barnstorming, traveling to different cities to play exhibition games. The quality of play of the independent Negro teams like the Homestead Grays or Kansas City Monarchs, a member of the Negro National League, equaled—and, according to many, surpassed—that played by white major leaguers. In 1922, the Monarchs swept a doubleheader playing the touring Babe Ruth All-Stars.

Helen Wills Moody

Despite gaining the right to vote, women gained little on the playing fields. Female athletes still had little to choose from besides tennis and golf. Even in these sports, Moody and Vare were slighted in comparison to their male counterparts, Tilden and Jones. Among all sportswomen, Ederle received the decade's biggest headlines when, in 1926, she swam across the English Channel in record time (for men or women).

The crash of the stock market in 1929 brought an abrupt end to the Golden Age of Sports. America's dreams of unlimited prosperity and fame crashed along with the market. The Great Depression had begun.

SPORTS CELEBRITIES:

Athletes Achieve National Fame

The development of mass media—magazines, newspaper chains, and radio—went hand-in-hand with the development of the advertising industry. The mass production of goods—begun in the late 19th century—led to a boom in advertising. At first, many magazines were reluctant to accept advertisements. Yet the money made by charging advertisers to run their ads made it possible for magazine publishers to print and sell more copies at a lower price to readers.

In 1920, KDKA in Pittsburgh became the first commercial radio station. Within two years of KDKA's first broadcast, the number of licensed stations had grown to 564. Since radio stations did not charge listeners any fee at all, they depended upon advertising for all the money they made.

The media and advertisers soon found both could profit from transforming sports heroes into celebrities. Stories that portrayed athletes as larger than life helped the media catch the eyes and ears of a wider audience. So magazines and radio spun legends about movie stars like Rudolph Valentino and Mary Pickford, national heroes like Charles Lindbergh, and sports figures like **Babe Ruth** and **Red Grange**. By linking their products to the celebrities, advertisers increased their sales. Savvy players took advantage of this celebrity-making partnership between the media and advertisers. Teams and individual athletes hired press agents to help mold a public image that they could better sell. By the end of the 1920s, the media, advertisers, leagues, teams, and players had all helped to create the first superstars in American sports.

CLARENCE DEMAR

June 7, 1888–June 11, 1958

KNOWN AS MR. MARATHON, Clarence DeMar ran over 100 marathons during his lifetime. In his 25 starts in the Boston Marathon, he completed every race, finished among the top ten 15 times, and won a record seven times!

In his first Boston Marathon (then 24.7 miles), DeMar finished second by less than a minute in 1910. Though warned by his doctor that he had a heart murmur and should stop running, DeMar won the next year's marathon. He set a new Boston record of 2:21:39, slicing nearly three minutes off the previous best time. He entered—and won—nine other distance races that year.

After finishing a disappointing 12th in the 1912 Olympics in Stockholm, Sweden, DeMar did not run another marathon for five years. In 1917, he finished third in Boston, but later won the Brockton Fair Marathon in record time. After serving overseas in World War I, DeMar finally won his second Boston Marathon in 1922. His time, 2:18:10, was a record for the old course. DeMar won again in 1923. On a longer 26.1-mile course in 1924, he won his third straight Boston Marathon, beating his nearest challenger by more than five minutes. He then won a bronze medal at the Paris Olympic Games. In 1926 and 1927, he won an incredible five straight marathon races, ending with his fifth win in Boston. The Boston champion again in 1928, he also won a 44-mile race from Providence to Boston. In 1930, an amazing 19 years after winning his first marathon, the 42-year-old DeMar won the Boston race for the seventh time. He would continue to run marathons until age 66.

"Mister Marathon" ran over 100 marathons in his career.

CAREER CAPSULE

An Olympic bronze medalist in 1924 and winner of the Boston Marathon seven times.

GERTRUDE EDERLE

born October 23, 1906

AN OUTSTANDING AMATEUR swimmer, Gertrude Ederle at one time held world records in every distance from 100 to 800 meters. But she is best known as the first woman to swim the English Channel.

The daughter of German immigrants, "Trudy" learned to swim as a way of escaping the summer heat of New York City streets. At 15, she won national swimming titles in both 220- and 440-yard races. The next year, Trudy entered and won her first distance race. She set a new record in defeating 50 world-class swimmers in a three-mile race across New York Bay. By the end of the following year, Ederle had already set

18 world distance swimming records. In the 1924 Olympic games in Paris, Trudy won two bronze medals in individual freestyle races and was part of the U.S. freestyle relay team that captured a gold medal. By the end of 1925, she held 29 national and world records.

That year, she announced that she would swim the English Channel, a feat that had been accomplished by only five people, all men. Although her first attempt failed, she completed the 20-mile swim from France to England on August 6, 1926. Despite stormy weather, rough waters, and a wave of seasickness, Ederle swam the channel in just 14 hours and 31 minutes. That was nearly two hours faster than the fastest male finisher's time!

For each long swim, Ederle had a support crew who provided nourishment.

The woman who challenged—and beat—men in a physical endeavor was an overnight hero all over the world. Ederle inspired thousands of women to swim both for fun and for sport. Her success in achieving a feat considered impossible for a woman paved the way for women's acceptance in the world of sports.

Career Capsule

The first woman to swim the English Channel, in 1926. Swam 21 miles from France to England in 14.31. Also won three medals at the 1924 Olympics.

Red Grange 

June 13, 1903–January 28, 1991

The legendary halfback for Illinois University and the Chicago Bears in the 1920s, Red Grange was football's greatest star during the Golden Age of Sports. "This man Red Grange of Illinois," sportswriter and short-story author Damon Runyon wrote in 1925, "is three or four men and a horse rolled into one for football purposes. He is Jack Dempsey, Babe Ruth, [singer and entertainer] Al Jolson, [champion distance runner] Paavo Nurmi, and [Kentucky Derby winner] Man o' War."

Harold Grange was born in Forksville, Pennsylvania, but grew up in Wheaton, Illinois. At age 15, Harold—called "Red" because of his flaming red hair—suffered a devastating leg injury. His doctors told him that he would never play football again. Yet Red did not let the injury stop him from achieving greatness as an all-around athlete. In all four years of high school, he won varsity letters in baseball, basketball, and track, as well as football.

Grange earned as many nicknames as Babe Ruth. Some called him the Wheaton Ice Man because he had worked part-time for an ice company in high school. Others knew Grange as Old 77, his uniform number. Many called him Red. But his most famous nickname came from famed sportswriter Grantland Rice. Rice called him the Galloping Ghost because when Grange ran, no one could touch him.

The legend of Red Grange began with his very first game for the University of Illinois (the Illini) in 1923. The swift and graceful running back scored three touchdowns, including one 65-yard run and another for 35 yards, against the Nebraska Cornhuskers. During his first season, he gained 1,296 yards and scored 12 touchdowns.

Grange had his greatest college game in October 1924. Illinois was facing previously undefeated Michigan. Grange began by running back the opening kickoff 95 yards for a touchdown. When the

Illini lined up for their first offensive play, Grange got the ball again. He raced 67 yards for another touchdown. Later in the first quarter, he rushed for touchdowns of 54 and 44 yards. In just 12 minutes, he had scored four touchdowns. He went on to score a fifth touchdown himself and toss a 20-yard pass for a sixth. Grange's 402 yards of offense in the game—including passes for 64 yards—crushed Michigan, 39–14.

Red was named to the All-American Football Team during all three of his years at Illinois. In just 20 varsity games, he scored 31 touchdowns and passed for six more. He rushed for 2,071 yards on only 388 carries, averaging 5.3 yards per rush.

In November 1925, he left the Illini in mid-season to sign a contract with the Chicago Bears. Grange joined the Bears on Thanksgiving Day. The team immediately went on a coast-to-coast tour, playing eight games in just 12 days. The tour—and Grange's stardom—greatly heightened interest in the professional National Football League (NFL), which had been organized five years earlier. At the time, the college game still drew all the attention—and almost all of the football fans. Grange became pro football's first great drawing card. He played before sellout crowds all over the country. Already the football idol of his generation, Grange instantly gave the new league credibility among sports fans. In just three months of play, Grange earned $100,000—an enormous sum for those days.

After a salary dispute, Grange left the Bears in 1926. With his manager, C.C. "Cash and Carry" Pyle, Grange formed the rival American Football League. A financial disaster, the league disbanded after just one season. Returning to the NFL, he played for the New York Yankees in 1927. After sitting out the entire 1928 season with a knee injury, he returned to the Bears in 1929. He remained with the team for the rest of his career. Named to the All-Pro Team in 1931, Grange became a noted defen-

Grange's running ability earned him the nickname "Galloping Ghost."

THE BIRTH OF THE NFL DRAFT

When Red Grange left college to pursue a pro career, his signing led to the creation of the NFL draft of college players. Illini coach Bob Zuppke protested the signing to longtime Bears owner and coach George Halas, a former Illinois student. Zuppke told Halas that taking players from college rosters in mid-season could ruin the college game. Halas found Zuppke's argument persuasive (but not forceful enough to convince him to release Grange from his contract).

After his meeting with Zuppke, Halas became the league's foremost backer of a new system of signing college players: the NFL draft. All of the teams' owners pledged not to sign a player until he had completed his college years. Every year, teams would take turns picking college players. A player could then sign a pro contract only with the team that had drafted him.

sive back in the 1930s. A second knee injury in 1935 ended his career.

Red next went to Hollywood, where he starred in a series of cliffhanger movies named after him: "The Galloping Ghost." From 1947 to 1961, he announced games on radio and television for the Bears. When the Professional Football Hall of Fame first opened its doors in 1963, Grange was among the first group of players selected for membership.

Yet through it all, Grange retained his modesty. Looking back at his stardom, Grange explained in his later years, "The country and writers were looking to make big names of people. They needed someone in football and I guess I was the one they picked. I was happy that I was, too."

Career Capsule

All-America three consecutive seasons with Illinois (1923–25), scoring 31 touchdowns in 20-game collegiate career. Signed by Chicago in 1925, attracted sellout crowds across the country.

Bobby Jones attracted large audiences on the golf course long before television.

Bobby Jones 

March 17, 1902–December 18, 1971

PERHAPS THE GREATEST golfer who ever lived, Bobby Jones was certainly the greatest of the amateur era. During the 1920s, the Golden Age of Sports, Bobby Jones was the Babe Ruth of golf. He had a picture-perfect swing and a matchless record. He won 13 major championships, including a record five U.S. Amateur titles and four U.S. Open trophies, in just eight years.

As a player, Jones earned a reputation for honesty and sportsmanship. Twice in his career, he called penalties on himself during the U.S. Open. Though no one else had seen it, he had accidentally moved the ball with his club while preparing to drive the ball. But Jones could not cheat. "To praise me for that is to congratulate someone for not robbing a bank," he joked. His sense of fair play led the U.S. Professional Golfing Association (PGA) to call its annual sportsmanship award the Bob Jones Award. Robert Tyre Jones, Jr., was born in Atlanta, Georgia. Because his father had starred on the University of Georgia baseball team, baseball was Bobby's first love. By age five, however, he had begun to play golf. A year later, he won a local six-hole tournament. A natural mimic, he never took golf lessons. Instead, he copied the style of the golf pro at the East Lake course of the Atlanta Athletic Club. By the time he was nine, Bobby had won the club's junior championship.

In 1916, Jones—just 14 years old—beat adult golfers to win the Georgia State Amateur championship. In his first trip to the U.S. Amateur championships that year, he defeated a former champion in the first round, but lost in the third round. Despite his strong showing in 1916, Jones failed to win a single major title during his teens. He did win the Southern Amateur championship three times (1917, 1920, and 1922). He also finished as

An action shot of Jones' almost perfect swing with a driver. He never took golf lessons, but he had the ability to duplicate the swings of other good players he watched. Eventually, other golfers tried to copy his swing.

runner-up in several events, including the U.S. Amateur and the Canadian Open in 1919, and the U.S. Open in 1922. But he did not win a major event until he got his temper under control. As a teenager, Bobby punished himself when he failed to live up to his expectations. He was not satisfied with a good shot; it had to be perfect. If he misplayed a shot, he would tear up his scorecard or throw a club. These outbursts invariably made it difficult for him to concentrate on his next shots.

Still just 21 years old, Jones kept his temper in check and began winning major tournaments in 1923. In a play-off, he won the U.S. Open (still an amateur event at that time). The following year, he won his first U.S. Men's Amateur title and finished as the runner-up at the U.S. Open. Jones repeated this performance in 1925, defending his amateur title and placing second at the Open. In 1926, Jones became the first golfer ever to win both major open titles in the same year. He won the British Open championship, tying the tournament record by completing the 72 holes in just 291 shots. He then won his second U.S. Open title. He also finished as runner-up in that year's U.S. Amateur.

In 1927, Jones defended his British Open crown to become the first American to win the event two years in a row. He shot a record-setting 285, six strokes under the previous mark. After a disappointing 11th-place finish at the U.S. Open, Jones won the U.S. Amateur tournament for the third time in his career. The following year, he returned to form at the U.S. Open, finishing as the runner-up. He then won his record-tying fourth U.S. Amateur title in five years. In 1929, Jones and Al Espinosa were tied for the lead after 72 holes at the U.S. Open. In a 36-hole play-off, Jones beat Espinosa by an incredible 23 strokes!

In 1930, Jones had the finest year any golfer has ever had. Though he failed to win the Savannah Open, he won the rest of the tournaments he entered. He began by winning the British Men's Amateur. Despite not playing his best, he then won the British Open. Next, he successfully defended his U.S. Open title. His victory gave him a record-tying four U.S. Open titles. Finally, he won his record-setting fifth U.S. Men's Amateur title. This victory completed Jones' Grand Slam, or as newspapers of the day called it, the "impregnable quadrilateral." No other golfer before or since has won the four biggest tournaments in golf in a single year.

At 28, Jones retired. He was at the height of his career, and his record during the previous eight years (1923-30) has never been matched. In eight U.S. Opens, he had won four titles and finished second three times. He had won five of eight U.S. Amateur tournaments and was runner-up in another. He played in the British Open three times—and won the title all three years! And after eight years of trying, he had finally won the British Amateur title.

To Bobby Jones—a member of the World Golf Hall of Fame, the PGA of America Hall of Fame, and the American Golf Hall of Fame— golf was just a game. He always said that his family came first, his profession (the law) second, and golf third. Yet Jones was not quite finished with golf. After designing the picturesque Augusta National Golf Course, Jones invited the world's top players to compete in a tournament that he called the Augusta National Invitational. Everyone else simply called it The Masters Tournament. The tournament quickly secured its place as one of the four major events on the professional golf tour.

CAREER CAPSULE

Achieved golf's only recognized Grand Slam (1930). Second all-time in major championships (13). Won U.S. Amateur 5 times, more than any golfer (consecutively 1924–25, 1927–28, 1930), U.S. Open 4 times (1923, 1926, consecutively 1929–30), British Open 3 times (consecutively 1926–27, 1930), and British Amateur (1930).

HELEN WILLS MOODY

born October 6, 1905

IN 1920, the year women won the right to vote in the United States, a 15-year-old California girl, her hair in pigtails, took the national junior tennis title in both singles and doubles. Over the next 13 years, Helen Wills Moody became the dominate and most popular female tennis player in the nation. She was a superb baseliner with hard-hitting ground strokes and a powerful, slicing serve. Moody won 19 Grand Slam singles championships, including eight at Wimbledon. (Not until 1990, when **Martina Navratilova** won her ninth Wimbledon crown, did this record fall.)

Though she dressed in the traditional long skirts, stockings and sleeves early in her career, Moody modernized women's tennis wear with shorter skirts, sleeveless blouses, and her trademark—the white sun visor.

Born in Centerville, California, Helen Wills learned to play tennis with her father, a doctor, at the nearby Berkeley Tennis Club. By age 13, Helen had won the Pacific Coast Juniors Championship. In 1922, still just 16, Helen reached the singles final of the U.S. women's championship. Though she lost in singles, she won the first of four U.S. doubles titles (1922, 1924, 1925, and 1928).

In 1923, Helen won the first of seven U.S. singles championships (1923–25, 1927–29, and 1931). A member of the first U.S. Wightman Cup team in 1923, she helped the United States defeat Britain and went on to win 18 of her 20 singles matches in ten years on the team. In the 1924 Olympic Games in Paris, Wills won gold medals in both singles and doubles. She also went for the first time to Wimbledon, where she won the first of three doubles crowns (1924, 1927, and 1930), but lost the final match for the singles championship—the only time she would come away from Wimbledon without winning the singles title! Back in the United States, she scored the first of two (1924 and 1928) "triple crowns"—winning the singles championship and both the women's and mixed doubles titles—in the U.S. Championships.

Though she hammered the ball, Wills was quiet and reserved both on and off the court. During a match, she focused so intently on her game that her face seldom changed expression. This earned her the nickname "Little Miss Poker Face."

After recovery from an appendectomy in 1926, which sidelined her for most of the year, Wills returned with a vengeance. From 1927 to 1932, Wills was invincible, not losing even a set in any singles match anywhere! Her streak of 158 consecutive matches would not end until 1933. In 1927, Wills became only the second American woman to win the singles title at Wimbledon. She would go on to win it four years in a row and eight times in her career (1927–30, 1932–33, 1935, 1938). In 1928, she captured the first of three straight and four career French championships (1928–30; 1932). In winning that year's U.S. championship, Wills became the first woman to win three Grand Slam tournaments in a single year (a feat she would repeat in 1929)—all without losing a single set.

Wills' success allowed her to be a fashion maverick on the court. In the 1920s, she and several other players stopped wearing long skirts, stockings, and sleeves—the standard outfit for women tennis players at the time. Instead, Wills often chose a sleeveless shift with a knee-length skirt, which she insisted allowed her more freedom of movement and improved the quality of her play. She complemented this with a white sun visor pulled low over her face.

Brilliant at anticipating her opponent, Wills Moody made it look easy, never seeming to waste any energy on the court. A true sports hero, idolized throughout the country, Helen Wills Moody helped make tennis one of the prime attractions of the Golden Age of Sports.

A Phi Beta Kappa graduate of the University of California (1928), Moody later wrote *Fifteen-Thirty* (her memoirs), instructional books on tennis, and several novels.

Career Capsule

Second all-time most women's Grand Slam singles titles (19). Her 8 Wimbledon titles are second most all-time (consecutively 1927–30, 1932–33, 1935, 1938). Won 7 U.S. titles (consecutively 1923–25, 1927–29, 1931) and 4 French titles (consecutively 1928–30, 1932). Also won 12 Grand Slam doubles titles.

Babe Ruth

February 6, 1895–August 16, 1948

THE BABE. THE BAMBINO. The Sultan of Swat. By any name, George Herman Ruth was probably the most famous sports hero ever, one of the first American athletes to achieve worldwide recognition. Ruth became the most famous baseball player of all time by refashioning the game in his own image. Before Ruth, baseball was a game of speed (singles, doubles, and stolen bases). Ruth single-handedly transformed it into a game of power hitting. And the Babe set the standard with 714 career homers. (The previous record, held by nineteenth-century first baseman Roger Connor, was 136.)

The son of a saloonkeeper, George Ruth had a difficult childhood. "We were very poor," he later recalled. "And there were times when we never knew where the next meal was coming from. But I never minded. I was no worse off than the other kids with whom I played and fought." He spent much of his youth at St. Mary's Industrial School for Boys, a boarding school for "unruly" boys in Baltimore, Maryland. The Catholic brothers who ran the school introduced George to the game of baseball. He quickly became the team's star pitcher and hitter.

In 1914, when he was 19, Ruth reached the major leagues. His teammates on the Boston Red Sox teased him about his chubby body and his round face. Because he looked and acted like a baby-faced kid, he soon became known as the Babe. Ruth became so famous as a slugger that few people today know that he began his career as a pitcher. Ruth was not merely a good pitcher, but a great one. Twice he won 20 games in a single season. In his career, he won 94 games and lost only 46. Ruth's .671 winning percentage would rank fourth on the all-time list if he had pitched another 300 innings (about one more full season). In 1916, Ruth allowed less than two earned runs per nine innings to lead the league in earned run average (ERA). Ruth also won all three World Series games he started. In 1916, he pitched all 14 innings for the Red Sox in a 2–1 win over the Brooklyn Dodgers. In 1918, he started twice in the series against the Chicago Cubs, winning 1–0 and 3–2. He finished with an impressive 0.87 ERA in the World Series. His pitching heroics included 29⅔ scoreless innings in a row—a World Series record that stood until another Yankee lefthander, Whitey Ford, tossed 32 straight shutout innings in 1960 and 1961.

As a pitcher, however, Ruth played only every fourth day. Despite this handicap, Ruth averaged three home runs a season during a time when the league leaders usually had less than ten. In 1918, the

Ruth earned the name Babe from his Boston teammates because of his chubby, youthful appearance.

In 1920 and 1921, Ruth hit a total of 113 home runs (this one in Washington, D.C.) and helped restore the popularity of baseball.

Boston manager, Ed Barrow, realized that Ruth was too valuable a slugger to play only once every four days. Beginning that season, Ruth began playing outfield or first base on many days when he wasn't pitching. While playing all three positions, he led the league in home runs with 11 in 1918. The next year, Ruth slugged 29 home runs, more than anyone had ever hit in one season. After the season, the Red Sox sold his contract to the New York Yankees for $125,000 (a small fortune at that time). Ruth's new team made him a full-time outfielder in 1920, and baseball was never again the same.

Baseball faced a serious crisis at the time Ruth started playing for the Yankees. Following the 1920 season, eight members of the Chicago White Sox were banned from baseball for life. Seven of the players had admitted that they had accepted bribes to lose the 1919 World Series to the Cincinnati Reds on purpose. The crooked White Sox players raised doubts about the honesty of all professional baseball. ("Say It Ain't So": The Black Sox Scandal, page 20.)

Ruth almost single-handedly saved the game. This larger-than-life heroic figure made baseball more popular than ever. In 1920, Ruth broke his own home run record by hitting 54, more than any other *team* in the American League! He had his best season in 1921, the year after the White Sox scandal came to light. He hit 59 home runs, again breaking his own record. He batted .378, drove in 171 runs (a career high), and scored 177 runs, more than anyone else in the twentieth century. His slugging average for the season, .846, was slightly lower than his record .847 a year earlier. His performance carried the Yankees into the World Series for the first time in the team's history. Led by Ruth, the Yankees became the most popular team in baseball. The first team to top one million in attendance in a season (1920), the Yankees averaged more than one million fans a year during the decade, nearly twice the average of the other fifteen teams. The team's success allowed the owner to build a new stadium. Yankee Stadium, often called the "house that Ruth built," opened in 1923. That year, the Yankees won their third straight American League title and, for the first time, the World Series.

In 1927, Ruth hit 60 home runs, again more than any other team in the league! This single-season record lasted until another Yankee outfielder, Roger Maris, hit 61 in 1961. The 1927 Yankees are regarded as the best baseball team of all time. Ruth, first baseman **Lou Gehrig** (47), and second baseman Tony Lazzeri (18) finished first, second, and third in home runs. Since almost every hitter on the team was dangerous to the opposition, the lineup became known as "Murderers' Row." The Yankees won 110 games that year and lost only 44. The team then won all four games with the Pirates in that year's World Series.

Ruth and Gehrig, the two most feared hitters in "Murderers' Row."

His performance and his worldwide renown made Ruth baseball's first highly paid superstar. His $80,000 salary in 1930 and 1931 was even higher than that of Herbert Hoover, the President of the United States. "Well," Ruth explained to a reporter, "I had a better year than he did." It was the height of the Great Depression, and Hoover got much of the blame.

Already a legend, Ruth became a mythic figure in the 1932 World Series. Standing at the plate in the fifth inning of the third game, Ruth seemed to point his bat out to centerfield as Cubs pitcher Charlie Root prepared to throw the ball. Whether he was just taunting the pitcher or actually predicting a home run remains unclear. On the next pitch, however, Ruth rocketed the ball into the Wrigley Field bleachers, right where he had apparently pointed! Ever since, Ruth has been credited with "calling his shot," a legendary feat of heroic bluster that typified his career.

Ruth was legendary off the field as well. He was a huge man with an enormous appetite for anything he enjoyed. Ruth drank heavily, openly breaking the law that prohibited alcohol in the United States throughout the 1920s. He also regularly defied managers, broke team rules, and showed up late for practice. He was fined heavily by the Yankees and by the American League for his misbehavior. Yet his fame and popularity only grew.

Despite his flaws, Ruth became a hero to all baseball fans, especially children. Ruth loved kids, and often visited sick children in hospitals in the cities where he played. Ruth was the greatest star in America's Golden Age of Sports. Americans began spending more and more of their growing leisure hours attending sporting events, listening to them on the radio, or playing sports. Groups like the American Legion began to sponsor baseball programs for children. These programs offered young boys the

Whether it was posing with a monkey as a publicity stunt or selling Christmas seals at a charity effort, Ruth understood the value of good public relations. By the time Ruth bid farewell to his fans in a packed Yankee Stadium in 1948, he had become a legend. The team retired the number 3 uniform so that no other Yankee player will ever wear that number.

hope that they could someday become the "next Babe Ruth."

Taking advantage of America's growing obsession with sports, the greatest athlete of the age also became the nation's first sports celebrity. He was the first sports star ever to hire a press agent. His press agent would give reporters stories that would add to the Ruth legend, stories like the one about the "called shot" in the 1932 World Series. Through shrewd management of the press and his own oversized body and personality, Ruth became a national symbol, a defining part of American culture.

Ruth's career record of 714 homers would stand until 1974, when the Atlanta Braves' **Henry Aaron** broke the record and went on to hit 40 more. Had Ruth played every day instead of pitching during his first five seasons, he might have hit more than 800 home runs. Although often considered a pure power hitter, Ruth hit for average, too. His career batting average of .342 is the tenth best of all time. Ruth also led the league in walks eleven times (and still holds the career record of 2,056), in runs scored eight times, and in runs batted in six times.

Appropriately, Ruth was one of five former players elected to the Baseball Hall of Fame in its first year, 1936.

Even after his playing days were over, Ruth's popularity with fans of all ages never faded. He had hoped to become a manager when his career ended, but his rowdy behavior and reputation for irresponsibility discouraged any team from hiring him. Ruth nonetheless remained active in baseball, returning to stadiums regularly for Old Timers' games and never failing to receive the longest and loudest applause from the fans. Long after he had died of cancer in 1948, Ruth remained the enduring symbol of the Yankees—and of baseball.

Career Capsule

All-time leader in slugging average (.690), HR frequency (8.5 HR every 100 at bats), and walks (2,056); second all-time most HR (714), RBI (2.211), and runs scored (2,174). Holds season record highest slugging average (.847 in 1920), 1923 MVP. Had .342 career batting average and 2,873 hits. 60 HR in 1927, 50+ HR 3 other times, and 40+ HR 7 other times. 100+ RBI and 100+ walks 13 times each; 100+ runs scored 12 times. Second all-time most World Series HR (15). Began career as a pitcher; 94 career wins and 2.28 ERA. Won 20+ games 2 times; ERA leader in 1916. Played on 10 pennant winners, 7 World Series winners (3 with Boston, 4 with New York). Career span 1914–35.

Bill Tilden

February 10, 1893–June 5, 1953

THE FIRST GREAT American tennis players, Bill Tilden and **Helen Wills Moody**, were heroes in the 1920s. And "Big Bill" Tilden was the Babe Ruth of tennis. No American man has won more Grand Slam titles than Tilden.

William Tatum Tilden II was born in Philadelphia, Pennsylvania. Though Bill was physically frail, he played tennis from a very early age. Teamed with Mary Browne, he won two straight U.S. mixed doubles titles in 1913 and 1914. After these early successes, however, he did not win another major title until 1918. That year, he won the U.S. men's doubles championship with Vincent Richards.

Tilden began to make his mark as a singles player in 1918. After winning the U.S. Clay Court singles title, he lost in the finals of the U.S. National Championships. This was the first of eight straight U.S. finals in which Tilden would play. After losing in the U.S. finals again in 1919, Tilden worked relentlessly all winter on improving his backhand. The effort proved worthwhile. In 1920, already 27 years old, he won his first major singles title at Wimbledon. In doing so, he became the first American man ever to win the All-England tournament. Tennis players did not often travel abroad to play in the 1920s. Tilden did so only twice (1920 and 1921)—and won the singles title both times.

After his first win at Wimbledon, Tilden became virtually unbeatable. He was ranked number one in the world for a record-setting six years from 1920 to 1925. He ranked number one in the U.S. for the entire decade (1920–29) to set another record. He won six straight U.S. singles titles from 1920 to 1925, a streak unmatched in the 20th century. He also captured six straight U.S. Clay Court singles titles from 1922 to 1927, giving him seven for his career. Tilden was not only the best U.S. player, but also a flamboyant showman with a proven ability to draw crowds. He won most of these singles titles after losing part of the middle finger on his right hand (his playing hand). Doctors surgically removed the finger above the upper joint following an infection in 1922. Yet Tilden simply changed his grip and kept on winning.

Tilden dominated doubles play during the first half of the decade, too. From 1921 to 1923, he won three straight U.S. men's doubles titles. In 1922 and 1923, he and Molla Mallory captured the U.S. mixed doubles titles, too. This made him the first man ever to win a "triple crown" (both doubles titles and the singles title) at the U.S. Nationals two years in a row. In 1927, Tilden added two more major doubles titles: at Wimbledon and the U.S. Nationals.

Tilden also led the U.S. Davis Cup team to a record seven straight victories in the international team tournament from 1920 to 1926. In Davis Cup play, he won 13 consecutive singles matches and eight of nine doubles matches from 1920 to 1925. Although he also helped the U.S. team reach the Davis Cup finals from 1927 to 1930, France won the tournament all four years.

As captain of the U.S. team in 1928, Tilden made worldwide headlines. Tilden had earned a few dollars by writing some articles about that year's Wimbledon tournament. Since anyone who made money from the sport was ruled ineligible to play, Tilden was suspended. The United States Lawn Tennis Association (USLTA) charged him with violating his amateur status and removed him from the team. All major tournaments in the 1920s were open to amateurs only.

Tilden was ranked number one in the world for six years.

The U.S. team defeated Italy and moved into the finals against France. French tennis officials were furious. They were hosting the Davis Cup for the first time and wanted Tilden to play. So at the request of the U.S. Ambassador to France, the USLTA put Tilden back on the team. Though Tilden scored the lone U.S. victory, France won the Davis Cup, four matches to one. The USLTA then barred him from playing again that year. The suspension prevented him from playing in the 1928 U.S. Championships, where he had reached the singles final in nine of the previous ten years.

In 1929, however, he regained the U.S. singles crown. His seventh and last U.S. title tied a record held by Richard Sears (1881–87) and William Larned (1901–02 and 1907–11). The following year, at age 37, he won his last two major amateur titles: the mixed doubles championship in France and the singles crown at Wimbledon.

After losing in the U.S. semifinals in 1930, Tilden retired from amateur tennis to make a series of instructional films. Tilden had always wanted to become an actor. He spent most of his family fortune—as well as his writing fees and later his professional earnings—financing and acting in plays. He appeared in everything from Shakespeare to Dracula. Yet he never had any success on stage.

In 1931, Tilden became a touring tennis professional. He won the pro singles title in his first year and the doubles title in 1932. His stardom helped establish professional tennis, which had begun five years earlier, as a major drawing card across the nation. Soon others left the amateur ranks to play for prize money. The first great pro tennis tour in 1934 pitted 41-year-old Tilden against 33-year-old Ellsworth Vines, who won the series 47 to 26. The following year, Tilden won the pro singles title for the second time. Professional tennis tours grew in size, prize money, and popularity throughout the 1930s and 1940s. Despite his age, Tilden remained the biggest star on the tour. At 52, he won his second pro doubles title in 1945. Five years later, the Associated Press overwhelmingly voted him the greatest tennis player of the half century.

In 1953, the 60-year-old Tilden was packing for a trip to yet another tournament when he died of a heart attack. Six years later, he was inducted into the International Tennis Hall of Fame.

Career Capsule

Won 7 U.S. singles titles, 6 consecutively (1920–25, 1929) and 3 Wimbledon titles (consecutively 1920–21, 1930). Also won 6 Grand Slam doubles titles. Led U.S. to 7 consecutive Davis Cup victories (1920–26).

GLENNA COLLETT VARE

June 20, 1903–February 2, 1989

PERHAPS THE BEST American woman ever to play golf, Glenna Collett Vare helped make the sport popular during the Golden Age of Sports. During the 1920s, almost every sport seemed to have a special star and Bobby Jones and Glenna Collett shone on the golf course. They not only attracted new fans to their sports, they inspired Americans to play these games themselves.

Glenna Collett grew up in Providence, Rhode Island, in the first decades of the twentieth century. In her time, few women played sports of any kind. But Glenna loved to play baseball and tennis with her brother, and also became an excellent swimmer and diver. Her father recognized her athletic talent and encouraged her to learn golf, his favorite sport. He brought her to a local golf course where she played for the first time when she was thirteen. Glenna loved the game. Within two years, she was practicing daily, sometimes on the golf course, where the golf professional would often watch, and sometimes in her own yard.

Glenna played well in her first tournament at sixteen. She first won a tournament—Philadelphia's Berthellyn Cup—in 1921. Collett demonstrated a degree of power and accuracy from the tee unusual for women of her generation. In 1922, she won her first Women's U.S. Amateur Championship. She repeated this feat in 1925, three straight years from 1928 to 1930, and again in 1935. In all, Collett won six U.S. Amateur Championships—more than any other golfer, male or female, in history. (Her contemporary, **Bobby Jones**, won five U.S. amateur titles.) She also finished as runner-up twice (1931 and 1932). During those same two years, she came in second at the British Amateur Championships, too. In 1924, her best year, Collett entered 60 events—and won 59 of them!

Vare played only as an amateur; however, the LPGA presents a trophy in her name to a professional golfer each year. She won a total of six U.S. championships.

Stylish, refined, and reserved, Collett never got the chance to play golf professionally. In her era, no women's golf tournaments offered prize money to the winners. She competed not for money but for the thrill of victory. She also played for fun, sometimes with the game's best male golfers. Her flawless golfing form allowed her to drive the ball as far as most male golfers in spite of being smaller than they were.

After her marriage in 1931, Glenna Collett Vare played less often. She captured one last national amateur title in 1935, but her skills dropped off. In 1959, Vare won the Rhode Island State Championship at age 56. She continued to play in golf tournaments until the age of 83.

Although Vare never earned any prize money playing golf, she earned the reputation as one of the best ever to play the game. In 1952, the Ladies Professional Golf Association began awarding the Vare Trophy in her honor. The trophy goes to the golfer who compiles the lowest scoring average on the women's pro tour for the year. In 1965, Vare received the Bobby Jones Award for a lifetime of exemplary conduct on and off the links. Vare was named to the World Golf Hall of Fame in 1981. In writing two books about her greatest matches, Vare inspired and advised the next generation of female golfers. Often called the "First Lady of American Golf," Glenna Collett Vare established a place for women on the golf course.

Career Capsule

Won U.S. Women's Amateur 6 times, more than any golfer (1922, 1925, consecutively 1928–30, 1935).

Johnny Weissmuller

June 2, 1904–January 21, 1984

THE MOST FAMOUS swimmer in history, Johnny Weissmuller became a Hollywood legend in the role of Tarzan. In his swimming career, Weissmuller never lost a race, won five Olympic gold medals, and set an incredible 67 world records.

From 1921 to 1930, Weissmuller held 52 national freestyle titles at distances ranging from 100 to 880 yards. In 1922, Weissmuller became the first person ever to swim 100 meters in less than a minute (58.6 seconds). In 1924, he broke his own record for 100 meters with a time of 57.4 seconds. This record would stand for 10 years.

At the 1924 Olympics in Paris, Weissmuller won three gold medals. In both the 100-meter and 400-meter freestyle races, he set new records. His third gold medal came as the anchor (final swimmer) of the United States 4 × 200-meter freestyle relay team. The team set a new world record in the event. Weissmuller also took home a bronze medal as a member of the U.S. water polo team.

Weissmuller (right) achieved as much fame in films as in sports.

Weissmuller set two Olympic records in 1924 in the 100-meter and 400-meter freestyle races.

Four years later, in 1928, he won two more gold medals at the Olympic Games in Amsterdam, the Netherlands. He broke his own Olympic record in the 100-meter freestyle race. As the anchor and only remaining member of the 1924 freestyle relay team, he helped set another world record in the 4 × 200-meter race.

Weissmuller ended his career as an amateur swimmer in 1932. Because of his handsome features and athletic body, he was often hired to model swimsuits. This lead to his discovery by Hollywood moviemakers who cast him in the role of the fictional character, Tarzan. Over the next 20 years, Weissmuller starred in twelve Tarzan movies. He was the most famous person to ever play the role of Tarzan. In 1950, the Associated Press named Weissmuller the greatest swimmer of the first half-century.

Career Capsule

Won 3 gold medals (including 100- and 400-meter freestyle) at 1924 Olympics and 2 gold medals at 1928 Olympics.

Chapter 5

The Depression

Sports as a Great Escape

1931–1945

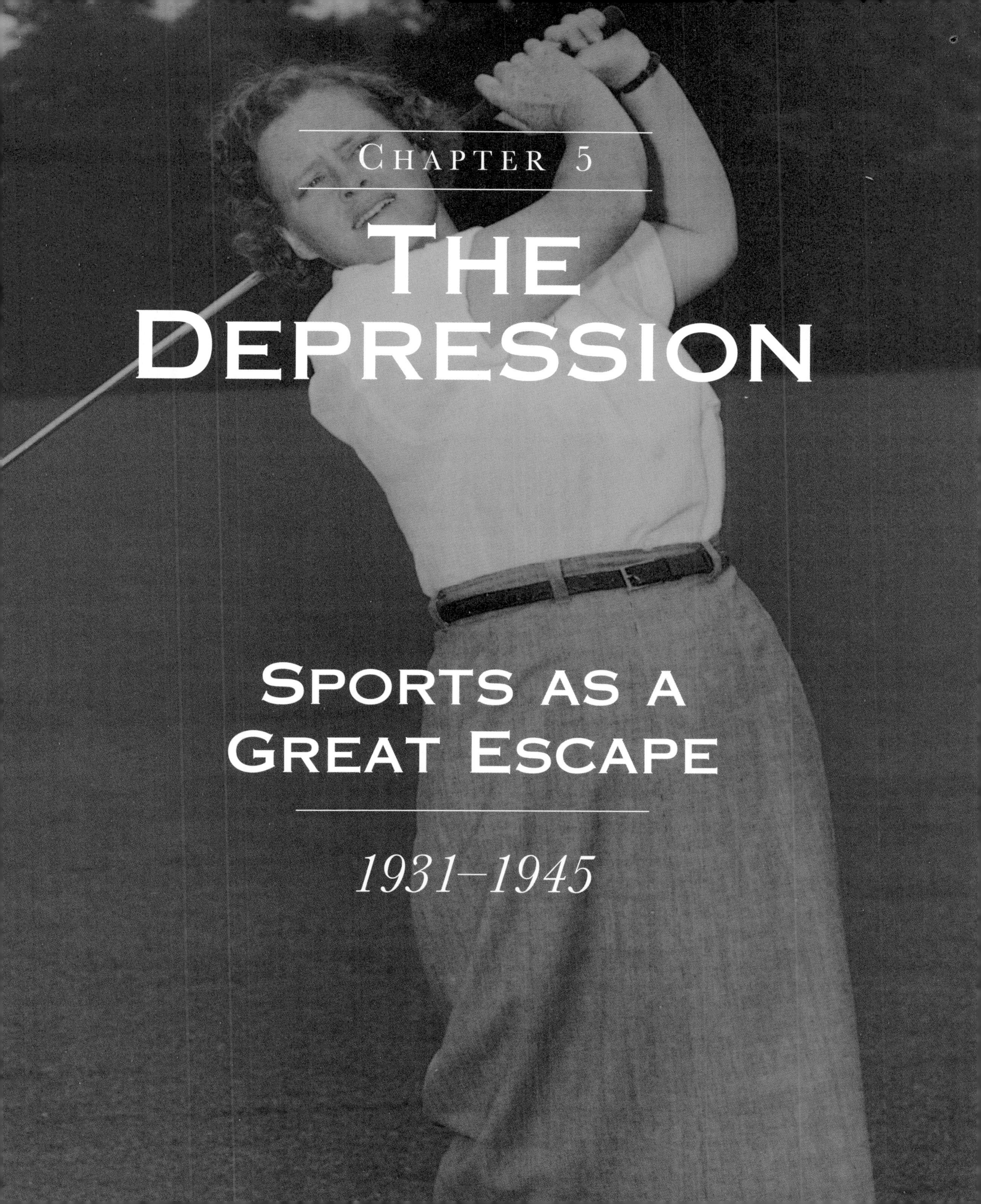

The Great Depression hit America hard. Five thousand banks failed. One out of four Americans—13 million people—lost their jobs. As crop prices fell, mortgage holders seized one out of four farms. Homeless people lived in shacks made of cardboard and discarded lumber. These communities came to be known as Hoovervilles, after President Herbert Hoover. Franklin Delano Roosevelt won a landslide victory in 1932 over Hoover, whom voters associated with hard times. Roosevelt quickly persuaded Congress to pass his New Deal legislation. These laws set up government agencies that provided relief and put eight million people to work. The Social Security Act offered financial support to the aged, the unemployed, and the disabled.

But Baseball Thrives

During the Depression, minor-league baseball entered an era of growth and stability. From 1933 through 1940, minor-league baseball grew from 14 leagues to 44. Young men who could not find regular jobs were hired to play baseball. By 1940, 20 million Americans spent their summer evenings watching baseball in minor-league ballparks. Baseball brought relief from their everyday hardships.

The radio became the information and entertainment center of most American homes. Roosevelt used the radio to speak directly to the nation in his "fireside chats." Those listening to the nation's first coast-to-coast radio news broadcast in 1937 heard the German airship *Hindenburg* explode over New Jersey. Orson Welles frightened the nation with "The War of the Worlds," a science-fiction drama.

In 1932, Jack Graney became the first athlete to become a broadcaster. Graney had played 14 years with the Cleveland Indians, compiling a lifetime .250 batting average. He was the first to broadcast "color"—to analyze the plays of the game.

Meanwhile whenever games were broadcast on the radio, attendance and interest in baseball rose. In 1938, Brooklyn Dodgers general manager Larry MacPhail brought sports broadcaster Red Barber to the microphone, and Mel Allen arrived in 1940 to became the legendary "Voice of the Yankees" for the next 30 years.

Sports offered relief from the hard realities of everyday life. More and more Americans used the athletic fields, tennis courts, baseball diamonds, and swimming pools built by the National Recreation Association.

Amateurs Compete

Winter sports got a boost when Lake Placid, New York, hosted the Winter Olympics in 1932. For the only time in history, the United States led in Winter Olympic medals. Skiing became popular, leading to a boom in trails, lifts, and resorts in New England and the Rockies. In 1936, a tour by three-time Olympic figure-skating champion Sonja Henie of Norway inspired Americans to take to the ice.

Interest in college sports remained high. Major college football bowl games began between 1935 and 1937. The first National Invitation Tournament brought the twelve best college basketball teams together in 1938. A year later, the National Collegiate Athletic Association sponsored its first championship tournament. The professional National Football League split into two divisions and staged its first championship game in 1933. Slingin' **Sammy Baugh** was the league's best player.

The Augusta National Golf Course, designed by **Bobby Jones**, opened in Georgia, and the first Masters Tournament was played there in 1934. In tennis, Californian Don Budge in 1938 became the first player ever to win the Grand Slam. He took all four major tournaments in a single year.

Baseball still dominated the professional sporting scene—and the Yankees dominated baseball. They won eight pennants and seven World Series between 1931 and 1945. The first All-Star Game in 1933 helped lift major league attendance figures that had dropped during the nation's hard times. Six years later, baseball opened its Hall of Fame—the nation's first sports museum—in Cooperstown, New York.

Blacks remained shut out of pro sports. Yet Negro League baseball became a fixture in the lives of African Americans. The Homestead Grays from Pittsburgh, led by such stars as catcher Josh Gibson—who hit perhaps 900 home runs—and first baseman Buck Leonard, dominated the Negro National League. The Grays won nine pennants from 1937 to 1945. Star pitcher **Satchel Paige** collected about 2,000 wins.

JESSE OWENS TRIUMPHS

In other sports, African-American track and field star Jesse Owens won four gold medals at the 1936 Olympic Games in Berlin, Germany, as the shadows of World War II gathered. This was an affront to Nazi claims about the superiority of non-Jewish whites, whom they called Aryans.

Following Japan's attack on Pearl Harbor in 1941, the United States joined Great Britain, France, and their allies in a war against Germany and Japan. More than 16 million Americans served in the armed forces during World War II. Among them were sports stars **Hank Greenberg**, **Joe DiMaggio**, and **Tom Harmon**.

At home, many women took the places of the men fighting abroad. The All-American Girls Professional Baseball League, formed in 1943, gave women their best opportunity ever to play organized baseball. The league lasted for 11 years. During the war, **Patty Berg** established herself as a golf legend. **Alice Marble**, the best woman doubles tennis player, worked as a spy for the United States.

For African Americans and women, the end of the war often spelled disappointment. But in their disappointment were the seeds of better things to come. Among those African Americans who served in the army was Lieutenant **Jackie Robinson**. The feats for which he would be remembered would not be military, but athletic.

After the Glory Days End:

Is There Life After Sports?

During their playing days, athletes bask in glory. Fans know their names and accomplishments. Some sports celebrities used their fame as springboards for further success. **Johnny Weissmuller** became a movie star. **Tom Harmon** became a top football sportscaster. **Patty Berg** taught at golf clinics. Quarterback **Sammy Baugh** coached for the New York Titans (later the Jets). **Hank Greenberg** became a baseball executive. Most of these opportunities were reserved for superstars.

Those athletes who achieved modest success often had to find their own way. Some took full-time jobs they had held during the off-season: as salespeople, insurance agents, bartenders. Some opened businesses. Sadly, some never found their way off the field. With few job skills and little education, they sank into poverty and sometimes alcoholism, and died alone and penniless.

Even star status did not guarantee success in later years. **Babe Ruth** couldn't get a job as a baseball manager. The hero of the 1936 Olympics, **Jesse Owens**, was forced to take a job as a playground instructor. (Fifteen years later, he achieved financial success through his own public relations business.) Free-spending **Joe Louis**, broke and in debt, unwisely returned to boxing. Tennis star **Bill Tilden** never made it in what he believed to be his true calling: acting. He squandered his tennis earnings, and his family fortune, trying to produce and star in a hit play. Personal tragedies worsened the emptiness felt by **Alice Marble** after her tennis playing days. Rocked by a miscarriage and her husband's death in World War II, she attempted suicide.

In the 1980s, athletes and former athletes created organizations to help retired athletes during hard times. The assistance and counseling that groups like the Baseball Assistance Team (B.A.T.) offer helps players and their families build new lives long after the glory days have gone.

SAMMY BAUGH 

born March 17, 1914

FOR ALL-AROUND PLAY, no football player has ever come close to the accomplishments of "Slinging Sammy" Baugh. The first great throwing quarterback in the National Football League (NFL), the Hall-of-Famer led the league in passing a record six times in 16 years as a pro. Baugh not only excelled as a quarterback, but was also the greatest punter of all time. He still holds the single-season and career records for average punting yardage. Even more, Baugh was a superb defensive back. He shares the record for most interceptions caught in a single game (4).

A two-time All-American, Baugh led Texas Christian University in 1937 to a 16-6 victory over Marquette in the very first Cotton Bowl. With the NFL's Washington Redskins, Baugh led the league in passing in 1937, his rookie season. Baugh would go on to lead the NFL in passing five more times (1940, 1943, 1945, 1947, and 1949). In 1945, he completed 70.3 percent of his pass attempts (128 of 182). This set the standard in the NFL for nearly 40 years.

The famous number 33 posed with his two sons. He was a triple threat who could pass, punt, and play defense.

As a punter, Baugh mastered the art of quick kicking, a surprise tactic in which an offensive player punts before the fourth down. Baugh would catch the defense off guard and send the ball over their heads. He led the league in punting four straight years from 1940 to 1943. In 1940, he averaged an NFL record 51.3 yards per punt. On defense, Baugh led the league in interceptions with 11 in 1943. In his first nine years, Baugh led the Redskins to five title games—and two NFL championships (1937 and 1942).

CAREER CAPSULE

Completed 1,693 passes in 2,995 attempts for a 56.5 completion percentage over 16 years. Threw for 21,886 yards and 186 touchdowns. Holds record for career punting average of 45.1 yards and highest season average of 51 yards. Led the league in passing six times and punting four times. Career span 1937–52 with Washington. All-American for three seasons at Texas Christian University.

PATTY BERG 

born February 13, 1918

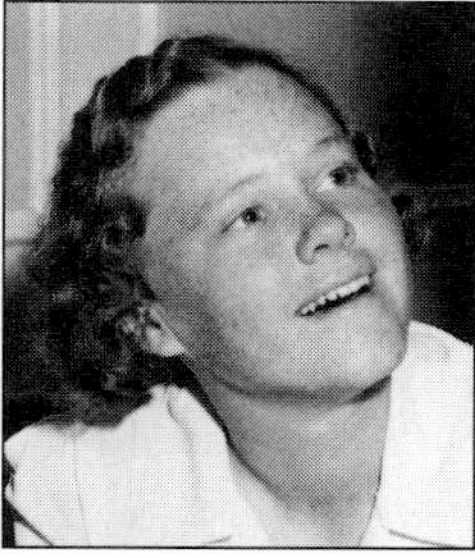

DURING HER TIME, Patty Berg was considered a tomboy. An all-around athlete, Patty won a Minnesota girls' speed-skating championship and finished third in the nationals. As a young girl, she played quarterback on a boys' football team. In high school, she ran track. But beginning in her teens, her best game was golf. An amateur and professional champion, and later founder and the first president of the Ladies Professional Golf Association (LPGA), Berg helped popularize women's golf.

A native of Minneapolis, the red-haired, freckle-faced Patty took up golf at age 12. When her father presented her younger brother with a golf club membership, Patty protested that she should get one, too. So he bought her a membership and a set of clubs. By 1935, Patty had won the first of three Minnesota State Championships. Patty reached the finals of the women's national tournament—held that year on her home course, Interlachen Country Club—before losing to **Glenna Collett Vare**.

Berg was known for her powerful drives, such as this one she hit in a 1959 tournament.

By 1938, Berg, just 20 years old, was considered the best woman golfer in the country. She won 10 of 13 tournaments entered that year, including the U.S. Amateur Championship. The Associated Press chose Berg as the Outstanding Woman Athlete of the Year, an honor she received again in 1943 and 1955.

Having won nearly 30 amateur titles, Berg turned professional in 1940. No professional golf tour for women had yet been established. Only three pro events, together offering about $500 in prize money, existed. Berg signed a contract with Wilson Sporting Goods to play exhibitions and teach at clinics and summer camps for about $7,500 a year.

In 1941, Berg won her first professional tournament, the Women's Western Open—an event she won again in 1943 and 1948. During World War II, Berg staged exhibitions for British War Relief and joined the Marine Corps Women's Reserve. The work done by women during the war led to greater acceptance of women's place in the economy. In sports, this acceptance helped create more professional opportunities for women. The first U.S. Women's National Open was held in 1946, and Berg was the event's first champion.

CAREER CAPSULE

Won first-ever Women's National Open in 1946. Founder and first president of LPGA.

ELLISON M. "TARZAN" BROWN

September 22, 1914–August 23, 1975

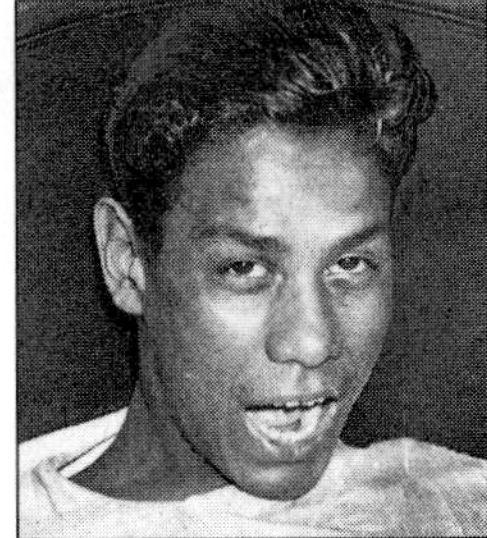

PERHAPS THE MOST COLORFUL marathoner ever, Tarzan Brown won the famed Boston Marathon twice. He also won the national amateur 25-kilometer race championships in both 1935 and 1938.

Born in Ashaway, Rhode Island, Ellison M. Brown was a member of the Narragansett tribe. He may have gotten the nickname Tarzan because he spent so much time in the woods as a boy. Tarzan first gained attention as a marathoner in 1935 in bizarre fashion. His mother had died just two days before the Boston Marathon. To honor her, he created a racing tunic from tatters of one of her dresses. Brown's shoes fell apart after 20 miles, forcing him to run barefoot for the last six miles. Despite all this, he finished a respectable 13th.

The following year, Brown was leading the Boston Marathon when John A. Kelley, the 1935 winner, caught up to him at the 21-mile mark. "Nice going, Tarzan," Kelley laughed, patting

Brown's bottom as he passed. The taunt revived Brown, who roared back and won easily in 2 hours, 33 minutes, and 40 seconds. Later that year, Brown won the New York Marathon in Port Chester in 2:36:57. Immediately after the race, he took an all-night train to Manchester, New Hampshire. That same day, he won the New England Championship in 2:45:52. This gave him an unprecedented two marathon victories in 30 hours!

The 1937 Boston Marathon took place on a sweltering hot day. Brown ran among the leaders until he arrived in suburban Natick. There, he abruptly jumped into Lake Cochituate. While he cooled off, he waved good-bye to the other runners. Eventually, he climbed out to finish 31st in the race. Two years later, Brown won his second Boston Marathon, setting a new record of 2:28:51.

Career Capsule

Winner of the 1936 and 1939 Boston Marathons, twice broke the world marathon record. Ran and won two marathons on consecutive days and was twice U.S. 25-kilometer champion.

Lou Gehrig

June 19, 1903–June 2, 1941

"I MAY HAVE BEEN GIVEN a bad break," Lou Gehrig admitted, "but I have an awful lot to live for. All in all, I can say on this day that I consider myself the luckiest man on the face of the earth." The words of the dying man echoed through Yankee Stadium, moving nearly 62,000 fans to tears. After 14 seasons, the legendary first baseman had been forced off the playing field in 1939 by a debilitating disease that now bears his name. Just two years later, Gehrig would be dead.

Today, Gehrig is best remembered as the "Iron Horse." He played in 2,130 consecutive games—a record that would last 56 years before **Cal Ripken, Jr.**, surpassed it. Yet Gehrig was more than just durable. Throughout most of Gehrig's career, he was overshadowed by his larger-than-life teammate **Babe Ruth**. But Gehrig, hitting cleanup behind Ruth, helped make the big man an even better slugger. Few opposing pitchers wanted to pitch around Ruth to get to Gehrig. For Gehrig was a brilliant hitter and worthy slugger in his own right. He hit .340 lifetime, drove in 1,990 runs, and holds the career record for most grand slams (23).

The "Iron Horse" had a career batting average of .340.

Gehrig and Ruth, slugging Yankee teammates for ten full seasons, could not have been more different. While Ruth was flashy, boastful, and loud, Gehrig was shy, modest, and reserved. Yet Gehrig, like Ruth, was one of the best-liked players in the game. He earned a reputation for honesty, reliability, and good humor.

Born in the Bronx, New York, Lou was the only one of his four siblings to survive childhood. Lou first played baseball with the members of Columbia University's Sigma Nu fraternity, where his mother worked as a cook and his father as a handyman. In 1920, he helped his Commerce High School team win the New York City public school championship. Later, in a game against Chicago's best high school team, Gehrig cracked a ninth-inning grand slam to put Commerce in the lead for good. After high school, he starred for the Columbia University baseball team and also played on the football team.

In a brief stay with the Yankees in 1923, Gehrig hit .423 with 9 RBIs in just 13 games. Yet Miller

In 1927, Gehrig batted .373, had a slugging average of .765, hit 52 doubles, 47 home runs, and was the league's MVP.

Huggins, the Yankee manager, wanted him to get some more experience in the minor leagues. So Gehrig was sent to Hartford, Connecticut, where he batted .304 and .369 in two seasons. Back with the Yankees on June 1, 1925, Gehrig pinch hit for Pee Wee Wanninger and singled. The next day, he started in place of first baseman Wally Pipp. This began the streak that would span more than 13 seasons.

Gehrig remained in the lineup for good reason. Beginning in 1926, he had at least 100 runs scored and 100 RBIs for a record 13 straight years. He also batted over .300 for the first 12 of those years.

Gehrig had his first great season as a member of the 1927 Yankee lineup known as "Murderers' Row." Every hitter was dangerous. Gehrig batted .373 with 52 doubles and 47 home runs (second only to Ruth's 60 that year). He had a slugging average of .765—the fourth best figure in baseball history, yet still behind Ruth's .772 that year. Gehrig led the league with 175 RBIs and won the league's Most Valuable Player (MVP) award.

After losing the World Series to the St. Louis Cardinals in seven games in 1926, the Yanks swept the 1927 and 1928 World Series. Gehrig's best series came in 1928. He batted .545—second all-time only to Ruth's .625 the same year. He set a record for a four-game series with 9 RBIs—more than the entire Cardinal team. In just four games, he hit four home runs. His slugging average was an unapproachable 1.727—an average of almost two bases per at bat! (The next best in World Series history is just 1.273.)

In 1931, Gehrig tied with Ruth for the league lead in home runs with 46. He also led the league with 163 runs scored and an American League (AL) record 184 RBIs. Gehrig was named the league's MVP for the second time. The following year, he accomplished something that Ruth never did: He hit four consecutive home runs in a single game. In

Gehrig was the 1934 Triple Crown winner, leading the league in batting average, home runs, and RBIs. He was a dependable fielder at first base as well as a dangerous hitter.

the World Series, his .529 hitting and 8 RBIs led the Yankees to a four-game sweep over the Chicago Cubs.

Gehrig won the only batting title of his career in 1934, when he hit .363. He also led the league in home runs (49) and RBIs (165) to win the AL Triple Crown. Two years later, Gehrig scored 167 runs, second best in this century behind—who else?—Ruth's 177 in 1921. Gehrig's 152 RBIs, .354 batting average, and league-leading 49 homers earned him his third MVP award.

In 1938, Gehrig's average dipped to .295, the lowest of his career. The Yankees won their third straight World Series title—and the sixth in seven appearances in Gehrig's career. Yet Gehrig batted only .286 in the series and failed to drive in a single run.

After just eight games in 1939, Gehrig—batting just .143—took himself out of the lineup. His teammates, sportswriters, and fans could all see that Gehrig had lost something. One month later, he discovered he had amyotrophic lateral sclerosis (ALS).

This disease hardens the spinal cord and cuts off pathways for nerves. Gehrig's ALS had already begun to paralyze some parts of his body. Gehrig was forced to retire at age 35.

On July 4, 1939, nearly 62,000 fans crowded into Yankee Stadium for Lou Gehrig Appreciation Day. Showered with gifts and surrounded by Ruth and other teammates, Gehrig delivered his heart-wrenching "luckiest man" speech. After the season ended, a special election made Gehrig the youngest man ever inducted into the Baseball Hall of Fame.

Career Capsule

Played in 2,130 consecutive games, all-time leader in grand slam home runs (23), third in RBIs (1,990) and slugging average (.632). MVP in 1927 and 1936 and won Triple Crown (home runs, batting average, and RBIs) in 1934. Career batting average of .340 and hit 493 home runs. Had over 100 RBIs 13 consecutive seasons, led the league in RBIs five times and in home runs three times. Played on seven World Series winners with the Yankees. Career span 1923–39.

Hank Greenberg

January 1, 1911–September 4, 1986

IN THE FALL OF 1948, Detroit Tigers slugger Hank Greenberg had a conflict of faith. The Tigers had gone into a tailspin and had almost squandered their lead over the New York Yankees. Greenberg's hitting had started to turn the team around again. In the middle of the heated pennant race, the Jewish high holidays were coming up—and Greenberg had never before played ball on the holidays. After consulting a rabbi, Greenberg decided to play on Rosh Hashanah (the Jewish New Year), but

Greenberg was one of baseball's first great Jewish players.

Greenberg won the MVP award in 1935 and 1940.

pray on the more somber Yom Kippur (the Day of Atonement). Although the Tigers lost on Yom Kippur, Greenberg's 10th-inning shot on Rosh Hashanah won the game—and helped lead the Tigers to the World Series.

One of the first great Jewish ballplayers, Hank Greenberg was one of the most powerful right-handed hitters ever to play baseball. The third of five children of Romanian immigrants, Hank was born in New York City, where he lived with his parents until his marriage at age 35. As a boy, he played baseball eight hours a day in the summer months until high school, when he began driving a truck for his father's textile company. After one semester at New York University, Hank dropped out to join the Detroit Tigers.

In 1933, his rookie season, the first baseman hit .301 and drove in 87 runs. The following year he led the league with an impressive total of 63 doubles. He batted .339, smashed 26 home runs, and drove in 139 runs to lead the Tigers to the World Series. In the series, Greenberg's .321 average and 7 RBIs were not enough as the Cardinals won in seven games.

In 1935, Greenberg led the league in homers (36) and RBIs (170). The .328 hitter was named the league's Most Valuable Player (MVP). In the World Series, he hit a two-run shot to help the Tigers win the second game, but broke his wrist later in the game and had to sit out the rest of the series. The Tigers nonetheless won the series over the Chicago Cubs, 4 games to 2.

Greenberg missed most of the 1936 season after breaking his wrist again in the Tigers' 12th game. But he came back stronger than ever. In 1937, he drove 183 runs home, falling just one RBI short of **Lou Gehrig**'s league record. Hammerin' Hank belted out 103 extra-base hits (40 homers, 14 triples, 49 home runs), fourth best of all time. The following year, Greenberg became the first player to challenge **Babe Ruth**'s single-season home run record of 60. Though he failed to connect in the final five games of the season, he finished with 58. He led the league in scoring (144) and was second in RBIs (146). In 1940, Greenberg won his second MVP award. He led the league with 41 homers, 50 doubles, 150 RBIs, and .670 slugging average—the seventh straight year in which he had slugged over .600. Despite Greenberg's .357 batting average and six RBIs, the Tigers lost the World Series to the Reds in seven games.

In the prime of his career, Greenberg became the first American League player drafted into the U.S. Army as the nation prepared for its entry into World War II. He was released due to his age (30) on December 5, 1941—just two days before the Japanese attack on Pearl Harbor. Greenberg immediately reapplied for active duty.

After missing four and a half seasons, he returned in time to lead the Tigers back to the World Series in 1945. In half a season, he cracked 13 homers and knocked in 60 runs. Greenberg's grand slam on the final day of the season gave the Tigers the pennant. He then led the team with 2 homers, 7 runs, and 7 RBIs to help the Tigers edge the Cubs in seven games in the World Series.

In 1946, Greenberg led the league in home runs (44) and RBIs (127), each for the fourth time. After the season, he applied for the job of Tigers' general manager. Instead, the Tigers' owner had him shipped to the Pittsburgh Pirates. Though the Pirates made Greenberg the first $100,000 player in the National League, he played just one more season before retiring.

In 1949, Greenberg became director of the Cleveland Indians' minor-league operations. He later bought a share in the team ownership and served as its general manager. In 1957, a year after his election to the Baseball Hall of Fame, Greenberg urged the team's board of directors to move the team to Los Angeles before the Dodgers did. The board instead voted to sell the club to a local banker, forcing Greenberg out. Although he briefly became a part owner of the Chicago White Sox in 1959, Greenberg retired from the front office in 1960.

Career Capsules

Hit 331 career home runs (58 in 1938) and was MVP in 1935 and 1941. League leader in home runs and RBIs four times each and had over 100 RBIs seven times. In four World Series, he batted .318, slugged .624, hit 5 home runs, and knocked in 22 runs in just 23 games. Career span 1933–41, 1945–47.

Tom Harmon

September 28, 1919–March 17, 1990

Tom Harmon is usually remembered as a sportscaster. But his media career was built on an award-winning college football career and his heroism as a fighter pilot in World War II.

Born in Gary, Indiana, Thomas D. Harmon grew up to be 6 feet tall and 195 pounds. Tom combined speed, agility, and great ball-handling skill to become an All-American at the University of Michigan.

In 24 college games, Harmon carried the ball 398 times for 2,134 yards, averaging 5.4 yards per carry. He also completed 101 of 233 pass attempts for 1,399 yards. He scored 33 touchdowns—two more than the legendary **Red Grange** had scored for the University of Illinois in the mid-1920s—and threw for 16 more. In addition, Harmon kicked 33 extra points and connected for two field goals. He scored 237 points in his career. As a rusher and passer, Harmon averaged 147 yards per game for a total of 3,533 yards. A good offensive blocker and efficient defensive tackler, Harmon also punted for the Wolverines.

As passer and runner, Harmon averaged 147 yards per game.

Legendary coach **Amos Alonzo Stagg** considered him the best football player of all time. "I'll take Harmon on my team," he said, "and you can have the rest." Selected for All-American teams in 1939 and 1940, Harmon won both the Heisman Trophy and the Maxwell Trophy—each given annually to college football's best player—in his senior year. He also won the Walter Camp Trophy, presented to the nation's outstanding halfback. The Associated Press named him Male Athlete of the Year in 1940.

Harmon saved his best for last. In his final college game against arch-rival Ohio State, Harmon stole the show. He ran for three touchdowns, passed for two more, kicked four extra points, and averaged more than 50 yards a punt. The Wolverines romped to a 40–0 victory.

In 1941, the Chicago Bears made Harmon the number one draft pick in the nation. But Harmon

At the University of Michigan, Harmon scored 237 career points.

had no intention of pursuing a pro football career. He did earn $1,500 by playing in one game for the New York Americans in a rival pro league. But he wanted to become a radio sports announcer more than he wanted to play. The handsome All-American first went to Hollywood, where he starred in "Harmon of Michigan," the story of his life. Though the movie flopped, Harmon earned enough to buy his parents a house in Ann Arbor, Michigan.

Later that year, the Japanese bombed Pearl Harbor, and the United States entered World War II. Harmon enlisted in the Army Air Corps. As a fighter pilot, he was twice missing in action. In 1943, his plane crashed into the jungle in Suriname (then called Dutch Guiana). He survived for four days in the swamps and rain forests before his rescue. Later that same year, Harmon bailed out of a crashing plane after it had been shot down. This time, Harmon was stranded in China (at that time under the control of Japan) for 32 days. Friendly Chinese finally smuggled him through enemy territory. His heroics earned Harmon both a Silver Star and a Purple Heart.

In 1946, the government presented the returning war hero with an overdue tax bill for $7,000—based on his earnings from the 1941 movie. To make some money, Harmon decided to go pro. He played with the Los Angeles Rams for only two seasons (1946–47). Sadly, leg injuries sustained during the war had stripped him of the speed and power he had displayed in his college years. After his retirement as a player, Harmon became a successful radio and television sportscaster, mostly in the Los Angeles area. His son, Mark, starred as a quarterback on the UCLA football team and then went on to become a successful movie and TV actor.

Career Capsule

Won Heisman Trophy in 1940 with the University of Michigan where he led the nation in scoring and was named All-American in 1939–40. Earned a Silver Star and a Purple Heart as a World War II fighter pilot. Played in NFL with Los Angeles 1946–47.

Joe Louis

May 13, 1914–April 12, 1981

Joe Louis, "The Brown Bomber," was the longest reigning heavyweight champion in boxing history. He dominated other boxers with his lightning-quick hands, his punishing left jab, and his crushing left hook. Louis held the title against all challengers for over eleven years.

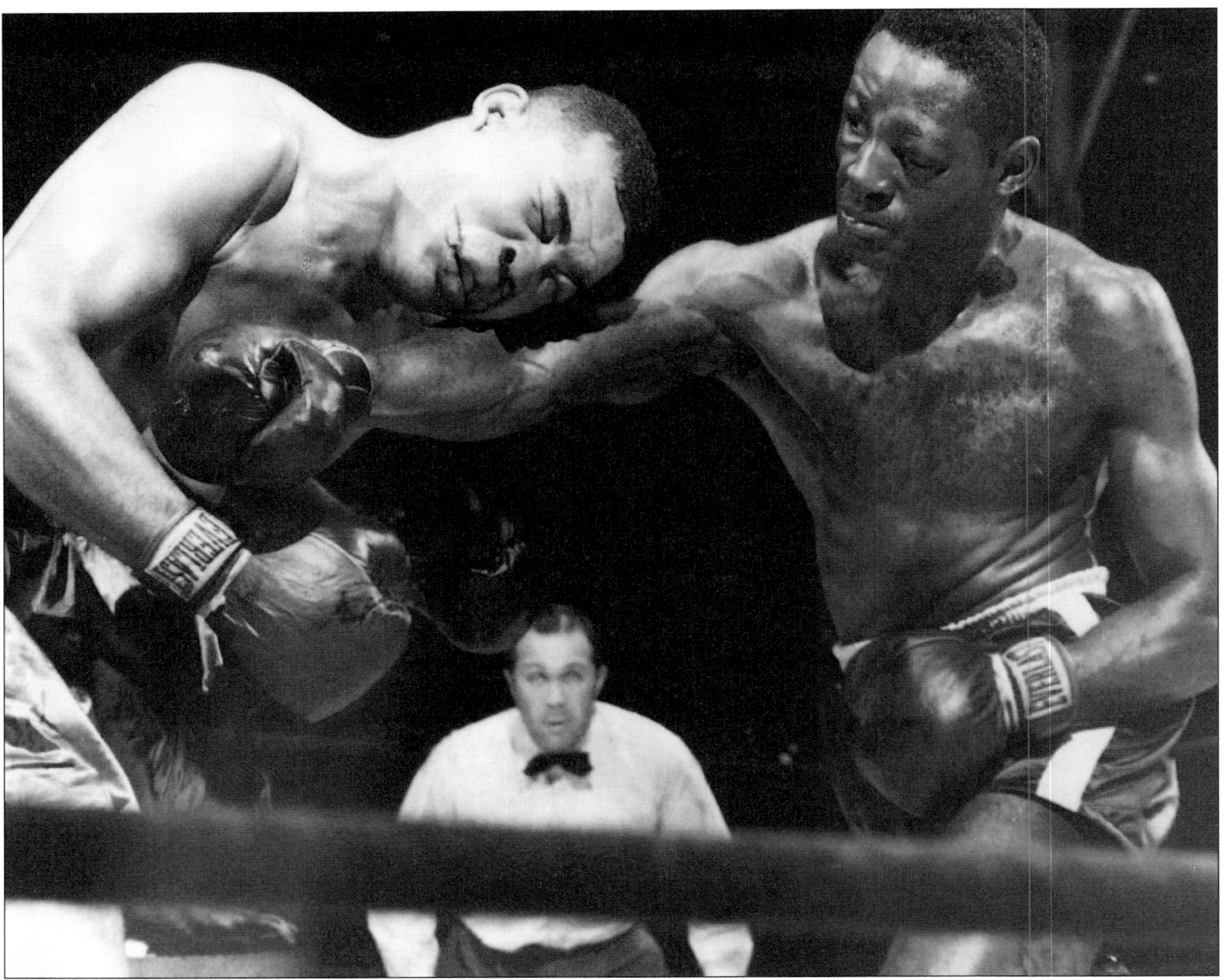

Even winning could be painful as Louis took a right from Ezzard Charles.

Joseph Louis Barrow, the eighth child of a cotton sharecropper, was born outside Lafayette, Alabama. Joe's father died when he was two. Throughout his childhood, Joe did odd jobs to help the family make ends meet, leaving little time for school. After his mother remarried and moved the family to Detroit, Michigan, Joe worked on an ice wagon (delivering ice in the days when few families had refrigerators) and in an auto factory. He later studied carpentry, intending to become a cabinet maker.

Joe first came to national attention in 1934, when he won the national Amateur Athletic Union light heavyweight title. Standing 6 feet, 1½ inches tall and weighing 200 pounds, Louis already displayed awesome punching power although barely out of his teens. He had won 50 of his 54 amateur fights, 43 by knockouts. Having won the amateur championship, Louis decided to turn pro.

Louis made a powerful first impression, connecting for a first-round knockout in his professional debut. Over the next two years, he won 27 consecutive bouts, 23 of them by knockout. Two of the boxers he knocked out were former heavyweight champions Primo Carnera and Max Baer. In 1935, he earned more than $350,000 from his 14 fights—a huge amount during the Great Depression. The Associated Press voted him Athlete of the Year, making him the first African American to receive this honor.

In 1936, Louis squared off against another former heavyweight champion, Germany's Max Schmeling. Surprisingly, Schmeling knocked down Louis in the fourth round and finished him off in the twelfth round with a right-hand blow to Louis' chin. The upset was the first loss in Louis' professional career.

Two months later, Louis quickly restored his status as a heavyweight contender by knocking out former champ Jack Sharkey in the third round. Six more victories, five of them by knockout, set the stage for a championship bout with James J. Braddock.

The title bout took place in Chicago on June 22, 1937. Braddock stunned Louis early, knocking him off his feet in the first round. But Louis bounced back up. In the eighth round, Louis knocked out the champion to win the world heavyweight crown.

After winning his first three title defenses, Louis faced a rematch with Schmeling in 1938. Since their first fight, Nazi Germany's infamous leader, Adolf Hitler, had touted Schmeling as an ideal example of racial purity. Schmeling himself heightened racial tensions with some ill-advised insults directed toward Americans, especially blacks. An enraged Louis charged out from his corner at the opening bell. Within a minute, he had knocked down the German boxer three times. The fight ended with Schmeling on the canvas in just two minutes and four seconds—at the time, the second fastest knockout in a heavyweight championship bout. Louis, who earned nearly $350,000 for the two-minute fight, had now knocked out all five heavyweight champions of the 1930s.

After boxing, Louis tried professional wrestling briefly.

Louis enlisted in the Army during World War II. Over the next four years in service, he fought 96 bouts.

After defeating Schmeling, Louis crushed all challengers. In 1939, he scored four knockouts. In 1940, he beat four challengers, three by knockouts. Most of his opponents were now afraid to even get into the ring with him. Psyched out from the start, they had no chance of winning. Louis demonstrated unshakable confidence in the ring. "After I won the title," he once recalled, "I didn't think about [the possibility of losing]. Oh, I knew that if I kept on fighting, some guy would come along and take the title away from me, but not this guy, never tonight."

At the end of 1940, Louis launched what reporters called his "Bum of the Month" tour. He defended his title at the unprecedented rate of nearly once a month. Louis had beaten six "bums" in six months when he faced light heavyweight Billy Conn in 1941. Many sportswriters thought Conn would be too swift for Louis. The champion silenced his doubters by warning, "He can run, but he can't hide." Yet Louis very nearly lost the fight. Conn jabbed and dodged for 12 rounds. But in the 13th, he unwisely gave up his winning strategy and decided to go for a knockout. Attempting to slug it out with the champ, Conn was floored before the round was over.

The bombing of Pearl Harbor brought the United States into World War II in December 1941. Louis immediately joined the U.S. Army. Over the next four years, he boxed in 96 exhibition bouts and made numerous public appearances to entertain the troops. He also won two title fights, both by knockout. The fights raised more than $80,000 for the Army and Navy relief funds.

Returning to the professional ring in 1946, Louis scored two knockouts. In 1947, Louis nearly lost his title, but won a hard-fought 15-round decision over Jersey Joe Walcott. Louis then knocked out Walcott in the 11th round of their 1948 rematch, his 25th and last title defense. Nine months later, Louis announced his retirement after 11 years and 9 months as the heavyweight champion.

Though Louis made millions of dollars as a boxer, he squandered much of it through big spending, unwise investments, generosity, and drinking in clubs and bars. Shortly after his retirement, the U.S. government told him that he owed more than one million dollars in taxes. Desperate for money, Louis returned to the ring in 1950. He lost a 15-round decision to new champion Ezzard Charles. His final fight came in 1951. Future heavyweight champion Rocky Marciano knocked Louis out in the eighth round.

After his retirement, Louis briefly tried a career as a wrestler. In the 1960s, he tried, unsuccessfully, to establish an interracial chain of food stores with Billy Conn and struggled to overcome a cocaine addiction. In his later years, Louis—still popular 20 years after giving up the crown—worked as a celebrity greeter in Las Vegas casinos and made countless other public appearances.

Career Capsule

Held the world heavyweight crown for a record 11 years and 9 months, from June 1937 through March 1949. Won 63 of 66 fights, 49 by knockout, and successfully defended his title a record 25 times.

Alice Marble

September 28, 1913–December 13, 1990

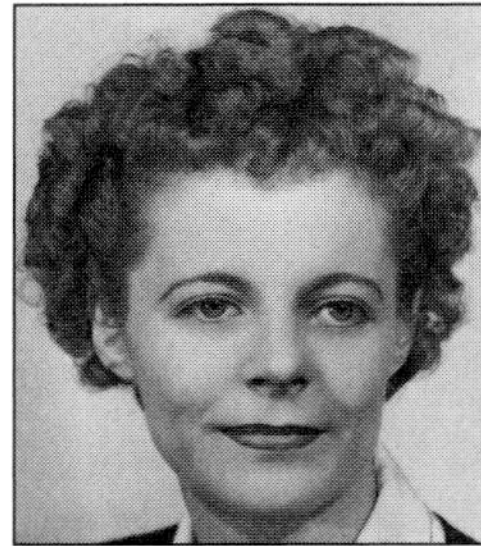

In the 1930s, Alice Marble introduced a revolutionary new style that would forever change the game of women's tennis: the serve-and-volley game. Prior to the 1930s, virtually all women tennis players stayed near the baseline during matches. Yet the generations who followed Marble embraced the new, aggressive power game she had championed. A devastating doubles player, Marble won 18 Grand Slam titles, 13 of them in doubles.

The daughter of a California cattle rancher, Alice grew up in San Francisco, where she was a fan of the city's minor-league baseball team, the San Francisco Seals. She often played catch with Seals players, such as **Joe DiMaggio**. Her parents, however, urged her to take up tennis, considering it more suitable for a girl. Alice began playing tennis on city courts at age 15. Her quick feet, excellent coordination, and keen athletic skills made her a formidable young player. However, since she did not have a coach during those early years, she had not yet learned to hit ground strokes properly. This flaw in her game caused her to rush the net and try to cut off her opponents' attempts to hit the ball past her. In time, this weakness became a strength. She became the best serve-and-volley woman player.

Marble's picture-perfect form enabled her to dominate women's tennis. Years later, Billie Jean King took lessons from Marble, learning her strong serve-and-volley style of play.

In 1930, Marble finally got a coach: Eleanor "Teach" Tennant. Though she greatly improved her baseline ground strokes, Marble retained the big serve and aggressive volley as her standard style of play. By 1933, Marble already ranked third in the United States. That year, however, in an East Hampton, New York, tournament, she played the semifinals and finals of the singles and doubles—four matches and an incredible 108 games—in a single day. Marble collapsed afterward. A year later, she collapsed again, this time on the court during a tournament in France. Variously diagnosed as having anemia, tuberculosis, a gall bladder disorder, or sunstroke, she was warned by her doctors never to play again.

Marble, however, would not quit. She recovered from her illness through a program of diet and exercise—including lots of tennis—and came back with a bang in 1936. At Forest Hills, New York, she won her first two Grand Slam titles: the U.S. singles championship and the mixed doubles title. She quickly regained her ranking as the number one player in the nation from 1936 to 1940.

For those five years, Marble dominated the U.S. and Wimbledon tournaments—especially in doubles matches. She won four straight U.S. women's doubles championships from 1937 to 1940 and three consecutive U.S. mixed doubles titles from 1938 to 1940. She also won the singles championship during those three years, giving her three U.S. "triple crowns" (both doubles titles and the singles championship) in a row!

Marble also performed well at Wimbledon. From 1937 to 1939, she won three straight mixed doubles titles in the All-England Championships. She also won two women's doubles titles in a row (1938 and 1939). Marble won a triple crown at Wimbledon by winning the 1939 singles title, too. By now, she ranked number one in the world and was twice named Female Athlete of the Year by the Associated Press (1939 and 1940).

World War II caused the suspension of the English, French, and Australian championship matches. Marble decided to turn professional, playing exhibition matches against Britain's Mary Hardwick while touring the country. (No professional tennis tour yet existed.) The end of her amateur career prevented her from competing in any more major tournaments, since all of them remained amateur events until 1968.

In 1944, Marble lost a child to a miscarriage. Later that year, she learned that her husband, army captain Joe Crowley, had died when his plane had been shot down over Germany. In despair, Marble attempted suicide, but was discovered by Teach Tennant in time to save her.

A year later, U.S. military intelligence recruited Marble as a spy. The Nazis, fearing they would lose the war, were beginning to smuggle stolen treasures out of the country. Working undercover, Marble reacquainted herself with Hans Steinmetz, a Swiss banker she had dated before the war. When he invited her to stay in his palatial mansion, she quickly accepted. Three weeks later, she found his private vault. There, she discovered stockpiles of gold bars, jewelry, paintings, and currency. She also found—and photographed—a ledger that listed the names of the prominent Nazis who had entrusted their stolen fortunes to Steinmetz. She barely escaped alive after being shot in the back by a double agent.

In 1950, Alice Marble wrote an impassioned editorial for *American Lawn Tennis* magazine. She urged the United States Lawn Tennis Association to invite **Althea Gibson** to play in the national championships. "If she is refused a chance to succeed or to fail," Marble wrote, "then there is an ineradicable mark against a game to which I have devoted much of my life, and I would be bitterly ashamed." One month later, the USLTA took her advice. Marble thus played an important role in breaking down the racial barrier that kept African Americans from playing in major tennis tournaments. For her many contributions to the game, Marble was inducted into the International Tennis Hall of Fame in 1964.

CAREER CAPSULE

The pioneer of the serve-and-volley game, Marble won 18 Grand Slam titles, including 13 in mixed or women's doubles. Was named Female Athlete of the Year by the Associated Press in 1939 and 1940.

JESSE OWENS 

September 12, 1913–March 31, 1980

WINNING FOUR GOLD MEDALS in track-and-field events at the 1936 Olympics ranks as one of the greatest athletic performances in Olympic history. Yet Jesse Owens' athletic feats become even more heroic when considered in the context of time and place. The Olympic Games that year took place in Berlin, Germany. For three years, Germany had been ruled by Adolf Hitler and the National Socialist (Nazi) Party. Hitler believed that what he called Aryans—Christian German and Nordic peoples—were superior to Jews, Africans, Asians, and gypsies. The Nazis had already begun rounding up non-Aryans—primarily Jews and gypsies—in Germany and neighboring countries and forcing

Part of Owens' success was due to his ability to stay low at the start of sprint races.

them into Dachau, Buchenwald, and other concentration camps. Hitler's goal was to make Germany a purely Aryan empire. He planned to use the 1936 Olympic Games to demonstrate Aryan supremacy to the world. Instead, Owens, a black man, showed the world that white supremacy was a lie. In this way, his Olympic victories had an impact that reached far beyond the arena to the worldwide political stage. Through it all, Owens maintained his grace and dignity.

One of seven children, James Cleveland Owens was born in Danville, Alabama. The grandson of slaves and son of sharecroppers, James picked cotton from the time he was seven. When he was nine years old, the family moved to Cleveland, Ohio. James got his nickname from a schoolteacher who asked the new student his name. When he replied, "J.C.," she thought he had said, "Jesse."

Jesse, who ran his first race at age 13, pumped gas and delivered groceries while attending East Technical High School. In high school, he became a nationally known sprinter. In 1933, he set national high school records in the 100-yard dash, the 220-yard dash, and the broad jump at the National Interscholastic Championships in Chicago. When he graduated, 28 colleges recruited him, offering athletic scholarships. Instead, Jesse chose to attend

Ohio State University in Columbus, even though the school had not offered him a scholarship. He wanted to stay close to home. Jesse paid his own tuition by working nights as an elevator operator for $100 a month. He later worked as a page in the Ohio state legislature.

On the Ohio State track team, Owens—fast, graceful, and a great jumper—became known as the "Ebony Antelope." Owens first gained worldwide attention at the 1935 Big Ten track-and-field championships in Ann Arbor, Michigan. A week before the championships, Owens had fallen down a flight of stairs while wrestling with a fellow fraternity member. He had injured his back so badly that he could not get dressed by himself. He could not get into or out of a car without help. On the day of the track meet, Owens did not warm up or even stretch. Yet when the competition began, Owens performed brilliantly. In a single day, he set or equaled six world track-and-field records—a feat no other athlete has ever matched. Owens ran 100 yards in 9.4 seconds to equal the world record. His only attempt at the long jump measured 26 feet, $8\frac{1}{4}$ inches—exceeding the old mark by six inches. He then ran the 220-yard dash in 20.3 seconds—a new world record. (This also broke the mark for the 200-meter dash, which is almost four feet shorter than 220 yards.) Finally, Owens became the first athlete ever to run the 220-yard low hurdles in less than 23 seconds. (His time, 22.6 seconds, also broke the record for the shorter 200-meter hurdles.) Five new world records had been set and one equaled—in about 45 minutes. His world record in the long jump would remain unbroken until 1960—making it the longest lasting (more than 25 years) record in track-and-field history. The crowd was stunned by Owens' perfor-

In 1935, Owens tied the world record for 100 yards at Ohio State. That same day, he set or equaled six world records.

mance. Tug Wilson, Commissioner of the Big Ten Conference, remarked, "He is a floating wonder, just like he had wings."

After the Olympic broad jump, Owens mounted the victory stand.

At the 1936 Olympic trials, Owens won the 100-meter and 200-meter sprints as well as the long jump. This performance guaranteed him a trip to Berlin for the 1936 Olympic Games.

Of the 66 athletes on the U.S. Olympic Track Team, ten were black. The Nazis scorned the U.S. team's reliance on athletes from what they called an inferior race. Yet those ten black athletes won six of the 11 individual gold medals won by the U.S. team. Owens won gold medals in both the 100- and 200-meter sprints, the long jump, and as leadoff runner for the U.S. 4 × 100-meter relay team. In three of these events, he set new Olympic records. In the fourth (the 100 meters), he tied the Olympic record.

In the final heat of the 100-meter sprint, Owens tied the Olympic mark of 10.3 seconds to defeat U.S. teammate Ralph Metcalfe by one-tenth of a second.

The next day, Owens almost failed to qualify for the broad jump. Having fouled on his previous attempts, he had one more chance to qualify. German contestant Luz Long—a true sportsman who rejected Nazi propaganda—then offered Owens some advice: To avoid fouling, Owens should make sure to jump a couple of inches *before* reaching the end of the takeoff board. That way he wouldn't cross the line and foul, yet the one or two inches he would sacrifice on his jump would not eliminate him from competition in the final round. The strategy worked. When Owens later won the event with a jump of 26 feet, $5\frac{1}{2}$ inches, Long—the silver medalist—was the first to congratulate him. Owens later wrote, "You can melt down all the medals and cups I have, and they wouldn't be a plating on the 24-carat friendship I felt for Luz Long at that moment."

The next day, Owens set another Olympic mark: 20.7 seconds in the 200-meter sprint. He beat Mack Robinson, the older brother of **Jackie Robinson**, by four yards.

The relay was marked by some controversy. Not until the morning of the race were Owens and Metcalfe named to the relay team. They replaced Marty Glickman and Sam Stoller, the only Jews on the U.S. Track Team and the only members of the team who did not get a chance to compete in the Olympics. U.S. officials seemed to be going out of their way to avoid offending their Nazi hosts. Nonetheless, the makeshift relay team set a new world record of 39.8 seconds.

The four gold medals Owens won at a single Olympiad went unmatched until **Carl Lewis** won the same four events in 1984. Owens' 200-meter time and the relay team's time remained Olympic records until 1956. His 100-meter time and his broad jump distance were the Olympic standards until 1960.

Like Luz Long, most German citizens greeted Owens warmly. People crowded around the Olympic hero to ask for his autograph or to take pictures of him. Hitler, however, who attended the games, did not congratulate any of the black gold medalists from the United States. Asked if the snub bothered him, Owens cracked, "It was all right with me. I didn't go to Berlin to shake hands with him, anyway."

Owens became a world symbol of the struggle against tyranny and racism, not only abroad but at home. He received a hero's welcome on his return.

Cleveland and New York staged ticker-tape parades in his honor. Yet doors of acceptance and opportunity did not open. "I came back to my native country," Owens later recalled, "and I couldn't ride in the front of the bus. I had to go to the back door. I couldn't live where I wanted."

The Associated Press recognized Owens as Male Athlete of the Year in 1936. But he did not receive that year's Sullivan Award, given by the Amateur Athletic Union (A.A.U.) to the nation's best amateur athlete. The A.A.U. had suspended Owens for refusing to run in a scheduled meet in Sweden.

Owens later became a playground instructor in Cleveland. He appeared in countless paid public exhibitions: racing against cars, trucks, motorcycles, horses, and dogs. He also toured for a while with basketball's Harlem Globetrotters.

In the 1950s, Owens opened his own public relations and marketing business. He arranged his own public-speaking appearances. Owens gave two or three speeches a week, usually on the subjects of patriotism, clean living, or fair play. He credited athletics with teaching him these values. In playing sports, he said, "you learn not only the sport but things like respect of others, ethics in life, how you are going to live, how you treat your fellow man, how you live with your fellow man." Inspiring audiences with his evangelical style, Owens made more than $100,000 a year as a public speaker.

Owens finally received long-overdue recognition from the White House in 1976. President Gerald Ford awarded Owens the Presidential Medal of Freedom. In 1984, four years after Owens' death, the avenue that leads to the Olympic Stadium in Berlin was renamed in his honor.

Career Capsule

In 1935, Owens set or tied six world track and field records in less than an hour at Big Ten Championship. He won a record four gold medals—in the 100- and 200-meter sprints, the long jump, and as a member of the 4 × 100-meter relay team—at the 1936 Olympics.

Satchel Paige

July 7, 1906–June 6, 1982

A legendary figure, Satchel Paige was the hero of many tall tales—many of them told by Paige himself. Yet he was also perhaps the greatest pitcher in the Negro leagues—and perhaps the best of all time. Paige had it all: speed, craftiness, a variety of curveballs, and deceptive deliveries. Hall-of-Fame centerfielder **Joe DiMaggio** called him the best pitcher he had ever seen.

Leroy Robert Paige, the sixth of eight children, was born in Mobile, Alabama. As a boy, Leroy delivered ice and later carried luggage at the Mobile train station. He frequently carried more satchels (bags) than seemed humanly possible—which led to his nickname, Satchel. He later said he learned how to pitch by throwing rocks at windows and boys from rival gangs. Satchel was placed in the Alabama Reform School for Boys when he was 12.

"One thing they told me in the reform school, they told me that all that wild-a'-loose feelin' I

Satchel Paige first pitched a game at Yankee Stadium while he was in the Negro Leagues.

put in rock throwin', I ought to put in throwin' baseballs," Paige later said. "Well, I listened to that."

When Satchel was released from reform school at age 16, he continued throwing baseballs. Within a year, he was playing for the Chattanooga (Tennessee) Black Lookouts, a team in the Negro leagues. Satchel loved to pitch. For the next 22 years, he played for anyone who could meet his price. In 1935, he pitched every day for 29 straight days—and lost only once. He pitched all year, playing in the Negro Southern Association, the Negro National League, and the American Negro League, as well as in Mexico, the Caribbean, and South America. He played for two years with a white semipro team in North Dakota. He even wore a false red beard (a team gimmick) for the otherwise white, barnstorming House of David team. In 1932 and 1933, Paige won 63 games with the Pittsburgh Crawfords, the best Negro team of the decade.

Paige was the first Negro League player in the Hall of Fame.

Paige was tall (6 feet, 3 inches) and skinny (180 pounds). But he could throw hard and fast. Some opposing hitters swore that the ball disappeared before crossing the plate. Although baseball was still racially segregated, Paige often faced major leaguers in exhibition games. In one game, he struck out Rogers Hornsby—a lifetime .358 hitter in the big leagues—five times. In another, Paige struck out 22 barnstorming major leaguers in a single game. In 1934, he pitched a six-game series against 30-game winner Dizzy Dean. Paige outpitched the future Hall of Famer and won four of the games, including a classic 1–0 win that took 13 innings. A year later, the Yankees arranged for Paige to pitch against a young prospect from San Francisco named Joe DiMaggio. They wanted to see whether DiMaggio could handle top-notch pitching. DiMaggio struck out twice, but managed a weak single in his fourth at bat. That convinced the Yankees that DiMaggio was ready; the team brought him up to the big leagues the next season.

Paige organized his own barnstorming tours, calling his team Satchel Paige's All-Stars. He traveled as many as 30,000 miles a year and made as much as $35,000—more than most white major leaguers at the time. He billed himself as Satchel Paige, World's Greatest Pitcher, Guaranteed to Strike Out the First Nine Men. And often, he did just that. More than once, he signaled his outfielders to leave the field, then calmly struck out the side.

Paige's career seemed over in 1938. He injured his arm so badly that he could no longer even lift it. He took a job as a coach with the famed Kansas City Monarchs. Paige hated not being able to pitch. But he went 14 months without even trying to pick up a ball. Then during a pregame warm-up one day in 1940, someone overthrew first base. Paige instinctively picked up the ball and tossed it back to the pitcher. Everyone on the field stopped and stared at the man whose arm was supposed to be dead. Paige picked up a glove and began throwing to the Monarchs' catcher, at first slowly, then harder and harder. Paige had somehow recovered—and continued to pitch for another 27 years!

Paige helped the Kansas City Monarchs win six pennants in the 1940s. With the Monarchs, Paige developed what he called the "hesitation pitch." As his front foot hit the ground, he would pause for a moment—less than a second—before delivering the ball. The hesitation baffled hitters, who never seemed to know just when the pitch would be coming. In 1942, Paige won three games as the Monarchs swept the Homestead Grays in the Black World Series.

In 1948, one year after **Jackie Robinson** broke the major-league color barrier, Paige got his chance to play in the big leagues. Bill Veeck, owner of the Cleveland Indians, signed him to a contract. By the time the majors let him play, though, Paige already had at least 22 years of experience. As a "rookie," Paige was at least 42 years old—and perhaps as old

Paige, who did not believe in running to get into shape, eventually made the major leagues at age 42.

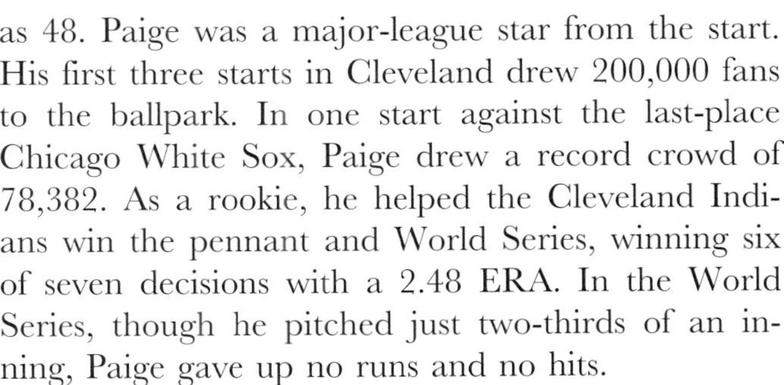

as 48. Paige was a major-league star from the start. His first three starts in Cleveland drew 200,000 fans to the ballpark. In one start against the last-place Chicago White Sox, Paige drew a record crowd of 78,382. As a rookie, he helped the Cleveland Indians win the pennant and World Series, winning six of seven decisions with a 2.48 ERA. In the World Series, though he pitched just two-thirds of an inning, Paige gave up no runs and no hits.

In Paige's second year with the Indians, he had an ERA of 3.04. He won four games, lost seven, and saved five. Yet when Veeck sold the Indians after the 1949 season, the new management let Paige go. "Everybody kept telling me he was through," said Veeck, explaining the new owners' thinking, "but that was understandable. They thought he was only human."

By 1951, Veeck had bought the hapless St. Louis Browns. He quickly signed Paige, who became the most effective pitcher on a poor staff. Capitalizing on Paige's fame, Veeck installed a rocking chair in the bullpen for him. Paige often showed up late to the ballpark and sometimes even missed games. Asked why he had missed a game against the Boston Red Sox, Paige patiently explained, "My feet told me it was gonna rain."

Paige also rebelled against the training methods used by Browns manager Rogers Hornsby. "With Mr. Hornsby, it's all running," he complained. "Now, I don't generally run at all. I believe in training by rising gently up and down from the bench. But old Mahjong had me flyin' around, shakin' my legs, and carryin' on until I very near passed. Now, what did all that do for my arm?"

Yet despite his antics, he pitched effectively. He led the league's relief pitchers in wins with eight in 1952. He finished that year with 12 wins, 10 losses, 10 saves, and the team's best ERA (3.07). The next year, he saved 11 with a 3.53 ERA. In both 1952 and 1953, Paige was named to the American League All-Star Team.

After his brief major-league career, Paige kept on barnstorming and playing in semipro games until 1967. He returned to the big leagues for one game with the Kansas City Athletics in 1965. The 59- or 65-year-old pitcher—the oldest man ever to pitch in a major-league game—tossed three innings of one-hit shutout ball.

In 1971, the Baseball Hall of Fame considered adding an exhibit to honor Negro League players. Paige was insulted by the suggestion that the Negro League stars be kept in a separate wing of the Hall of Fame. "I was just as good as the white boys," Paige argued. "I ain't going in the back door of the Hall of Fame." Several months later, Satchel Paige was granted full membership in the Baseball Hall of Fame. He was the first player admitted into the Hall based on his career in the Negro Leagues.

Career Capsule

Pitched 55 career no-hitters and won an estimated 2,000 of the 2,500 games he pitched over 20 years in the Negro Leagues. Entered Major Leagues at age 42 and won 28, lost 31, and saved 32 with a 3.29 ERA over five years. Returned to American league at age 59 to start one game for Kansas City.

Paige's Tips on Staying Young

1. Avoid fried meats which angry up the blood.
2. If your stomach disputes you, lie down and pacify it with cool thoughts.
3. Keep the juices flowing by jangling around gently as you move.
4. Go very light on the vices, such as carrying on in society. The social ramble ain't restful.
5. Avoid running at all times.
6. Don't look back. Something might be gaining on you.

Helen Stephens

February 13, 1918–January 17, 1994

TRACK AND FIELD star Helen Stephens first attracted notice in her high school gym class in Fulton, Missouri, in 1934. In an informal setting, the school's track coach clocked her at 5.8 seconds in the 50-yard dash—matching the world record! A year later, at the U.S. national track and field championships, Stephens won the 50-meter dash, the standing long jump, and the shot put. She also took

In three years of competition, Stephens never lost a race. Here she won at 100 meters in the 1936 Olympics.

Amateur Athletic Union (AAU) titles in 100- and 200-meter races.

Six feet tall, Stephens successfully defended her titles in all three events at the 1936 nationals. She took the AAU championship in javelin throwing (121 feet, 6½ inches). She set a world record of 11.6 seconds as the AAU champion in the 100-meter race. As a member of the 1936 U.S. Olympic Track and Field Team, Stephens then won the gold in the Olympic 100-meter dash in just 11.5 seconds. Though she had shaved one-tenth of a second off her own record, her time was wind-aided and so not considered a world record. But it remained the Olympic record until 1960, when **Wilma Rudolph** ran the distance in 11 seconds flat. Stephens won a second gold medal in Berlin as a member of the 4 × 100-meter relay team. The Associated Press chose Stephens as Female Athlete of the Year in 1936.

At the 1937 nationals, Stephens won the 50-meter dash and shot put titles for the third straight year and added a victory in the 200-meter dash. After a brief but sparkling career, Stephens retired from amateur athletics. In three years of track and field competition, she had never been defeated.

After joining the Marines during World War II, Stephens worked for many years as a research librarian for the Defense Mapping Agency.

Career Capsule

Won two gold medals at the 1936 Olympic Games in the 100-meter sprint and throwing the javelin. In less than three years, she earned 13 national or AAU titles in six different track and field events. She never lost a race at any distance.

Chapter 6

After World War II

An End to Segregation

1946–1958

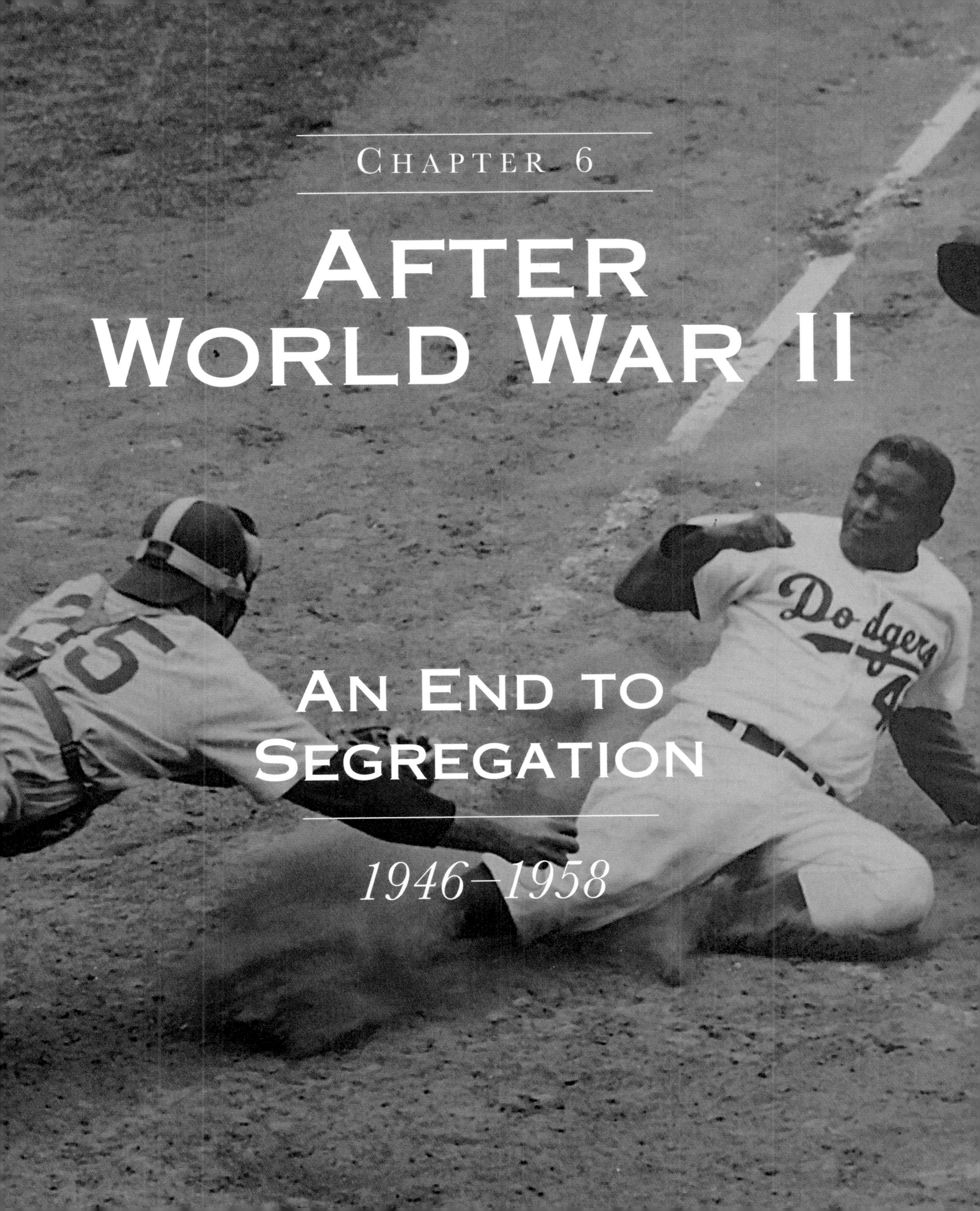

The end of World War II brought peace and prosperity. Yet a cloud hung over this new peace. Nazi Germany and Japan were defeated. But the United States was locked into a rivalry with its former ally, the Soviet Union. The Soviets now had their own atomic bomb. For more than 40 years, the United States and the Soviet Union fought to dominate each other. Since they never fought each other directly, that period is called the Cold War.

The Helsinki Olympics

The rivalry was about military strength, but it was also about ideas of how people should be governed. The United States had become the world's strongest democracy. The Soviet Union was under communist dictatorship. Under communism, every part of a nation is supposedly shared by all the people. In the Soviet Union, people were assured of work and enough money to live, but in return for that security, they gave up much of their freedom. Both nations felt that their way of governing was right. And both were willing to put military muscle behind those nations whose governments they supported.

Because the rivalry was about ideas and not just military power, it showed up in many different places. In the 1952 Olympics in Helsinki, Finland, the Soviet Union took part for the first time in 40 years. Soviet athletes won nine gold medals in gymnastics and another nine in wrestling and weight lifting. However, U.S. athletes won more points than Soviet athletes, 614 to 553.5. To many Americans, the competition seemed unfair. The Soviet government supported its athletes. The capitalist United States did not pay its athletes. U.S. amateur rules also prevented Olympic athletes from endorsing products and playing professionally. So U.S. Olympians supported themselves by working at ordinary jobs and training as best they could.

Not more than a handful of Americans would have chosen life in the Soviet Union over life in the United States. But many people were disappointed that their efforts in World War II had not brought them the equal opportunities they thought they had earned. The most disappointed of these groups were African Americans. In the South, laws prevented them from sharing schools, hospitals, public events, and even water fountains with whites. In the North, there were few laws separating the races. But by custom, black people were kept out of certain housing, certain neighborhoods, many schools, and the best jobs. Strange as it may seem today, African Americans did not play on professional sports teams or on most college teams. In many cases, they sat in separate sections when they went to watch these teams.

More Players and Fans

Brooklyn Dodgers' president Branch Rickey knew this was unfair. He also knew it was bad business. Before World War II, three million African Americans had moved to northern cities from the South. Rickey thought that if he hired black players, he could draw crowds of African-American fans. He was right.

In 1947, Rickey hired **Jackie Robinson** to play for the Dodgers. The Dodgers became the team of African Americans. Black fans flocked to National League stadiums. Robinson was followed by other great black athletes, such as **Roy Campanella**, New York Giants centerfielder Willie Mays, and Chicago Cubs shortstop Ernie Banks. It took 14 years, until 1961, before the last professional team in football—the Washington Redskins—accepted black players. Nevertheless, integrated teams still played sometimes in segregated stadiums.

Bobby Mitchell

Change in other sports was just as slow—or slower. But in 1956, tennis player **Althea Gibson** became the first black player, male or female, to win a Grand Slam singles title. The achievements of black athletes added momentum to the civil-rights movement. In 1954, the Supreme Court ruled that public schools could not provide "separate but equal" education to black students and white ones. American public schools were ordered to integrate. Two years later, a year-long boycott of Montgomery, Alabama, buses led to a Supreme Court ruling that segregation of city buses was illegal.

Althea Gibson

Women's gains during World War II were less enduring, but there were notable exceptions. The All-American Girls Professional Baseball League folded, but **Babe Didrikson Zaharias** founded the Ladies Professional Golf Association, the first professional women's sports association, in 1949. A year later, 18-year-old Joan Pflueger defeated a field of men to win the Grand American Trapshoot championship. In 1952 skier **Andrea Mead Lawrence** and diver **Pat McCormick** each won two Olympic gold medals (a performance McCormick repeated in 1956). And **"Little Mo" Connolly** became the first woman to win tennis' Grand Slam in 1953.

Living Room Sports

In 1949, fewer than one million American families owned televisions. Ten years later, nearly 90 percent of homes had at least one. Television brought the sights and sounds of live sports events into America's living rooms. Families gathered around the television to watch Robinson steal home or Tenley Albright glide across the ice on her way to Olympic gold. Unlike radio, television hurt ticket sellers everywhere. Attendance at minor-league baseball games, for example, dropped from 42 million in 1949, to just 15 million in 1957.

Still, television brought dollars to major-league sports. Money paid for the right to broadcast games or tournaments to national audiences dramatically increased the profits of owners and promoters. Broadcasters earned vast amounts of money from advertisers who sponsored televised sports events. Golfer **Arnold Palmer** became the first sports hero of the television age. Handsome and personable, Palmer earned millions endorsing products. His business savvy set the standard for the generations of athletes to follow.

TEAMS ON THE MOVE:

The Sports Market Expands

New York baseball fans suffered a crushing blow in 1957. Both of the city's National League teams—the Brooklyn Dodgers and the New York Giants—were headed for California. The owners of the two teams moved the clubs to Los Angeles and San Francisco.

Three baseball teams had already moved. The Boston Braves left for Milwaukee in 1953; the St. Louis Browns became the Baltimore Orioles a year later; and the Philadelphia Athletics packed up for Kansas City in 1955. Three basketball teams and one football team had left their home cities.

Although these cross-country shifts left fans feeling hurt and angry, more and more owners of sports teams hoped to rake in greater profits by operating elsewhere. The owners of the five baseball teams that moved in the 1950s, for example, no longer wanted to share their market with competing clubs. Boston, St. Louis, Philadelphia, and New York all had more than one major-league team before the moves. By 1958, only Chicago had two pro teams.

Most club owners seeking to increase their profits looked westward. New markets had opened up in growing cities west of the Mississippi River.

Beginning in 1961, sports owners developed another way to take advantage of these new markets: league expansion. Between 1960 and 1995, both baseball and football grew from 16 to 28 pro teams. Basketball grew from just 8 teams to 29 during the same period. Fewer teams have moved since league expansion began. But the grass often looks greener in other cities.

TENLEY ALBRIGHT

born July 18, 1935

COMBINING GRACE, ARTISTRY, and skill, Tenley Albright became the women's world figure skating champion in 1953. The first American woman to win the world competition, Albright inspired a generation of skaters that followed her. Three years later, Albright became the first American woman to win an Olympic gold medal for figure skating. Her performance helped establish the United States as a world power in women's figure skating.

Born in Newton Center, Massachusetts, nine-year-old Tenley received her first pair of ice skates as a gift from her parents and joined the Skating Club of Boston. After suffering from poliomyelitis, a disease also known as infantile paralysis, at age 11, Tenley was urged to continue her ice skating as therapy for her weakened muscles. Just four months after her recovery, she won the Eastern U.S. Junior Ladies Championship in 1947. Two years later, she won her first national title, the U.S. Ladies Novice Singles Championship. Moving up to the next age class, she won the U.S. Ladies Junior Singles championship in 1950.

Albright kept up the demanding schedule required to improve her skills while still in school. On weekends, she would skate almost all day; on weekdays, she practiced compulsory figures at four o'clock in the morning, long before breakfast and school. Yet she always preferred the creativity of free skating to the compulsories that ice-skating competitions demand. "There's such a wonderful feeling of freedom when you free skate," she explained. "It's a feeling of gliding like a bird."

Albright's first international competition came in the Winter Olympics in Oslo, Norway, in 1952. There, she won the silver medal in figure skating—the first time since 1924 that an American woman had finished as high as second place in Olympic figure-skating competition. Later that year, Albright won the U.S. ladies singles championship for the first time. She would successfully defend her national title in each of the next four years.

In 1953, she outclassed all her rivals to become the first American woman ever to win the world figure-skating championship. She also retained her national title in the U.S. ladies singles and won the North American figure-skating championship. Albright was the first American woman to hold all three titles in the same year. Although she lost the world title in 1954 to West German Gundi Busch, she recaptured the world figure-skating crown the following year.

In a fall just two weeks before the 1956 Winter Olympics in Cortina, Italy, Albright injured her right leg, severing a vein with her skate blade. Despite the handicap, Albright's display of grace and strength won the first place votes from 10 of 11 judges, carrying her to victory over her 16-year-old teammate **Carol Heiss**. The Olympic gold medal—the first won by an American woman in figure skating—was hers. Two weeks later, still hampered by her ankle injury, Albright lost her world title to Heiss in a very close contest.

Hours of practice paid off for Albright with Olympic gold.

After she won her fifth consecutive national title in 1956, Albright retired from skating competition to study medicine. One of just six women accepted at Harvard Medical School in 1957, Albright—who received a bachelor's degree from Radcliffe College—went on to become a skilled surgeon and an expert on sports medicine. Albright was elected to the United States Figure Skating Association Hall of Fame in 1976 and the International Women's Sports Hall of Fame in 1983. In 1979, she became the first woman to serve as an officer on the U.S. Olympic Committee.

CAREER CAPSULE

Gold medalist at 1956 Olympics, silver medalist at 1952 Olympics. World Champion twice (1953 and 1955) and U.S. Champion five consecutive years (1952–56). First woman to win an Olympic gold medal and a world championship in figure skating.

ROY CAMPANELLA

November 19, 1921–June 26, 1993

THE FIRST AFRICAN AMERICAN to catch in the major leagues, Roy Campanella demonstrated courage and dignity both on and off the field. Campanella was a clubhouse leader on Brooklyn Dodger teams, featuring future Hall of Famers Pee Wee Reese, Duke Snider, and **Jackie Robinson**. The Dodgers won five National League pennants during Campanella's ten years on the team. An excellent defensive catcher and dangerous power hitter, Campanella won three National League Most Valuable Player (MVP) awards.

Roy's father was an Italian immigrant and his mother was African American. He was born in Homestead, Pennsylvania, where his father sold fruits and vegetables. Growing up during the Great Depression, Roy and his brother Lawrence delivered milk to add to the family income. In high school, Roy starred not only in baseball but also football, basketball, and track.

Campy set a record, for catchers, of 807 putouts.

In 1937, when he was only 15 years old, Roy joined the Baltimore Elites of the Negro National League. Except for one season in the Mexican League, he remained with the Elites for the next nine years. A few months after Jackie Robinson broke baseball's color barrier by playing minor-league ball in the Dodgers farm system, Campanella signed on, too. "Campy" was sent to the Dodgers' farm team in Nashua, New Hampshire. One night later that year, Nashua manager Walter Alston was tossed out of the game for arguing with an umpire. Before leaving, Alston chose Campy to manage the team for the rest of the game. Without any warning, Campanella became the first black man ever to manage in the minor leagues. He led his team to a 7–5 win.

When he came up to the big-league Dodgers in 1948, Campanella was a 27-year-old rookie. In just over half a season, he pounded out nine home runs and knocked in 45 runs to win the job as the Dodgers' starting catcher. In 1951, Campanella hit .325 with 33 homers, 90 runs, and 108 runs batted in. Though the Dodgers lost the pennant to the Giants in an unforgettable three-game playoff series, Campy won his first National League Most Valuable Player award.

Two years later, Campy had his best season—and again was named his league's most valuable player. He hit .312 with a .611 slugging average. He scored 103 runs and set records for most home runs (41) and RBIs (142) by a catcher in a single season. On the field, he set a record for most putouts in a season at his position (807).

Campanella won his record-setting third MVP award in 1955, the year the Dodgers won their only World Series in Brooklyn. He batted .318 with 32 homers and 107 RBIs. Campanella and the Dodgers had lost to the Yankees in 1949, 1952, and 1953 (and would lose to them again in 1956). When the Yanks won the first two games in 1955, it looked like the Dodgers would lose again. But in the third game, Campanella had three hits, one of them a home run, and three RBIs as the Dodgers won, 8–3. Campy's homer in the fourth game triggered a rally that helped the Dodgers tie the series at two games each. They went on to win the series, four games to three.

An auto accident cut short Campanella's career after the 1957 season. The crash left him partly paralyzed. Despite being confined to a wheelchair, Campanella served as a spring training instructor and made countless public appearances on behalf of the Dodgers for the next 35 years. In the 1970s, he also served on a special committee that selected the best players from the Negro Leagues for membership in the Baseball Hall of Fame. Campanella himself was elected to the hall in 1969.

Career Capsule

A three-time MVP, with a career batting average of .276, with 242 home runs and 856 runs batted in. Played on five pennant winners and one World Series winning team. Career span 1948–57 with the Brooklyn Dodgers.

Florence Chadwick

November 9, 1918–March 15, 1995

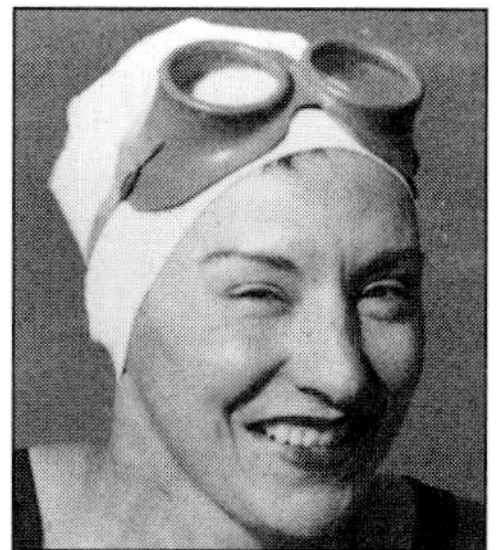

In 1926, Florence Chadwick, at seven years old, was inspired to take up distance swimming by **Gertrude Ederle**, the first woman to swim across the English Channel from France to Great Britain. Florence vowed to do the same someday. Though it would take her 24 years to keep this promise, Chadwick swam the channel four times. With each crossing, she set a new record.

An uncle, Mike Lacko, entered her in her first swimming race, which she lost, at age 6. "I decided to work harder," Chadwick later recalled, "and prove somehow that his confidence was not misplaced." By age 10, Florence had won the six-mile San Diego Bay Channel race. The first ever to complete the swim, Florence would win this race ten times in the next 18 years. She was the student body president at Point Loma High School, where she continued to swim competitively. When she finished fourth in the 1936 Olympic trials, however, she failed to make the U.S. team.

Chadwick's competitive swimming career seemed finished. Yet she remained committed to her pursuit of distance swimming. She especially wanted to swim the English Channel. During World War II (1941–45), she directed aquatic shows for the military and appeared in a movie with swimmer-turned-star Esther Williams. In 1948, Chadwick took a job in Saudi Arabia with the Arabian-American Oil Company. Chadwick trained in the rough waters of the Persian Gulf, swimming as much as ten hours a day on weekends.

In 1950, the London *Daily Mail* sponsored a contest to swim the channel. Yet the newspaper rejected Chadwick's application because she was an unknown: She had no record as a distance swimmer and had trained on her own with no publicity. Chadwick decided to complete the swim at her own expense. She failed in her first attempt. But on

August 8, 1950, escorted by a party of 15 in a fishing boat, Chadwick set out again. Eating nothing but sugar cubes during the crossing, she swam the 20 miles from Cape Gris-Nez, France, to Dover, England, in just 13 hours and 23 minutes. Her performance chopped more than an hour off Ederle's record time of 14:31! "I feel fine," she announced as she emerged from the water. "I am quite prepared to swim back."

Chadwick was welcomed home to San Diego with a ticker-tape parade. Though completely out of money, she soon signed contracts to endorse various products, to appear on radio and TV shows, and to swim in exhibitions. She also toured the country teaching children how to swim and promoting physical fitness and sports.

An exhausted Chadwick, covered with grease to protect her, staggers ashore at Dover, England.

In 1951, seeking even greater distance-swimming challenges, Chadwick became the first woman to swim the channel from England to France. Swimming this other direction, against the tide, was a much more difficult task. Yet Chadwick again set a record time (16:22), becoming the only woman ever to swim the English Channel in both directions.

The following year, she became the first woman to swim the 21 miles across the Catalina Channel from the southern coast of California to Catalina Island. Again, she did it in record time (13:47). In 1953, Chadwick undertook four marathon swims—the English Channel, the Straits of Gibraltar between Morocco and Spain, a round trip across the Bosporus Strait from Europe to Asia and back, and the Turkish Dardanelles—in a span of just five weeks! She set a new world record at each site. In 1955, she again broke her own record for the English Channel swim, completing the distance against the current in just 13:55.

Chadwick did not retire from long-distance swimming until 1969. At age 50, she established a successful career as a stockbroker. In recognition of her dedicated efforts, her unparalleled accomplishments, and her inspiring example, Chadwick was inducted into the International Swimming Hall of Fame in 1970.

Career Capsule

First woman to swim the English Channel in both directions and to swim the Catalina Channel. Set four world records in 1953 swiming the English Channel, Straits of Gibralter, Bosporus (round trip), and Turkish Dardanelles.

Maureen Connolly

September 17, 1934–June 21, 1969

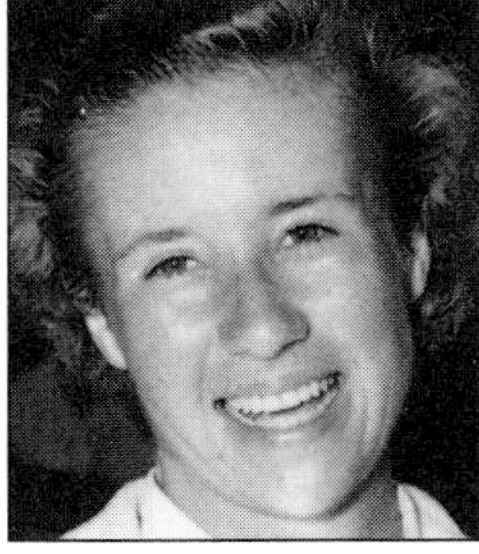

Easily among the top ten women tennis players of all time, Maureen Connolly was virtually unbeatable in the early 1950s. A devastating baseline player with quick feet, an outstanding backhand, powerful ground strokes, and remarkable accuracy, Little Mo almost never needed to go to the net. She won the Grand Slam in 1953, and ranked first in the world from 1951 to 1954.

Born and raised in San Diego, California, Maureen began playing tennis at age 10 on the concrete public courts of the city. She loved the game, often continuing to practice after the courts had closed by hitting a ball against her garage until the dead of night. After finishing second in the first tournament she entered, Maureen became a student of renowned tennis coach Eleanor Tennant in 1947. (Tennant had previously coached **Helen Wills Moody** and **Alice Marble**, two other U.S. champions.) In 1949, at age 14, Connolly became the U.S. junior champion. This began an astonishing streak in which the teenager won 56 straight matches without a loss. By 1950, she ranked 10th in the world. Sportswriters began calling her "Little Mo," comparing her explosive shots to those from the cannons of the battleship *Missouri.*

Though small, Little Mo could cover a lot of ground.

Beginning with the U.S. championships in 1951, Connolly dominated women's tennis, losing only four more matches during the rest of her career! That year, Connolly won the first of three consecutive singles titles, breezing through the tournament without losing a single set. The title made her, at 16 years and 11 months, the youngest U.S. champion (until Tracy Austin won in 1979). A favorite of both the crowds and the media, Connolly was named by the Associated Press as Female Athlete of the Year from 1951 to 1953 and as Woman of the Year in 1951.

In winning the first of three consecutive all-England singles titles in 1952, Connolly became the youngest winner at Wimbledon in nearly 50 years. A year later, she hit her peak, becoming the first of only three women ever to win the Grand Slam of tennis, capturing the Australian, French, Wimbledon, and U.S. singles titles in one calendar year. In these four major tournaments combined, she lost only one set. For the year, Connolly won 61 of 63 matches to take singles titles in 10 of the 12 tournaments she entered, including the first of two straight U.S. clay court championships.

In addition to her singles championships at Wimbledon and the U.S. clay court tournaments in 1954, Connolly won singles titles at both the Italian and French Opens. She also teamed up to win championship titles in U.S. clay court doubles, Australian doubles, French women's doubles, and French mixed doubles—becoming one of only five players ever to win all three French titles in the same year.

Connolly also represented the United States in Wightman Cup matches against Great Britain and Ireland from 1951 to 1954. Connolly won all seven singles matches and both doubles matches in which she played, helping the U.S. team defeat Britain all four years.

Two weeks after her third win at Wimbledon, Connolly—just 19 years old—suffered a career-ending leg injury when a truck struck the horse she was riding. Although unable to continue playing competitively, Connolly became a tennis instructor and coach and devoted herself to the Maureen Connolly Brinker Foundation, established to promote junior tennis. Elected to the International Tennis Hall of Fame in 1968, Connolly died of cancer a year later.

Career Capsule

In 1953 became first woman to win the Grand Slam. Won the U.S. singles title in 1951, at age 16. After that, lost only four matches until retiring in 1954. Never beaten at Wimbledon, winning three consecutive titles (1952–54). Won three consecutive U.S. singles titles (1951–53), two consecutive French titles (1953–54), and Australian title (1953).

Joe DiMaggio

born November 25, 1914

Although his 56-game hitting streak overshadowed his other accomplishments, Joe DiMaggio was more than a model of on-field consistency. A graceful and talented centerfielder as well as an awesome hitter, DiMaggio possessed a picture-perfect swing. He had an uncanny ability to anticipate where a pitch would be thrown or where a ball would be hit. His encyclopedic knowledge of opposing hitters and keen timing allowed him to make every fielding play look easy.

Off the field, DiMaggio became an American icon. Popular among New York's cafe society and theater crowd in the late 1930s, DiMaggio was named one of the world's ten best-dressed men. He opened his own restaurant and nightclub on Fisherman's Wharf in San Francisco. In 1939, more than 30,000 people tried to crowd into the church where DiMaggio married Hollywood starlet and nightclub singer Dorothy Arnold. His second marriage, to movie star Marilyn Monroe in 1954, made him half of America's most famous couple. In *The Old Man and the Sea*, Ernest Hemingway used DiMaggio as a symbol of consistency and perfection. Decades after he retired, DiMaggio would be held up as the idealized figure of his era in Paul Simon and Art Garfunkel's "Mrs. Robinson" and Billy Joel's "We Didn't Start the Fire." Yet despite his huge stardom, DiMaggio was a shy and private man. He always seemed reluctant to be a public figure and was uncomfortable with his fame.

The eighth of nine children, Joseph Paul DiMaggio, Jr., was born in Martinez, California. DiMaggio's parents had emigrated from an island near Sicily. Joe grew up in San Francisco, where his father worked as a commercial crab fisher. As a boy, Joe sold newspapers to boost the family income. In junior high school, Joe often cut classes to watch his older brother Vince work out with the minor-league San Francisco Seals. (Two of Joe's four brothers, Vince and Dom, would each play more than 1,000 games as major-league outfielders.) When Joe started playing, his family could not afford a team uniform. Nevertheless, he led his Boys' Club team to a local championship in 1929.

When Joe was 17, he joined Vince on the Seals for the last three games of the 1932 season. Joe smashed a double and triple in his first game to assure himself a spot on the team. His manager, however, moved him to the outfield because his throwing was too wild to leave him at shortstop. In 1933, his first full season with the Seals, Joe had an incredible 61-game hitting streak—the longest ever in the minor leagues. He hit .340 for the season.

Despite a knee injury, the New York Yankees paid a whopping $25,000 and sent five players to the Seals for rights to DiMaggio in 1934. To gain more experience, however, he played one more season with the Seals. That year, 1935, DiMaggio hit .398 with 34 home runs and 154 runs batted in (RBIs).

In 1936, his rookie season with the Yankees, DiMaggio batted .323 with 29 homers. He tied for

In 1941, DiMaggio maintained a 56-game hitting streak that is still a record.

The "Yankee Clipper" had a career batting average of .325.

the league lead in triples, with 15. He also fielded .978 and led the league in outfield assists. The Yankees, who finished in second place in each of the previous three seasons, made it back to the World Series. DiMaggio hit .346 to help the Yankees defeat the New York Giants in six games—the first of four straight World Series victories for the Yankees! DiMaggio became the only player in major-league history to play on championship teams during each of his first four years.

In 1937, DiMaggio led the league in home runs (46), runs scored (151), and slugging average (.673). He also knocked in 167 runs, second in the league behind **Hank Greenberg**'s near-record 183. All four figures would represent career highs for the "Yankee Clipper." The following year, he became baseball's most famous salary holdout. DiMaggio wanted $45,000 a year, but finally settled for the original club offer of $25,000. Yankee fans booed him when he returned two weeks into the season. Yet he transformed the catcalls to cheers by batting .324 with 32 home runs. In 1939, he led the American League with a career-high .381 batting average. He also hit 30 homers—and slugged another in the All-Star game. For his efforts, DiMaggio was given the league's Most Valuable Player (MVP) award. In 1940, he batted .352 to lead the league for the second straight year.

Already a star, DiMaggio became a legend in 1941. From May 15 to July 16, he got at least one hit in every game he played. His incredible 56-game hitting streak, a major-league record, was stopped only by two terrific plays in the 57th game by Indian third baseman Ken Keltner. The next day, DiMaggio started another streak that went 17 more games. Overall that year, he batted .357 with 30 homers and a league-leading 125 RBIs. Again he was named the league's MVP as the Yanks won their fifth World Series in his six years.

DiMaggio, married and at 28 years old well past the draft age, volunteered for military service in 1943, fourteen months after the United States entered World War II. Newspapers praised him for giving up his $43,500 salary for a soldier's pay of $50 a month. DiMaggio would miss three full seasons while in the military. Upon his return in 1946, his batting average dipped below .300 (to .290) for the first time in his career.

The following year, however, his average was back up to .315. He won his third MVP award, tying a record set by Jimmie Foxx in the 1930s. In the fifth game of the 1947 World Series, DiMaggio's fifth-inning home run gave the Yankees a 2–1 win and a series lead of three games to two. DiMaggio might have won the sixth game, too. But with two runners on base in the sixth, Dodger leftfielder Al Gionfriddo made a spectacular catch of DiMaggio's 415-foot drive. In a rare display of on-field emotion, DiMaggio kicked up a cloud of dirt in disgust as Gionfriddo caught the ball. The Yankees went on to win the series the next day.

In 1948, DiMaggio led the league in home runs (39) and RBIs (155), each for the second time in his career. He had now knocked in at least 95 runs in each of his first ten seasons. The Yankees rewarded him with baseball's first $100,000-a-year contract in 1949. Although he missed the first half of the season with various injuries, he batted .346 for the second half. In mid-August 1950, it looked like DiMaggio—hitting only around .270—would have his worst season ever. But he hit .370 over the final six weeks of the season to lift his average to .301.

DiMaggio used his speed in the field as well as on the base paths.

His tenth-inning home run won the second game of that year's World Series.

By 1951, however, DiMaggio was no longer playing up to his high standards. He hit just .263 with 12 homers and 71 RBIs—all career lows. In spite of his poor season, he was selected for the American League All-Star Team for the 13th time in 13 years. He also helped the Yankees to their third straight World Series triumph. These three championships gave DiMaggio's teams nine World Series titles in ten appearances over just 13 years.

DiMaggio then turned down another six-figure contract and retired. "I feel that I have reached the stage," he explained, "where I can no longer produce for my ball club, my manager, my teammates, and my fans the sort of baseball their loyalty to me deserves." DiMaggio was a class act all the way, refusing to embarrass himself on the field.

Career Capsule

A lifetime .325 hitter with a 56-game hitting streak in 1941. MVP in 1939, 1941, and 1947. Batted over .300 11 times, had over 100 RBIs nine times, and was league leader in batting average, home runs, and RBIs two times each. Played in 10 World Series of which the Yankees won nine. Drove in 1,537 runs, scored 1,390 runs, and hit 389 doubles and 361 homers while striking out only 369 times.

The Clipper and the Splinter

During their playing days, the two best outfielders in the American League were Joe DiMaggio and Ted Williams of the Boston Red Sox. Who was better? The answer depended on whether you asked a fan in Boston or one in New York. Though Williams, the "Splendid Splinter," was a better hitter and slugger, DiMaggio, the "Yankee Clipper," was a better all-around player.

MVP voters gave DiMaggio the edge. In 1939, Williams' rookie year, he had one more homer and 16 more RBIs than DiMaggio. But DiMaggio outdistanced him in hitting, .381 to .327, and won the MVP award. In 1941, Williams became the last man to hit over .400 for a season (.406). He led DiMaggio in virtually every statistical category.

Yet DiMaggio had the hitting streak, the Yanks won the pennant, and Joltin' Joe took home another MVP award. In 1947, Williams won the Triple Crown—leading the league in hitting, homers, and RBIs. But somehow DiMaggio won the MVP by one point, the closest vote in league history. By this time, Red Sox fans felt that Williams had been cheated.

Curiously, both men achieved greatness while playing in parks ill-suited to their talents. The right-handed DiMaggio would have loved the "Green Monster"—the close, high, left-field wall in Boston's Fenway Park. And the left-handed Williams would have knocked countless balls into the short porch in right field at Yankee Stadium.

The last word on this debate comes from the players themselves. Williams called DiMaggio the greatest player he had ever seen. DiMaggio, in response, called Williams the greatest left-handed hitter he had ever seen.

ALTHEA GIBSON

born August 25, 1927

IN 1949, ALTHEA GIBSON broke the color barrier in the segregated sport of tennis, just as **Jackie Robinson** had done in 1947 in baseball. Tall and strong, Gibson was an aggressive serve-and-volley player with an overpowering serve. She would become the first African American to win the U.S. championship, as well as the first black athlete to win the All-England title at Wimbledon.

Gibson was born in Silver, South Carolina, where her father worked as a sharecropper on a cotton farm. At age three, Althea and her family moved to the Harlem neighborhood of New York City. She grew to love all sports, excelling at basketball, baseball, bowling, and paddle tennis. Althea was introduced to tennis in 1941. Her local Police Athletic League supervisor saw how well she played paddle tennis and bought her two used tennis rackets. Within weeks, the 14-year-old was beating experienced male players at the local Harlem River Tennis Courts.

Blacks barred from playing in events sponsored by the United States Lawn Tennis Association (USLTA) had formed their own group: the American Tennis Association (ATA). At 16, and again at 17, Althea won the national ATA girls' division championship. In 1946, two ATA officials, Dr. Hubert Eaton and Dr. Robert Johnson, offered her a deal. Althea, a high-school dropout, would complete her education while living with Eaton's family in Williston, North Carolina. In return, Eaton and Johnson would help her improve her game. Gibson accepted their offer; and by 1953, she had earned a bachelor of science degree at Florida A & M University.

Under their coaching, Gibson won the first of 11 straight ATA national women's championships in 1947. Her powerful overhead smash and aggressive play allowed her to dominate the competition. She won singles titles in all 18 ATA events held in 1947 and 1948. Teamed with Johnson, Gibson also won eight of nine mixed doubles titles in 1947. In addition to holding the ATA singles title from 1947 to 1957, Gibson and Johnson won the ATA mixed doubles championship seven times between 1948 and 1955.

Despite her success in ATA tournaments, Gibson was unwelcome on the USLTA tour. Racist policies barred blacks from playing in invitation-only tournaments, including the U.S. Championships and England's Wimbledon tournament. In 1948, years of effort by the ATA finally resulted in an African-American player (Dr. Reginald Weir) competing in a USLTA event (the U.S. Indoor Championships). The next year, Gibson played in both the Eastern and National Indoor Championships. She reached the quarterfinals in both events. In 1950, she did even better, winning the Eastern title and reaching the finals of the National Championships.

The door to integrated play had not yet fully opened, however. No blacks had yet played in any of the four Grand Slam tennis tournaments. Gibson received support from former champion **Alice Marble**, who wrote an editorial for *American Lawn Tennis* magazine in July 1950, urging the USLTA to admit Gibson. A month later, the USLTA finally invited Gibson to become the first African American to play in a major event: the U.S. Championships. Gibson breezed through the first round. But in a tough, rain-delayed, second-round match against Louise Brough, that year's Wimbledon champion, she lost, 6–1, 3–6, 9–7. The next summer, Gibson became the first black to play in the All-England Tennis Championships at Wimbledon, where she reached the quarterfinals.

Gibson ranked among the Top Ten U.S. women in both 1952 and 1953. Yet despite her success on the court, she was still not welcome in many country clubs that held major tournaments. Though she continued to dominate the ATA, Gibson did not perform as strongly in USLTA events. By 1954, she had dropped out of the Top Ten rankings. The following year, however, she regained her stride. She moved back into the Top Ten and remained there through 1958. In 1956, she won 16 of the 18 events she entered. She lost only at Wimbledon (in the

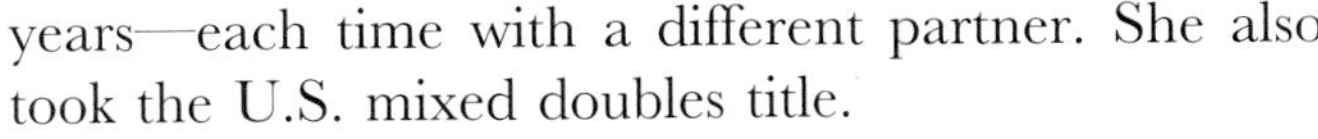

quarterfinals) and Forest Hills (in the finals). She became the first black player to win a Grand Slam tennis tournament when she took the French women's singles title. She also won both the French and Wimbledon women's doubles crowns. By the end of the year, Gibson ranked number two in the world.

For the next two years, Gibson dominated women's tennis to claim the number one ranking. She won both the Wimbledon and U.S. singles titles two years in a row (1957 and 1958). Gibson also won the women's doubles championships in Australia in 1957, and at Wimbledon both years—each time with a different partner. She also took the U.S. mixed doubles title.

With her triumphs, Gibson was embraced by much of the U.S. public and media. New York welcomed her home from her first Wimbledon victory with a ticker-tape parade. She has said that the most moving experience of her life was "returning to Harlem and seeing all those people come out of their tired old apartment houses to tell me how glad they were that one of the neighbors' children had gone out into the world and done something big." The Associated Press recognized her as Female Athlete of the Year in both 1957 and 1958.

Gibson's height and long arms earned her many points.

The rangy Gibson retrieved many shots opponents lobbed over her head.

Gibson retired from amateur tennis after 1958, choosing to quit while she was on top. Since no professional women's tennis tour existed in the 1950s, Gibson played exhibition matches during halftime of Harlem Globetrotters' basketball games. She earned over $100,000 in a single year.

Gibson later took up golf, breaking the color barrier in another largely segregated sport. She became the first black woman to earn a Ladies Professional Golf Association player's card in 1964. Though Gibson never achieved greatness in her seven years as a pro golfer, she had undeniably demonstrated it on the tennis courts. There, her dignity, grace, and exemplary play paved the way for many other African Americans to play top-level tennis.

CAREER CAPSULE

The first African American to win a Grand Slam tennis title, winning consecutive Wimbledon and U.S. singles titles (1957–58) and French title in 1956. Won 11 major titles—5 singles and 6 doubles—between 1956 and 1958.

BEN HOGAN

born August 13, 1912

A DEDICATED PERFECTIONIST, golfer Ben Hogan spent countless hours on the practice range working on his swing. His booming drives became the trademark of one of the greatest golfers of the "modern" era. Hogan is one of only four players to win golf's Grand Slam: the U.S. and British Opens, the Masters, and the U.S. PGA Championship. (The others are Gene Sarazen, Gary Player, and **Jack Nicklaus**.)

Born in Dublin, Texas, Ben Hogan had a difficult childhood. His father died when Ben was ten. As a boy, Ben sold newspapers to help his family make ends meet. He then became a caddie at a Fort Worth country club. He soon came to see golf as a way to escape his life of poverty. Hoping to make his fortune, Hogan turned pro at the age of 19. His early years on the tour were unsuccessful. Hogan could not even make a living. It took him more than seven years to win his first PGA event in 1938.

Finally, Hogan began to make a name for himself on the pro tour. In 1940, he won five events and more than $10,000 in prize money to became golf's leading money winner. He also led the tour in earnings in 1941 and 1942. In both 1940 and 1941, Hogan won the Vardon Trophy, given annually to the pro with the lowest scoring average for the year. Yet he had still not won a major tournament. His best finish before World War II was second place at the 1942 Masters.

World War II interrupted Hogan's newfound success. The war caused the suspension of most tournaments from 1942 to 1945. Only four of the 16 major events that would have been held during those years were actually played.

After the war, Hogan finally won his first major tournament at age 34: the 1946 U.S. PGA Championship. With his second-place finish at the Masters and victories in 13 of 32 events, Hogan earned more than $42,000 as golf's top money winner that year. Two years later, he won two major events: his second PGA title and the U.S. Open. At the Riviera Country Club in Los Angeles, California, he shot a record-breaking 276 over 72 holes. This would remain the U.S. Open record for almost 20 years, until Jack Nicklaus carded a 275 in 1967. Hogan won his third Vardon Trophy and was the top money winner in golf for a record fifth time. The PGA gave Hogan its first annual Player of the Year award in 1948.

Hogan was on top of the golf world when a terrible auto accident nearly claimed his life. After his car crashed into a Greyhound bus near Pecos, Texas, Hogan spent more than a month in the hospital. He had broken his pelvis, his collar bone, an ankle, and a rib. His doctors predicted that he would never walk again. Yet Hogan refused to give

Hogan's form made up for his small size and he hit with power.

Even from a sand trap, Hogan could blast onto the green.

up. Through countless hours of hard work, he gradually learned to walk again.

Surprisingly, he became a more dominant player on the professional tour after the accident than he was before it. In his first tournament after the accident, the 1950 Los Angeles Open, he tied the 1949 Player of the Year, Sam Snead, for the lead after 72 holes before losing by four strokes in a playoff. He then won the White Sulphur Springs tournament with an astonishing score of 259. Later that year, Hogan won a three-way play-off by four strokes to capture his second U.S. Open title at the Merion Golf Club in Ardmore, Pennsylvania. Recognizing his amazing comeback, the PGA again named him Player of the Year. The following year, he won the Masters Tournament for the first time. Hogan also successfully defended his U.S. Open title and was named PGA Player of the Year for the second straight year.

Hogan received the Player of the Year award for the fourth time in 1953. He entered only six tournaments that year, but won five of them—including three of the four major events. First, he won his second Masters title with a score of 274, breaking the previous Masters record by five strokes. (This would remain the tournament record until 1965, when Nicklaus shot a 271.) Next he won the U.S. Open for the fourth time in six years. This tied the record (shared by Willie Anderson and **Bobby Jones**) for most U.S. Open titles. Finally, he prevailed at the British Open in Scotland. This victory made Hogan one of only five players ever to win both Open titles in the same year—and only the second golfer ever to complete the Grand Slam. Hogan might have become the first golfer ever to win all four majors *in the same year*, but at that time, the PGA Championship conflicted with the British Open, making it impossible to play in both events. (The PGA later changed the date of its championship to allow players to compete in both tournaments.)

Hogan remained a strong competitor, but he never won another major tournament after 1953. He was runner-up at the Masters in both 1954 and 1955, and at the U.S. Open in 1955 and 1956. His last great triumph was in 1956, when he and Snead teamed to win the Canada Cup (now called the World Cup) for the United States. In addition to winning the team title, Hogan recorded the best individual score at the event.

Hogan retired from the tour in 1967. He was inducted into the World Golf Hall of Fame, the PGA

A parade was held in Hogan's honor in 1953.

of America Hall of Fame, and the American Golf Hall of Fame. The PGA now presents the Ben Hogan Award every year to a golfer who makes a courageous comeback from injury or physical disability. Yet no golfer since has ever come back as strongly as Ben Hogan himself.

Career Capsules

Third all-time career wins (63). Won U.S. Open four times (1948, 1950–51, 1953), the Masters (1951 and 1953), PGA Championship (1946 and 1948), and British Open (1953). PGA Player of the Year (1948, 1950–51, and 1953). Captured 63 professional titles, including nine majors and a Grand Slam.

Andrea Mead Lawrence

born April 19, 1932

THRILLING AUDIENCES with her speed and skill, Andrea Mead Lawrence became the first American skier ever to win two gold medals at a single Olympiad.

When Andrea was a child, her parents ran a ski resort, Pico Peak, near Rutland, Vermont. Andrea began skiing almost as soon as she began walking. She loved to rocket down the mountain making sharp, slaloming turns. Although Andrea never had any formal racing instruction, she entered her first junior races at age eight. In her first major senior race, 11-year-old Andrea placed second in the Women's Eastern Slalom Championships.

In 1947, Andrea won the slalom race at the U.S. Olympic trials. This win made her, at just 15 years old, the youngest member of the U.S. Women's Olympic Alpine Skiing Team. (Alpine skiing events include downhill racing and slaloms, both of which place an emphasis on speed, control, and precision.) At the 1948 Winter Olympics in St. Moritz, Switzerland, Mead placed eighth in the slalom (just over one-tenth of a second behind the bronze medalist) and a disappointing 21st in the combined Alpine. In the women's downhill skiing competition, Mead went too fast, lost control, and suffered a bad fall before completing the event in 35th place. Later that year, however, Mead bounced back, finishing third in the Alberg-Kandahar Downhill Race—Alpine skiing's most prestigious event—in Chamonix, France.

At the 1949 national championships near Whitefish, Montana, Mead swept the Alpine events, winning the combined downhill, downhill, and

Andrea competed without a helmet or synthetic outfits.

slalom events. By 1951, she was at her peak. Competing throughout Europe, she dominated the international field. Mead won ten of sixteen international events—including the Arlberg-Kandahar Downhill Race—and was the runner-up in four others. She also placed first in the International Week competition in Chamonix, France.

Tuning up for the Olympics in 1952, she again won the women's Alpine combined race at the nationals. Now married to skier David Lawrence, Andrea earned two gold medals at that year's Winter Olympics in Oslo, Norway. After winning the giant slalom by an impressive three seconds, Lawrence—despite a stumble that forced her to the edge of the course—scored the fourth-best time in the first of two slalom runs. Then, in the second run, the determined skier outperformed the competition by so wide a margin that her combined time for both runs won her the gold. Although she again fell in the downhill event and finished in 17th place, Lawrence's two gold medals made her the most successful American skier in Olympic history. In recognition of her performance, Lawrence received the Beck Trophy, awarded to the best U.S. skier in international competition.

Lawrence continued her U.S. dominance in 1953, again winning all three Alpine events at the nationals. In 1955, she received her third White Stag Trophy as the winner of the National Women's Alpine Combined. The hometown favorite at that year's internationals in Stowe, Vermont, Lawrence won three events. Despite giving birth to her third child just four months before the Winter Olympic games, Lawrence competed in her third Olympiad in 1956. She just missed a medal in the giant slalom, finishing in a fourth-place tie just 0.1 seconds behind the bronze medalist.

During the opening ceremonies of the Winter Olympics in Squaw Valley, California, in 1960, Lawrence, America's best Alpine skier, had the honor of skiing into the stadium carrying the Olympic flame.

After retiring from competitive skiing, Lawrence—a member of both the National Ski Hall of Fame and the International Women's Sports Hall of Fame—became an environmental activist. A lawsuit she brought to prevent overdevelopment of the Sierra Mountain village of Mammoth Lakes led to a landmark California environmental law. She later served three terms as Mono County supervisor, overseeing responsible zoning and development plans for the region.

Career Capsule

Won two gold medals at the 1952 Winter Olympics in slalom and giant slalom. Member of National Ski Hall of Fame and International Women's Sports Hall of Fame.

Mickey Mantle

October 20, 1931–August 13, 1995

The most powerful switch-hitter of all time, Mickey Mantle combined a thunderous bat with a country boy's smile to captivate the hearts of American baseball fans.

From the day he was born in Spavinaw, Oklahoma, Mantle was destined to play baseball. His father, Mutt, named him after his favorite ballplayer, Hall of Fame catcher Mickey Cochrane. Fearing he would spend the rest of his life working in the local mines in Commerce, Oklahoma, Mickey spent hours practicing to develop one of the most powerful swings in baseball. His father pitched to him daily and taught him to bat both right-handed and left-handed. Mutt pitched to Mickey right-handed while his grandfather threw left-handed. "Some day, major league managers will platoon their players," Mutt said. "The right-handed hitters will face left-handed pitchers and vice-versa."

Diagnosed with a bone disease called osteomyelitis, Mantle nearly lost his leg while in high school. Fortunately, a new "wonder drug" called penicillin saved his leg. At Commerce High, Mantle became an exceptional athlete, starring in three sports: football, basketball, and baseball.

Mantle's mammoth swing and country-boy charm made him a larger-than-life sports hero.

Although the osteomyelitis flared up on occasion throughout the rest of his life, Mantle possessed blazing speed. His swiftness on the base paths, matched with the arm strength he developed swinging a sledgehammer in the coal mines and milking 16 cows twice a day, helped him become a pro baseball player. At age 17, Mantle signed a contract to play in the New York Yankees' farm system. Scout Tom Greenwade described Mantle as "the best prospect I have ever seen."

In his first minor league season, Mantle hit .313, but committed 47 errors at shortstop. The following year, he won the Western Association batting title hitting .383 while clouting 26 homers. His defensive play continued to plague him as he made 55 errors in 137 games. "They had to put a chicken wire screen behind first base as a backstop," he said about his throwing errors. "They needed it to prevent somebody in the stands from getting killed."

Mantle moved up to the Yankee team in 1951. He played right field next to centerfielder **Joe DiMaggio** in the Yankee Clipper's final season. Mired in a hitting slump in mid-season, Mantle was sent down to a minor-league team for 40 games, but returned to the Yankees by the end of August.

The Yankees squared off with the New York Giants in the World Series that October, but Mantle suffered a severe knee injury during the second game. In the hospital, he was joined by his father, who had Hodgkin's disease and died later that year.

In 1952, Mantle hit .311 with 23 home runs in his first full season in the majors. His career took off as he became the most feared switch-hitter in the game. His tape-measure blasts were legendary. His best year was 1956, when he won the Triple Crown with a .353 batting average, 52 home runs, and 130 RBIs. Mantle won back to back Most Valuable Player awards in 1956 and 1957.

In 1961, both he and teammate Roger Maris made a run at **Babe Ruth**'s single-season record of 60 home runs. Maris broke the record with 61 while Mantle finished with 54. Mantle won his third Most Valuable Player trophy the following year.

During the 18 seasons Mantle was with the Yankees, the team played in 12 World Series, winning the championship seven times. He retired in 1968, with 536 career home runs, and 1,509 RBIs, and having played in 20 All-Star games. He was inducted into the Hall of Fame in 1974.

As a result of excessive drinking both during and after his baseball career, Mantle developed liver cancer. He received a liver transplant on June 8, 1995, but died on August 13, 1995, at the age of 63. During his final days, Mantle heightened public awareness of the importance of organ donorship and acknowledged that abusing alcohol shortened his career. "Don't be like me," he cautioned young athletes. "God gave me a body and the ability to play baseball. He gave me everything. I just wasted it."

Career Capsule

Hit 536 career home runs and drove in 1,509 runs. Won three MVP awards 1956, 1957, and 1962. Slugged longest ever recorded home run, 565 feet. Led American League in home runs four times and runs scored six times and won Triple Crown in 1956. Holds all-time World Series records for HR(18), RBI (40), runs scored (42), and walks (43). Appeared in 20 All-Star games.

PAT McCORMICK

born May 12, 1930

PATRICIA MCCORMICK was the first woman to win gold medals in both diving events at two consecutive Olympiads (1952 and 1956). Her grace, daring, agility, and hard work set the standard for all divers that followed her. Since 1924, U.S. men and women had won every Olympic diving gold medal—in both platform and springboard diving. McCormick continued the U.S. dominance in diving and took it to a new level.

Born Patricia Keller in Seal Beach, California, she grew up in the waters of the Pacific coast. The local surfers enjoyed her company—and the somersaults and twists she would practice after they tossed her into the air from their surfboards. As a teenager, Pat refined her diving technique by training at the Los Angeles Aquatics Club. She practiced six days a week, performing 80 to 100 dives a day. Her hard work paid off when she finished second in the national platform diving competition in 1947. She missed making the 1948 Olympic team by less than one point.

Shortly after marrying airline pilot Glenn McCormick—who would later serve as coach of the U.S. diving team—Pat McCormick won her first national championship in platform diving in 1949. The next year, she defended her platform title and won the national springboard championship, too. By 1951, no one could beat her. McCormick won all five of that year's U.S. indoor and outdoor events, becoming the first diver ever to sweep all five Amateur Athletic Union titles. At that year's Pan-American games in Buenos Aires, Argentina, she won the gold medal in platform diving and the silver in the springboard competition.

At the 1952 Olympic Games in Helsinki, Finland, McCormick, the leader of the U.S. swimming and diving team, took gold medals in both the platform and the three-meter springboard events. She clearly outperformed the competition, executing her dives almost flawlessly. A one and one-half gainer from the springboard was the highest scoring dive in competition. From the platform, she performed a running, one and a half somersault with a pike and a handstand into a forward half gainer.

McCormick continued to outshine all other divers over the next four years, winning 77 national championships. In the 1955 Pan-American games in Mexico City, she improved on her 1951 performance by taking the gold in both diving competitions. Though pregnant that year, she maintained a rigorous training schedule, swimming a half-mile every day until two days before giving birth.

Just five months later, McCormick returned to competition at the 1956 Olympic Games in Melbourne, Australia. Once again, she executed difficult dives to near perfection. McCormick became the first diver, male or female, to defend her Olympic gold medals in both the platform and the springboard. (Greg Louganis would match this feat in 1984 and 1988, twice winning Olympic gold in both the men's platform and springboard events.) Named Female Athlete of the Year by the Associated Press, McCormick also became only the second woman honored with the Sullivan Award, presented to the nation's best amateur athlete of the year.

McCormick won gold in both platform and three-meter springboard events.

After completing her competitive career, McCormick established a diving camp to train future champions. The first woman ever elected to the International Swimming Hall of Fame in 1965, McCormick was also inducted into the Women's Sports Hall of Fame in 1984, and the U.S. Olympic Hall of Fame a year later. She has also served as a member of the U.S. Olympic Committee and the 1984 Los Angeles Olympic Organizing Committee. In 1984, McCormick was invited to join a select group of American Olympic heroes in escorting the Olympic flag into the Los Angeles Coliseum. She then watched with pride as her daughter Kelly, one of her diving students, won a silver medal.

Career Capsule

Gold medalist in platform and springboard in two consecutive Olympics (1952 and 1956). Won three gold medals and one silver in the Pan-American Games. Received Sullivan Award in 1956.

Jackie Robinson

January 31, 1919–October 24, 1972

JACKIE ROBINSON WAS the first African American to play baseball in the major leagues in this century. Robinson changed the game of baseball as much through the style of his play as the color of his skin. A fiery competitor, Robinson was a clutch hitter and a brilliant, thrilling baserunner. He brought hustle and daring onto the field, breathing new life into the game. Robinson's success opened the doors for blacks in other sports as well as baseball.

Jack Roosevelt Robinson was born in Cairo, Georgia. After his father deserted the family when Jackie was 18 months old, his mother packed up her five children and moved to Pasadena, California. Jackie sold hot dogs at the Rose Bowl and delivered newspapers to help the family make ends meet. Jackie was a brilliant athlete. He starred in football, basketball, baseball, and track in high school. At Pasadena Junior College, Jackie set a record with a long jump of 25 feet, 6½ inches. In his second year, Jackie led all junior-college baseball players with a .466 batting average.

Jackie's athletic achievements won him a scholarship to the University of California at Los Angeles (UCLA). Again, he starred in four different sports. In football, Jackie averaged 12 yards per carry and was the nation's leading punt returner. In basketball, he twice led the Pacific Coast Conference (PCC) in scoring. In baseball, he stole five bases—including home—in his first college game. In track, he won the national collegiate title with a long jump of 24 feet, 10.25 inches.

While serving in the army during World War II, First Lieutenant Robinson demanded equal treatment and civil rights for black soldiers and demonstrated his willingness to stand up for his principles. Robinson challenged the illegal segregation of an army bus. He was court-martialed (tried by the army) for his refusal to move to the back of the bus. Yet Robinson would not back down. He was found not guilty. After the war ended in 1945, he coached for one semester at the all-black Samuel Houston College in Austin, Texas. He then batted .340 for one season as a shortstop with the Kansas City Monarchs of the Negro National League.

Late that season, Branch Rickey, general manager of the Brooklyn Dodgers, came to watch Robinson play. Rickey claimed to be looking for players for a new Negro league team, the Brooklyn Brown Dodgers. After the season ended, Rickey shrewdly signed Robinson to a contract with the major-league Dodgers. Some people thought Robinson was an odd choice to break baseball's color

After a year at first base, Jackie moved to second for the next five years.

Robinson was a fast base runner who could steal home. When he was on base, he distracted pitchers with his base-running ability.

barrier. In college, he had excelled more in other sports than in baseball. He had only one year of experience in the Negro Leagues. And he was already 26 years old. *The Sporting News* wrote a nasty scouting report: "Robinson is reported to possess baseball abilities which, if he were white, would make him eligible for a trial with, say, the Dodgers' Class B farm at Newport News (Virginia)—if he were six years younger." But Rickey chose Robinson not just for his athletic skills. Rickey recognized the kind of man Robinson was: fiercely competitive, mentally tough, and keenly intelligent.

Before joining the Dodgers, Robinson spent a year on the team's top farm club, the Montreal Royals. Robinson led the International League in hitting (.349) and won the league's Most Valuable Player (MVP) award. He had proved that he belonged.

As the first black to play in the major leagues, Robinson made history. But to do so, he had to endure racial insults, deliberate spikings, and even the coldness of some teammates. "I had to fight hard against loneliness, abuse, and the knowledge that any mistake I made would be magnified because I was the only black man out there," he later commented. Rickey had urged him to hold his temper in check for at least the first year, and Robinson agreed. Robinson unflinchingly took the insults and attacks. He played his game and was strong enough *not* to fight back. He did receive support from some teammates. Shortstop and team captain Pee Wee Reese, in particular, made a point before one game of putting his arm around Robinson's shoulder in a sign of solidarity.

The Dodgers instantly became the favorite team of African Americans throughout the nation. As basketball player **Bill Russell** once noted, "They picked up 20 million fans instantly." When the Dodgers came to town, attendance skyrocketed.

Robinson played a smart, aggressive game. He created runs not only with his hitting but with his baserunning. He would steal any base, including home. He regularly raced from first to third on a single. He would tag up and score on short fly balls to the outfield. Indeed, as a baserunner, Robinson probably caused more opposing teams to beat themselves than anyone else in the game. By dancing off first base, Robinson rattled pitchers into making countless balks and wild throws. His ability to distract a pitcher also helped improve his teammates' hitting. Robinson would routinely break for the next base to pull infielders and outfielders out of position. He would then suddenly stop and let the hitter find the holes he had created in the defense. Or he would go halfway to the next base on a shallow pop fly, daring the outfielder to throw him out. Often, the outfielder would end up embarrassing himself. This style of play—aimed at rattling the opposing team—was well known in the Negro Leagues, where it was called "tricky ball." But the white major leagues had never seen anything like it before.

As the Dodger first baseman, Robinson led the league in stolen bases (29) in 1947. He batted .297 with 125 runs scored. *The Sporting News*, which had doubted his abilities, selected him as the National League (NL) Rookie of the Year.

In his second season, Robinson switched to second base—a position he would hold for the next five years. He became one of the leaders of the Boys of Summer—the Dodger team that won six NL pennants in Robinson's ten seasons. Robinson usually batted cleanup—an honor on a team that boasted such sluggers as Duke Snider, Gil Hodges, and **Roy Campanella**.

Robinson had his best year in 1949. He led the league with a .342 average and 37 steals. He also drove in 124 runs. All three figures were career highs for him. The Dodgers won the NL pennant for the second time in three years. And Robinson was named the league's MVP.

Baseball's First Black Players

Jackie Robinson is often mistakenly considered baseball's first black player. However, in 1884, catcher Fleet Walker and his brother Welday had played for Toledo in the American Association. (The American Association was a major league from 1882 until 1891, when it merged with the National League.) Little is known of Welday Walker, who batted just .222. Fleet Walker, however, played in 42 games and batted 152 times. He hit .263 with 23 runs scored.

The unwritten rule that banned blacks from playing in the majors originated with Cap Anson, baseball's biggest star of the 1880s. As player-manager of the Chicago White Sox, Anson refused to let his team take the field against Toledo until Walker was removed from the team. Anson's racism—and the willingness of other teams to go along with it—laid the groundwork for baseball's 63-year ban on black players.

Two years later, the Dodgers went into the final game of the season needing a win. They had blown a 13-game lead over the New York Giants. If they lost again, the Giants would win the pennant. In the ninth inning, Robinson made a spectacular rolling catch to keep the game tied. Then in the 13th, he homered to win the game. The Dodgers and Giants ended the regular season in a tie. The Giants went on to win a memorable three-game playoff series.

By the mid-1950s, Robinson felt he had turned the other cheek long enough. With the presence of black players in the major leagues established, he began to speak his mind. He criticized the continuing racism in the game. He complained that black players still had to be better than—rather than just as good as—whites in order to play in the majors.

Robinson played primarily third base and the outfield after 1952. In 1954, he batted over .300 and made the All-Star team, both for the sixth straight year. The next year, the Dodgers won their fifth pennant in Robinson's nine years with the club. All four of his previous World Series appearances had ended in defeat to the New York Yankees. In 1955, however, the Dodgers finally edged the Yankees in seven games. The following year, the Dodgers won their fourth pennant in five years—but lost the World Series to the Yankees again. After the season ended, the 37-year-old Robinson was traded to the Dodgers' crosstown rivals, the Giants. Rather than accept the trade, Robinson chose to retire.

Robinson was elected to the Baseball Hall of Fame in 1962, his first year on the ballot. After his retirement, he became an executive with the Chock Full O' Nuts chain of coffee shops. He served as head of the board of the Freedom National Bank in Harlem (New York). In 1994, baseball honored his memory by renaming the Rookie of the Year Award the Jackie Robinson Award.

Career Capsule

Rookie of the year in 1947, the year he broke Major League Baseball's color barrier. National League MVP in 1949, batted .311 in his 10-year Dodger career.

BABE DIDRIKSON ZAHARIAS

June 26, 1914–September 27, 1956

BABE DIDRIKSON ZAHARIAS was one of the greatest athletes, male or female, in history. One of the best women basketball players in the country, Zaharias also won Olympic gold medals in track and field. But she gained her greatest fame as a champion golfer. No matter what sport she tried, she always wanted to be the best.

Mildred Didrikson grew up in Beaumont, Texas, during the Golden Age of Sports. Athletes and athletics surged in popularity in the 1920s. Despite the nation's enthusiasm for sports, few organized opportunities then existed for a budding female athlete. Yet Mildred took advantage of every opportunity. Using broomsticks and flatirons, she rigged up a weight-lifting machine in her back yard to help increase her strength and fitness. In the parks of Beaumont, she played baseball and football with boys—and outplayed most of them. Mildred also excelled at basketball, running, high-jumping, hurdling, swimming and diving, figure skating, even mumblety-peg and billiards. In baseball, she once hit five home runs in a single game. Since her powerful hitting reminded her friends of baseball's best player, **Babe Ruth**, they gave Mildred the nickname of "Babe." In high school, she played every sport that had a girls' team: basketball, golf, volleyball, baseball, tennis, and swimming. She even won a blue ribbon in sewing at the Texas State Fair.

Babe Didrikson Zaharias combined almost perfect form with power.

Babe's high school basketball team won every game in which she played. The star of the team, Babe once scored 104 points in a single game. An insurance company in Dallas quickly gave Didrikson a job as a typist so that she could play for the company's team, the Golden Cyclones. Didrikson was named an All-American basketball player three times with the Golden Cyclones. She led the team to three straight national finals from 1930 to 1932—and the national championship in 1931.

Didrikson also joined the Golden Cyclones track team. She had never competed in track and field before. At her first meet with the Cyclones, she won four events to lead her team to the overall trophy. At the 1930 national Amateur Athletic Union (AAU) meet, she set new American records in both the javelin throw and the baseball throw. The following year, she won three events in the national championships. At the AAU nationals in 1932, Didrikson won five events (long jump, javelin throw, shot put, baseball throw, and 80-meter hurdles) and tied another (high jump)—in a single day! Her marks in the javelin, hurdles, and high jump set new world records. The only member of her team, the Employers Casualty Insurance Company of Dallas, she scored 30 points at the meet to win both the individual and team championship. The second place team, 22 women from the University of Illinois, scored just 22 points combined!

Didrikson's amazing performance at the AAU nationals won her a spot on the U.S. Olympic team. Olympic rules, however, limited her to just three events. So Didrikson chose the three events in which she had just set world records. At the 1932 Olympic Games in Los Angeles, California, Didrikson won the gold medal in the javelin throw. Though the javelin slipped out of her hand, she still managed to hurl it more than 143 feet. Two days later, she set a world record of 11.7 seconds in winning the 80-meter hurdles. Didrikson then tied for first place in the high jump, setting a new world's record of 5 feet, 5¼ inches. In a "jump-off" with U.S. teammate Jean Shiley, both women cleared 5 feet, 5¾ inches. But the judges ruled that Didrikson had "dived" because her head crossed the bar before her body. Though Didrikson's style would become common in the high jump several years later, she was awarded only the silver medal. However, the height she and Shiley had cleared would remain a world record throughout the decade and an Olympic record until 1948.

Her Olympic medals made Didrikson the nation's best known female athlete. Almost everywhere she went, parades were held in her honor. She was heralded in the nation's newspapers. The Associated Press (AP) named her Female Athlete of the Year. When she allowed a photograph of herself to be used in an automobile ad, however, the AAU stripped her of her amateur status. As a professional, she toured the country with the Babe Didrikson All-American Basketball Team. She also barnstormed with the House of David baseball team. (As a gimmick, all the members of the team had to grow beards or wear false ones—all except Didrikson.) In a spring training game, she once pitched for the St. Louis Cardinals against the Philadelphia Phillies. She also toured giving billiard exhibitions. In addition, she offered demonstrations of so-called "womanly arts," such as needlework and typing. (She could type 86 words per minute.)

After the Olympics, Didrikson turned her attention to golf. She loved the game and worked hard to improve her play. She practiced by driving up to 1,000 golf balls a day. Often, her hands were so tired and sore by the end of the day that they had to be taped. By 1935, she had won her first tournament: the Texas Women's Golf Association Amateur championship. The United States Golf Association (USGA) then ruled that she could no longer compete as an amateur. Her years playing exhibition basketball and baseball games had made her a professional athlete. Yet few professional golf tournaments for women existed in the 1930s and 1940s. For this reason, amateur events offered much more recognition. After marrying professional wrestler George Zaharias in 1938, Babe Didrikson Zaharias worked to regain her amateur status. She entered a few professional tournaments, but refused cash prizes whenever she won.

In 1944, the USGA again recognized Zaharias as an amateur. She won the Women's Western Open Championship that year and the next. The AP again selected her the Female Athlete of the Year in 1945. This made her the only athlete ever awarded this honor in two different sports. Zaharias then went on a tear, winning 17 straight tournaments in 1946 and 1947. She captured the national championship at the U.S. Women's Amateur tournament in 1946. The following year, Zaharias became the first American woman to win the British Ladies' Amateur championship. Twice more named AP Female Athlete of the Year, she was the first person, woman or man, to win the AP Athlete of the Year award three years in a row. (**Maureen Connolly** [1951–53] and **Michael Jordan** [1991–93] have since matched this feat.)

After winning the best known amateur events, Zaharias turned pro again. In her first year, she won more money than any other woman in golf. She won the 1948 U.S. Women's Open and the first of four straight world championship titles. The following year, Zaharias helped organize the Ladies Professional Golf Association (LPGA). The LPGA still sponsors most of the major professional golf tournaments for women throughout the world. On the new LPGA tour, Zaharias continued to be the

She threw the javelin in the 1932 Olympics in Los Angeles.

Babe is still the only athlete ever to be named Female Athlete of the Year in two different sports.

leading money winner from 1949 to 1951. After finishing as runner-up in the 1949 U.S. Women's Open, she regained the title again in 1950. That year, she captured the Titleholders Championship, a major pro event that she had already won as an amateur in 1947. She was selected as the AP Female Athlete of the Year for the fifth time in 1950. By the end of the year, Zaharias had won every golf title available at least once. She also became the first female professional athlete to earn more than $100,000 a year through exhibitions, endorsements, and other activities related to sports.

Zaharias won her third Titleholders Championship in 1952. The following year she won the first "Babe Zaharias Open" in her hometown of Beaumont, Texas. Soon afterward, she discovered she had cancer. Yet she returned to golf less than four months after undergoing surgery. The Golf Writers of America applauded her heroic comeback from cancer by awarding Zaharias the first Ben Hogan Trophy, which honors golfers who overcome serious physical hardships to play. Her inspiring comeback continued through the U.S. Women's Open, which she won for the third time—by an incredible 12 strokes! Zaharias also won that year's Vare Trophy, given annually to the woman with the lowest average score on the pro tour for the year. The Associated Press named her Female Athlete of the Year for a sixth time, a record among all athletes. (**Chris Evert** is second with four selections.) Zaharias, whose 31 professional wins included 12 major events, died when the cancer returned in 1956.

Babe Zaharias was one of the first famous female athletes in the United States. Her successes in basketball, the Olympics, and golf led the Associated Press to name Zaharias the Female Athlete of the Half Century in 1950. Zaharias showed what a determined, hard-working woman could accomplish in sports. And she inspired a generation of female athletes to follow her example of excellence.

Career Capsule

As a basketball player, named an All-American three times (1930–32). During those same three years, she won 11 track and field titles at the annual AAU nationals. She won two gold (80-meter hurdles and javelin) and silver (high jump) medals at the 1932 Olympic Games. Became a golfer in 1935, and won 12 major titles, including the U.S. Open three times (1948, 1950, and 1954). Later became a founder and star of the LPGA tour, winning 31 events in her career.

CHAPTER 7

UPHEAVAL

SPORTS IN A TIME OF CHANGE

1959–1970

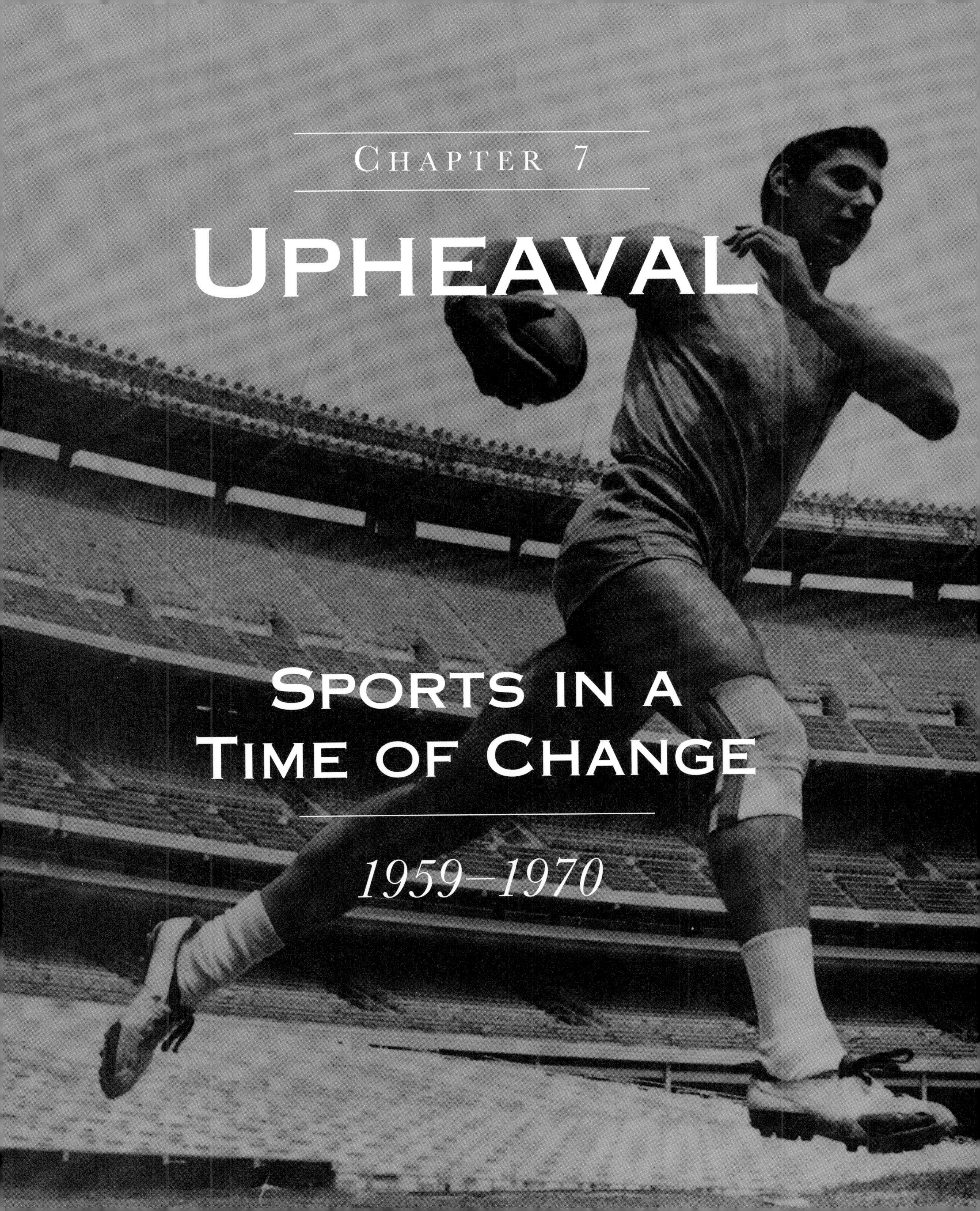

When John F. Kennedy was elected President in 1960, America seemed full of the idealism and youthfulness that he personified. In 1961, Kennedy challenged the nation to put a man on the moon by 1970. Toward that goal, in 1961, the United States sent its first astronaut, Alan Shepard, into space. Kennedy also founded the Peace Corps to send volunteers to help out in developing nations. Yet the idealism and youthful spirit of the age brought increasing demands at home for social change.

The civil rights movement made great strides in the early part of the Sixties. In 1963, Martin Luther King, Jr., led 250,000 protesters—black and white—in a March on Washington to demand new civil rights laws. With President Lyndon B. Johnson's strong support, the Civil Rights Act of 1964 made it illegal to consider a person's race in hiring decisions or to segregate public places. The principles practiced in professional baseball by Branch Rickey were now the law.

Black Athletes Spotlighted

Whether or not they wanted the role, African American athletes became symbols of the advancement of their race. The dramatic expansion of televised sports put athletes increasingly in the public eye. Heavyweight boxing champ Cassius Clay shocked the world when he announced that he had converted to the Black Muslim religion and changed his name to **Muhammad Ali**.

In 1962, **Jackie Robinson** became the first African American elected to the Baseball Hall-of-Fame. In 1967, Charles Sifford became the first African American to win a Professional Golf Association (PGA) tour event, the Hartford Open. In 1968, **Arthur Ashe** became the first African American man to win a major tennis title. Pro basketball was dominated by the rivalry of two outspoken young black men: **Wilt Chamberlain**, who broke almost every NBA record, and **Bill Russell**, a dedicated team player. In 1966, Russell became the first black head coach of a professional team. In 1970, another black, **Curt Flood**, fought against what he called the "slavery" of baseball's player contracts. He took baseball's owners to court, challenging their right to control a player for the life of his career.

For many, change was not coming fast enough. Russell, for example, remained the only African American to head a team for nearly a decade. The slow pace of racial progress prompted the birth of the radical Black Power movement. In the 1968 Mexico City Olympics, U.S. sprinting medalists Tommie Smith and John Carlos raised their fists in the Black Power salute while "The Star Spangled Banner" was played for them. This offended many Americans but inspired many others.

Women, too, demanded equal rights. Tennis star **Billie Jean King**, a champion of women's rights on and off the court, almost single-handedly established women's sports as a profitable business. In 1967, **Kathrine Switzer** became the first woman to run officially in the Boston Marathon. However, officials hadn't known that they issued a number to a woman when they accepted K.V. Switzer. When **Kathy Whitworth** became president of the LPGA in 1970, she greatly increased the sponsorship and the size of championship purses on the women's tour. Her aim: to get women's prizes on a par with those on the men's tour.

VIOLENT TIMES

Tragically, violence was often paired with social change. Assassins killed John F. Kennedy, Black Muslim leader Malcolm X, Nobel Peace Prize winner Martin Luther King, Jr., and Senator Robert F. Kennedy (John's brother).

The Southeast Asian country of Vietnam was engaged in a civil war against the communists. Under Presidents Kennedy and Lyndon Johnson, the U.S. backed South Vietnam. By 1967, 400,000 United States troops were there.

The war soon became controversial in the United States. Across the nation, demonstrators protested the war. One of the most controversial of the war's opponents was boxer Muhammad Ali. He announced that his beliefs as a Black Muslim prevented him from serving in Vietnam. He claimed he was a "conscientious objector." Although some conscientious objectors served out their military terms in peaceful pursuits, Ali's request was denied. In 1968, he was found guilty of avoiding the draft. Two years later, the Supreme Court reversed the decision.

Antiwar protests often met with violence or caused it. In 1970, National Guardsmen killed four students protesting the war at Kent State University in Ohio. Demonstrators gathered in Washington to protest. President Richard Nixon left the White House at early dawn one May morning to try to reason with the demonstrators. Nixon attempted to find a common ground with them by talking about football and surfing. He misunderstood. Sports were no longer the main concern of America's college students. They wanted the war ended. Eventually, Nixon supported peace negotiations, and the United States left Vietnam.

Sports also came under attack. Critics charged that sports served those in power. They said football taught militarism to American youth. Sport's defenders claimed that they represented the American way of life. By the mid-1960s, sports was no longer sacred and unexamined.

Despite all the unrest, the 1960s ended with hope. Astronauts Neil Armstrong and Edwin "Buzz" Aldrin met Kennedy's challenge by walking on the moon in 1969. As awareness of the planet's environment increased, Americans celebrated Earth Day for the first time.

In October 1969, the "Miracle" New York Mets won their first baseball world championship. The Mets were one of three champions in New York City that year. The New York Jets, behind the passing of quarterback **Joe Willie Namath**, won the professional football championship, and the New York Knicks, inspired by unselfish players such as **Bill Bradley**, won the national basketball championship.

SPORTS AND PRIDE:

The Special Olympics

The physical, mental, and emotional benefits of sports and exercise for both children and adults had long been recognized by the 1960s. Yet most people believed that the mentally retarded could handle neither the physical demands of sport nor the emotional stress of competition. Eunice Shriver, the sister of President John F. Kennedy, set out to challenge these stereotypes. (Like 7.5 million other Americans, Rosemary Kennedy, one of their sisters, was mentally retarded.)

In 1968, Shriver founded the Special Olympics. The organization offers athletic training for people with mental disabilities. It also sponsors regional, national, and international Olympic-style competion. In addition to improving physical conditioning, competitive sports has helped retarded participants develop self-confidence and has led them to perform better in school and on the job.

The first Special Olympics games, held that year at Chicago's Soldier Field, featured 900 athletes from 26 states and Canada competing in track and field, swimming, and floor hockey. The success of the first games soon prompted other states—and other countries—to open their own Special Olympics chapters. By the mid-1990s, the organization was working with more than one million mentally disabled people in 130 different countries.

HENRY AARON

born February 5, 1934

HANK AARON IS BEST remembered for eclipsing **Babe Ruth**'s home run record. Though he was much more than just a power hitter, Aaron left his mark by hitting 755 home runs during his illustrious Hall-of-Fame career.

Hank was born and raised in Mobile, Alabama. One of eight children, he learned to play baseball by hitting bottle caps with a broomstick. He began developing his arm and wrist strength by hauling 25-pound blocks of ice at an early age.

Signed by the Indianapolis Clowns of the old Negro American League, Aaron began playing semi-pro ball at age 16. A scout advised him to switch his cross-handed batting grip, and he responded by hitting two home runs in his first game.

The Milwaukee Braves bought Aaron's contract in 1952, just five years after **Jackie Robinson** broke baseball's color barrier. They sent him to play in the minor leagues where he hit .336 the first season. He won the league batting title the next season with a .362 average while accumulating 125 RBIs, and 115 runs scored. The Braves' regular left fielder broke his ankle early in 1954, which gave Aaron the opportunity to play regularly at the age of 20.

In 1956, Aaron won his first of two National League batting titles with a .328 average. He earned National Most Valuable Player honors in 1957 batting .322 with 44 homers and 132 RBIs. Aaron led the Braves to the pennant that year and then to the World Series, where they defeated the New York Yankees in seven games. Aaron hit .393 during the series, while launching three home runs.

During Aaron's major-league career, he was the model of consistency. He may not have been the most glamorous player of his time, but he was certainly the most reliable with the bat. Fourteen times during his career, he batted over .300. He hit 30 or more home runs during 15 seasons, and 40 or more in eight of those years. He led the league in homers four times, RBIs four times, batting average twice, and total hits twice. Aaron played in 24 All-Star games and won three Gold Glove awards.

The key to Aaron's success at the plate was his exceptionally quick wrists and powerful forearms. Even when pitchers could fool Aaron by changing the speed of the pitch, he was able to hit the ball with power. Pitchers were afraid to throw him fastballs because of his quick reflexes. "Throwing a fastball by Henry Aaron," pitcher Curt Simmons said, "is like trying to sneak sunrise past a rooster."

The Braves moved to Atlanta, Georgia, in 1966, and to a stadium where it was easier to hit home runs. By his late 30s, he was getting close to Babe Ruth's career record of 714 home runs. He hit 40 homers in 1973, giving him 713 for his career—one

Aaron displays the powerful wrists that made him a home-run threat every time he came to the plate.

April 8, 1974—Aaron hit his 715th homer against the Los Angeles Dodgers, breaking Babe Ruth's career record.

shy of Ruth's record. Aaron hit number 714 on opening day of the 1974 season to tie Ruth. On April 8, at Atlanta's opening home game against Los Angeles, Aaron drove an Al Downing fastball over the left-center field fence for his 715th career home run. Circling the bases before the Atlanta fans was a moment that Aaron will never forget.

"I was in my own little world at the time. It was like running in a bubble and I could see all these people jumping up and down and waving their arms in slow motion," he said. "I was told I had a big smile on my face as I came around third. I purposely never smiled as I ran the bases after a home run, but I suppose I couldn't help it that time."

Aaron finished his major league career with 755 home runs and 2,297 RBIs; both are still records. He hit 245 homers after he turned 35 years of age, which is also a record.

Following his retirement as an active player in 1975, Aaron joined the Braves' front office as Vice President and Director of Player Development. He was appointed to Senior Vice President and Assistant to the President of the Braves in 1989. Aaron is also vice president of the board of directors of Turner Broadcasting and serves on the National Board of the National Association for the Advancement of Colored People.

Career Capsule

Baseball's all-time home run leader. Also holds career records for Most Long Hits (1,477) and Most Total Bases (6,856). Ranks second on the all-time list in at-bats (12,364) and runs scored (2,174), third in games (3,298) and hits (3,771), ninth in doubles (624), and 11th in singles (2,294). Became the first player to ever compile both 3,000 hits and more than 500 home runs. He was the National League's Most Valuable Player in 1957, and named Player of Year by *The Sporting News* in 1956 and 1963.

Muhammad Ali

born January 17, 1942

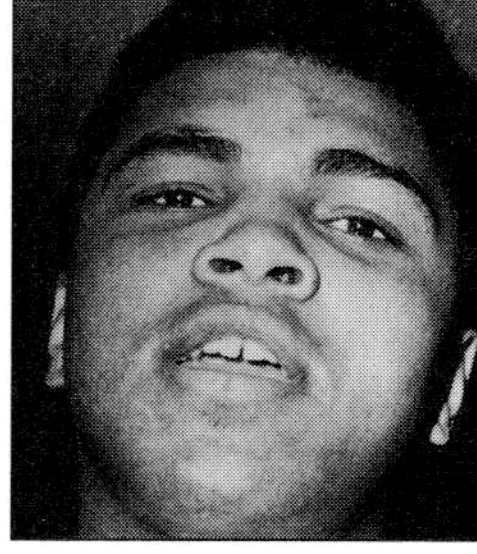

"I AM THE GREATEST," Muhammad Ali used to boast. "I'm bigger than boxing." As usual, Ali's boast proved genuine. In the 1960s, Ali's personal struggles mirrored the explosive social issues of the day: the clash between racism and racial pride, the fight against religious intolerance, and the movement to end the military draft and the Vietnam War. His personal decisions made Ali a symbolic figure. Ten years later, the most recognized man in the world was neither a national leader nor a movie star. He was Muhammad Ali.

As a fighter, Ali drew attention to himself through his clowning, poems, taunts, and predictions of the rounds in which his opponents would fall. But

Ali, who began his career as Cassius Clay, defeated former two-time champ, Floyd Patterson, in 1965. Ali won in 12 rounds.

the clowning stopped once he stepped into the ring. He combined quickness, grace, power, and intelligence as a boxer. Daring and self-confident, Ali fought professionally for more than two decades. And he won the heavyweight championship three different times.

Cassius Marcellus Clay, Jr., who later took the name Muhammad Ali, was born in Louisville, Kentucky. His father worked as a sign painter and his mother as a domestic worker. They brought up Cassius and his younger brother Rudy as Baptists. When Cassius was 12 years old, his bicycle was stolen from the local youth center. He found a police officer supervising boxers in a nearby gym. When the officer invited him to join the boxers, Cassius stepped into the ring for the first time.

Between 1954 and 1960, Cassius won 100 amateur bouts and lost only 8. He won six Kentucky Golden Gloves titles and two national championships. In 1960, Cassius also captured the International Golden Gloves crown in the heavyweight division. At the 1960 Olympic Games in Rome, Italy, Cassius won the light heavyweight gold medal.

He returned to Louisville a hero. Yet he found that even an Olympic medal did not ensure he could get into a "whites-only" restaurant. One ugly racial incident grew into a fight with the head of a white motorcycle gang. After the brawl ended, Cassius considered throwing his gold medal in the Ohio River in disgust. Racism made him feel like an outsider in his own country. He no longer felt proud to be an American.

After winning every title he could as an amateur, Cassius—standing 6 feet, 3 inches tall and weighing 200 pounds—decided to turn pro in 1960. He won his first professional bout, a six-round decision, later that year. Over the next four years, he won each of his 20 bouts. Ali credited his early success as a pro to his quickness, which allowed him to avoid his op-

Ali's self-confidence was obvious wherever he went.

ponents' punches and tire them out. "It takes a lot out of a fighter to throw punches that land in thin air," he wrote in his 1975 autobiography, *The Greatest: My Own Story*. "Throughout my amateur days, old boxers think I'm easy to hit, but I'm not. I concentrate on defense. I concentrate on timing and motions and pulling back. When I throw a jab, I know my opponent will throw a punch, and I pull back."

By 1964, Clay had won the right to fight the champ, Sonny Liston, for the heavyweight title. Liston was a heavy favorite to win the bout, which took place in Miami, Florida, on February 25. But the younger boxer danced in circles around the champ, taunting and pounding him for six rounds. When the bell rang to signal the start of the seventh round, Liston could not come out from his corner. Clay had become the new heavyweight champion of the world.

Shortly after winning the title, Cassius Clay accepted a new religion, the Nation of Islam, and adopted a new name: Muhammad Ali. His decision to convert was not popular with many of his fans. Many whites mistakenly saw the religion as based in racial hatred.

Ali and Liston met for a rematch in Lewiston, Maine, 15 months later. Ali flattened Liston in one minute and 42 seconds—the second quickest knockout ever in a heavyweight title bout. Later in 1965, Ali fought two-time champ Floyd Paterson in Las Vegas. When the referee stopped the fight and declared Ali the winner after 12 rounds, Ali had kept Paterson from becoming a three-time champion.

In 1966, Ali made another decision that was widely critized. The United States was fighting in Vietnam, and Ali had learned that his local draft board would soon be calling him up to serve in the military. Ali refused to go, formally notifying the draft board that he was a "conscientious objector." (This means a person whose deepest beliefs prevent her or him from killing or other warfare.) "I ain't got no quarrel with them Vietcong," he explained. (The Vietcong were enemy soldiers in the war.) The backlash from those who questioned Ali's patriotism forced the cancellation of his next fight. For most of the rest of the year, promoters scheduled Ali's fights outside of the United States.

Despite the turmoil, Ali had perhaps the greatest year of his boxing career in 1966. He overcame five challengers, knocking out four of them, to hold on to his title. The following year, he won two fights, one by knockout.

Ali was ordered to report to the U.S. Army base in Houston, Texas, in April 1967. When he refused to join the army for religious reasons, Ali was charged with failing to comply with the draft. Within hours, the New York Boxing Commission (NYBC) and the World Boxing Association (WBA) stripped Ali of his title—and his license to fight in the United States. A court in Houston found him guilty and Ali was sentenced to five years in prison and a $10,000 fine. He remained out of prison while his lawyers appealed the verdict—all the way to the U.S. Supreme Court.

Though many people in mainstream America now hated Ali, he became a folk hero among blacks, those who protested against the Vietnam War, the poor, and people in less developed nations. For the next three years, Ali drew crowds lecturing on college campuses or speaking before peace rallies.

In Ali's absence, the heavyweight crown was split. The WBA gave its title to Jimmy Ellis, who had won a tournament featuring the eight top-ranked boxers. The NYBC and five other state boxing commissions recognized "Smokin' Joe" Frazier—who had been ranked number one but had refused to box in the WBA tournament—as the champ. The title remained split until 1970, when Frazier stopped Ellis in five rounds.

In 1970, the U.S. Supreme Court reversed Ali's conviction. The court recognized his right to refuse to serve in the military for religious reasons. A Federal judge also ruled that the NYBC had been wrong to strip Ali of his boxing license.

With Ali back in the ring, the stage was set for what was billed as the "Fight of the Century." Ali met Frazier for the first time in New York's Madison Square Garden in March 1971. Although he was smaller, Frazier landed countless left hooks. In the 15th round, he knocked Ali down for only the third time in his career. Frazier won a unanimous decision to retain the heavyweight title.

During the next three years, Ali won 12 of 13 bouts, six by knockout. His only loss came in a split decision to Ken Norton. But Ali had come back to beat Norton in a rematch. His long-awaited rematch with Frazier came in January 1974. Frazier had lost

Ali trained hard before defending his title against Sonny Liston. The extra work paid off when Ali won in the first round.

Ali was as much a showman as he was an athlete.

the heavyweight crown to George Foreman a year earlier, but was still a tough fighter. Though Frazier landed some punishing blows in the middle rounds, Ali won the 12-round fight by a unanimous decision of the judges.

Nine months later, Ali again fought for the heavyweight title in the African nation of Zaire. Foreman, the favorite, pounded Ali's body for seven rounds while Ali braced himself against the ropes. But Ali avoided any head blows and let Foreman wear himself out. Ali's savvy "rope-a-dope" strategy worked perfectly. He knocked out an exhausted Foreman in the eighth round. His victory made Ali only the second man in boxing history to regain the world heavyweight championship.

After three successful title defenses in 1975, Ali again fought Frazier. Ali called it the "Thrilla in Manila" (the Philippines). Their third and most exciting bout was a slugfest. Ali pounded Frazier for four rounds. In the fifth and sixth, Frazier came back to connect with a flurry of punches. By the tenth, the fight was even and Ali seemed finished. Yet in the 11th, he landed several crushing blows and saw that Frazier had no energy left to defend himself. Ali poured everything he had into the next three rounds. Though Frazier never fell, his manager kept him in his corner at the opening of the 15th round. Ali had won the most grueling fight of his career.

Ali defended his title in six more bouts over the next two and a half years. After surprisingly losing a 15-round split decision—and the title—to young Leon Spinks in 1978, Ali regained the title in a rematch seven months later. The only boxer to win the heavyweight title three times, the 36-year-old Ali soon announced his retirement from the ring and gave up his title.

Ali unwisely returned for two more fights, quitting in the 11th round against champion Larry Holmes in 1980, and losing a decision to Trevor Berbick in 1981.

Although Ali earned more than $50 million in his career, boxing badly damaged his body. He revealed in 1984 that he had Parkinson's Syndrome. Repeated blows to the head had left him with slurred speech, facial immobility, poor balance, and difficulty walking. In 1990, *Life* magazine selected Ali as one of only four athletes included among the "100 Most Important Americans of the Twentieth Century." Four years later, when *Sports Illustrated* celebrated its 40th anniversary, Ali was chosen as the single most influential sports figure of the previous 40 years. He was, in his own words, the greatest.

Career Capsule

Heavyweight title a record three times (1964–67; 1974–78; 1978–79). Won 56 of 61 professional fights, 37 by knockout. Also won Olympic gold as a light heavyweight in 1960.

Mario Andretti

born February 28, 1940

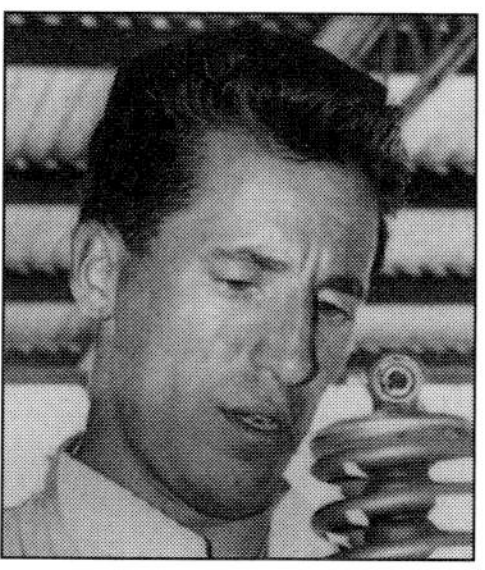

CHAMPION AUTOMOBILE racing driver Mario Andretti was the most versatile driver of all time. "I figure I was put on this earth to drive race cars," he once said. And drive them he did. Andretti achieved success in all types of racing. He drove stock cars, Indy cars, endurance cars, and Formula One racers—and won in each class.

Mario Gabriel Andretti was born in Montona, Italy, today part of Slovenia. After World War II, Mario, his twin brother, Aldo, and his older sister Anna Maria spent three years living in a refugee camp near Florence. The young twins developed a passion for auto racing. They loved watching the Mille Miglia, Italy's 1,000-mile cross-country road race. By age 13, Mario and Aldo were both studying auto mechanics and driving Formula One junior racing cars. (Formula One races are run mainly in Europe.)

When the twins were 15, the Andrettis immigrated to the United States and settled in Nazareth, Pennsylvania. Within three years, Mario and Aldo had bought and rebuilt their first stock car, which they took turns racing. Since their parents disapproved of auto racing, the twins kept their training a secret. When Aldo quit auto racing, after being severely injured in a crash in 1959, Mario left home rather than yield to his father's demand that he too give up racing. By 1960, Mario had already won 20 stock car races. He then switched to sprint cars—performance cars that race short distances—in the early 1960s. He also raced midget cars—drastically scaled-down racers—and won 11 midget car races in 1963.

A year later, Andretti began racing in the championship-car division of United States Auto Club (USAC)—later called Indy car races. The USAC sponsors speedway races, including the best known racing event in the country: the Indianapolis 500. Although Andretti won only one race in 1965, he took the USAC Championship (awarded on points earned through a driver's finishes in all USAC races). Andretti finished second six times and did not finish lower than fourth in any race that year. At the Indianapolis 500, he finished third and was voted the race's Rookie of the Year.

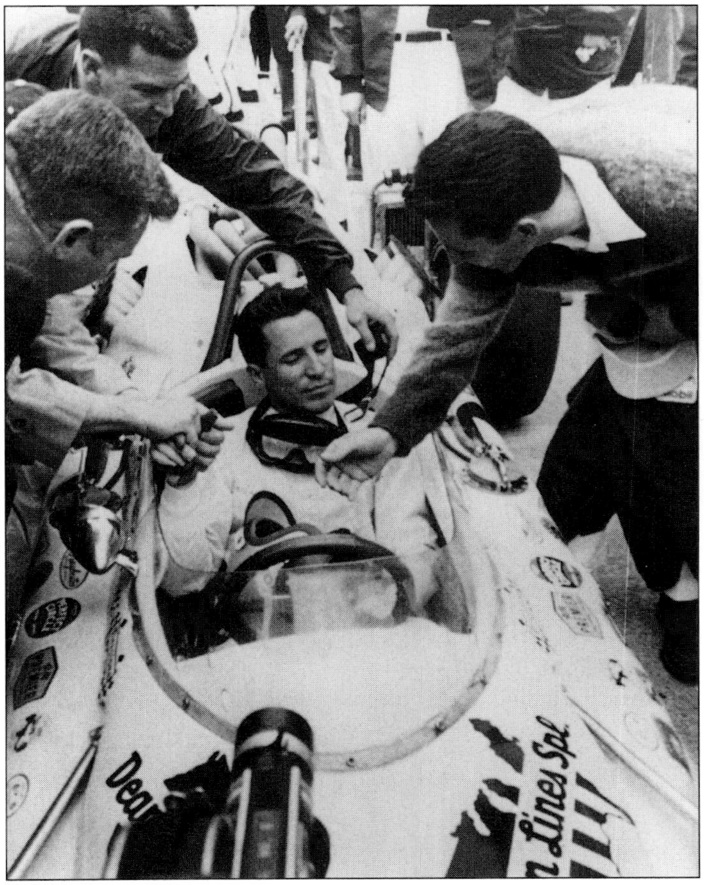

In 1966, Andretti's Indianapolis Speedway run was 165.9 mph.

Andretti won eight of 15 races in 1966 to earn his second straight USAC Championship. In 1967, he began competing in stock and sports car races, too. The USAC schedule did not offer enough action for Andretti. "If I stay home one weekend, I get irritable," he once explained. "If there's a race in Timbuktu, I've got to be there."

In 1967, Andretti won six Indy car races, five sprint car races, the Daytona Beach 500 (the premier NASCAR stock car event), and the 12-hour Grand Prix of Endurance race at Sebring, Florida. By the mid-1960s, Andretti was earning $90,000 in prize money and another $200,000 to endorse cars and tires. Among athletes in all sports, only golfer **Arnold Palmer** was earning more money at that time.

From 1966 to 1969, Andretti won 29 USAC races, including the big one, the Indy 500, with an average speed of 156.9 miles per hour in 1969. That year, he also won his third USAC Championship. Though he entered the Indy 500 twenty-five more times, Andretti never again won.

Daring and aggressive, Andretti won almost every other race at least once. In 1974, he won the USAC Dirt Car Championship. In 1978, driving a Lotus-designed car, Andretti became only the

Formula One gear offers plenty of protection.

second U.S. driver to win the Formula One world driving championship. He won his fourth Indy Car points Championship—second only to A.J. Foyt's seven titles—in 1984. His final Indy Car win, in 1993, made him the only driver ever to have won races in five different decades.

Though he retired from Indy Car racing in 1994, Andretti continued to race. In 1995, Andretti's team finished second, just three minutes behind the winner, in the 24 Hours of Le Mans in France.

Career Capsule

Only driver to win Daytona 500 (1967), Indy 500 (1969), and Formula One championship (1978). Twelve career Formula One victories, USAC/CART champion four times (1965–66, 1969, 1984). Won the pole position—given to the driver with the highest average speed in qualifying trials—a record 67 times.

Arthur Ashe

July 10, 1943–February 6, 1993

ALTHOUGH **Althea Gibson** had broken the color barrier in tennis in the 1950s, there had never been an outstanding black male tennis player until Arthur Ashe began to make his mark in the 1960s. Intelligent and witty, Ashe displayed a quiet dignity that—along with his powerful serve—commanded attention and respect.

Arthur was born in Richmond, Virginia, the son of a parks police officer. His mother died in 1949. A year later, at age seven, Arthur began playing tennis in a segregated (blacks only) playground next to his home. Arthur showed talent on the courts very early. Yet he never played in Virginia's junior tournaments, since blacks were not allowed to compete in them.

In his teens, Arthur improved his playing at Dr. Walter Johnson's tennis camp. Johnson, a fine player himself, had helped Gibson refine her game ten years earlier. Johnson helped Arthur evolve from a base line player to a savvy power hitter. Arthur developed a powerful serve, a brilliant backhand, and hard-hit, topspin ground strokes. By 1958, the

Ashe was the first black man playing top-level tennis at the time.

skinny 15-year-old had improved enough to reach the semifinals of the national junior championships. Johnson later introduced Arthur to tennis official Richard Hudlin. Hudlin offered to coach Ashe if he would move to St. Louis, where he could get more tournament experience. (Unlike Virginia, Missouri allowed blacks to compete in the state's junior tournaments.)

In 1961, Arthur helped Sumner High School win the U.S. Interscholastic Tournament. Black players had never been allowed to compete in the event before. His play earned him a full athletic scholarship to the University of California at Los Angeles (UCLA). Other racial barriers were about to fall. In 1963, Ashe won the U.S. Hard Court singles title. This made him the first black man to win a United States Tennis Association (USTA) tournament. Later that year, he became the first African American to play on the U.S. Davis Cup team. In 1965, Ashe became the first black to win the men's singles title in the U.S. Intercollegiate Championships. Ashe graduated from UCLA the following year with a degree in business administration and joined the U.S. Army. Ashe served for three years as a lieutenant in the Adjutant General's Corps, a position that allowed him to continue competing as an amateur tennis player.

In the finals of the first U.S. Amateur Singles Championship in 1968, Ashe lost two of the first three sets. But he came back to win the final two sets—and the national amateur title. The new amateur tournament had been created that year by the USTA because the open era of tennis had begun. Until 1968, most tournaments—including the four major events—had been open only to amateurs. In 1968, however, many tournaments became open to both amateur and professional players. The U.S. National Singles Championship became known as the U.S. Open.

Despite his amateur victory, Ashe was "seeded," or ranked only fifth among the male players at the new U.S. Open held at Forest Hills, New York. Few people expected him to perform as well in an event open to professionals. Yet Ashe served and volleyed brilliantly in the tournament. In the final match, Ashe beat Dutch pro Tom Okker in a hard-fought first set, 14 games to 12. He went on to serve 26 aces and win the first U.S. Open in five sets. In doing so, he became the first American to win the U.S. men's singles title since 1955. It was the first time an African-American player had won a major singles title since Althea Gibson in 1958. Ashe was the only player ever to win both national titles (U.S. Amateur and U.S. Open) in a single year.

In order to retain his amateur status, Ashe had to refuse the U.S. Open prize money. The Davis Cup was still open only to amateurs, and Ashe wanted to preserve his position on the U.S. team. He also needed to remain an amateur to get time away from his army duty for important tournaments. (The army did not give soldiers time off to make money.) So Okker received the $14,000 first prize, while Ashe took home $28 a day to cover his expenses.

By the end of 1968, Ashe was ranked number one among U.S. players. (He stayed among the top five from 1964 to 1976, holding the top ranking again in 1975.) Overall, he won ten tournaments and 72 of 82 matches that year. He had won 11

Ashe's tennis ability earned him an athletic scholarship to UCLA.

Though slender, Ashe generated power with his flawless form.

straight Davis Cup singles matches to help the United States to its first international victory in five years. Ashe, who turned pro in 1969, helped the United States retain its Davis Cup title for two more years. He won the longest final-round singles match in Davis Cup history in 1970. Ashe lost the first two sets before coming back to beat West Germany's Christian Kuhnke, 6–8, 10–12, 9–7, 13–11, 6–4. Later that year, he became the first black ever to win the Australian Open singles championship. In 1971, he won the French Open doubles title.

Ashe was virtually the only black man playing top-level tennis in the 1960s. He once observed, "I am often invited to clubs where other Negroes are admitted only as busboys." Despite his comment, Ashe did not enjoy being a symbol of the rise of African Americans in sports. He supported equal rights and opportunities for all races. But he did not feel that he had to be the spokesperson for the cause of black advancement just because he was black. Some people, blacks and whites, criticized him for being too soft spoken about racial issues.

Ashe's commitment to justice and equal opportunity was firm. He simply refused to limit his activism to issues defined by his race. For example, he spoke out much more against poverty than racism. He called for the improvement of living conditions for inner-city children. After retiring as a player, he set up tennis programs in several U.S. cities.

Ashe also strongly opposed apartheid—the laws in South Africa that until the 1990s offered almost no civil rights to people of color. In 1973, he received a visa to South Africa. He had applied twice before to play in the South African Open, but had been barred because of the color of his skin. In South Africa, Ashe could not stay in a hotel. South African hotels did not admit blacks. A young boy told Ashe that he had never seen a free black man before. Ashe then became the first black to reach the South African Open final, which he lost to Jimmy Connors.

In 1975, he had his most dramatic victory. Seeded sixth, Ashe upset the defending singles champion Jimmy Connors to win the All-England singles title at Wimbledon. The first black man to win at Wimbledon, Ashe constantly changed the pace and spin of the ball to win the four-set final, 6–1, 6–1, 5–7, 6–4. Two years later, he won his final Grand Slam championship: the Australian doubles title (with partner Tony Roche).

In 1978, Ashe helped the United States win the Davis Cup for the fifth time in his ten years on the team. Only three players (**Bill Tilden**, Stan Smith, and John McEnroe) have represented the United States in Davis Cup play more times than Ashe. Overall, he won 27 of 32 singles matches for the U.S. team.

Ashe suffered the first of three heart attacks in 1979. He retired from tennis the following year. The first African-American millionaire in tennis, he had earned more than $1.5 million in prize money. In addition, he had become the first black player to earn significant money from companies that hired him to endorse their products.

After retiring as a player, Ashe was captain of the U.S. Davis Cup team from 1981 to 1985. He also continued his work to promote positive social change. He served as the head of the National Heart Association from 1981 to 1982. Shortly after his election to the International Tennis Hall of Fame in 1985, Ashe was arrested for protesting against apartheid. He helped create tennis programs for poor children in several cities. In 1988, he published *A Hard Road to Glory*, a three-volume history of African Americans in sports.

That same year, he discovered he had contracted the AIDS virus. Ashe had undergone surgery after his second heart attack in 1983. During the operation, he received some HIV-infected blood. (At that time, blood was not screened for HIV, the virus that causes AIDS.) Ashe did not want to reveal publicly that he had AIDS. He hoped to avoid the media spotlight as he and his family privately dealt with the fatal disease.

However, in 1992, a reporter told Ashe that he had found out that Ashe had AIDS, and he was going to print the story. Ashe acknowledged that he had the disease. After the story came out, Ashe became outspoken about the need for education to prevent the spread of AIDS. He organized the Arthur Ashe Foundation for the Defeat of AIDS. He asked tennis stars to help raise $5 million for the foundation. *Sports Illustrated* named Ashe Sportsman of the Year, making him the first non-active athlete chosen for the award. Six weeks later, Ashe died as he had lived: with grace, courage, and dignity.

On the anniversary of Ashe's birthday in 1996, the city of Richmond unveiled a memorial to him along Monument Avenue, which was lined with statues of the leaders of the Confederacy. Although some whites and African Americans criticized the location, others felt it was just the right place to honor a man who had worked to end the discrimination that was a legacy of the Civil War. Paul DePasquale created a 12-foot bronze statue of Ashe in a warm-up suit with a book in one hand and a tennis racket in the other. Figures of three children look up at him from a base of polished black granite.

Career Capsule

The first African-American man to win a Grand Slam title (U.S. Open—1968 as an amateur, Australian Open—1968, and Wimbledon—1975). Won 35 amateur titles and 33 professional events, member of Davis Cup team 1963–78, captain 1980–85.

BILL BRADLEY 

born July 18, 1943

BILL BRADLEY HAS LIVED the storybook life of an all-American hero. He achieved success in nearly everything he attempted—as a star basketball player, a respected scholar, and a United States Senator.

Born in Crystal City, Missouri, William Warren Bradley was the only child of a wealthy bank president and a junior high school teacher. His mother insisted that Bill have a well-rounded education. She signed him up for lessons in three musical instruments, French, typing, dancing, and six sports. Bill began playing basketball at the local YMCA at age nine. His mother soon put a backboard and net up over the garage. Bill loved the game and practiced up to four hours a day. He would weigh down his shoes to improve his footwork. He also wore blinders to teach himself how to dribble the ball without looking at it. The reward for all this work was the 3,066 points he scored in high school. *Scholastic Coach* magazine twice selected Bill for its All-America team.

A straight-A student, Bill received offers of athletic scholarships to 75 schools. Yet he chose to go to Princeton University, an Ivy League school in New Jersey, that did not offer athletic scholarships. "It came down to the education being more important than the basketball," he later explained. "Students [at Princeton] hold as much respect for a musician as for an athlete." On the freshman team, Bill set a record by sinking 57 straight free throws. A brilliant play maker, passer, and scorer, Bill stood 6 feet, 5 inches tall. In 1963, he led the Tigers varsity team to the first of three straight Ivy League titles. He averaged 27.3 points per game, fifth highest in the nation. The following year, he improved his average to 32.3 points per game. Against Dartmouth, he set an Ivy League single-game record of 51 points. He then became the only college junior to make the U.S. Olympic Basketball Team. In Tokyo, Japan, Bradley helped the U.S. team sweep all nine games—and win the gold medal.

At Princeton, Bradley practiced shots from many different locations on the court.

In 1965, his senior year, Bradley averaged 30.5 points per game and shot 88 percent from the foul line to lead the Tigers to a 23–6 record and a berth in the NCAA Final Four. Though the Tigers lost to powerhouse Michigan in the semifinals, 93–76, he was superb in the consolation game against Wichita State. In his final college game, Bradley scored a national record 58 points (since broken). His NCAA tournament total of 177 points, however, remains a record today. Bradley was named the tournament's Most Valuable Player and College Player of the Year. He also became the first basketball player honored as the nation's top amateur athlete with the James E. Sullivan Award.

Bradley graduated from Princeton with honors in American history later that spring. The New York Knicks then selected Bradley in the first round of the National Basketball Association (NBA) draft. Because he disliked the media hype that had grown around him, Bradley initially turned down the Knicks' offer of $20,000 a year. Instead, he escaped to Oxford University in England, where he continued his studies on a Rhodes Scholarship. At Oxford, he studied politics, economics, and philosophy. Yet after two years, he realized he missed basketball. He returned to the United States and joined the Knicks for the 1967–68 season.

In his third season in the NBA, Bradley became the play maker for a great Knicks team. After losing the second

His last year at Princeton, Bradley was named to the All-America team and received a Rhodes Scholarship. He graduated in 1965 with honors.

game of the season, the Knicks went on a tear. They won 18 straight games—an NBA record at the time—to start the year at 19–1. The Knicks won a team record 60 games that season. The team went on to reach the 1970 NBA Finals. The Knicks beat the Los Angeles Lakers in seven games to capture its first NBA Championship.

Bradley was unlike most star athletes. Uncomfortable with his celebrity, he turned down offers to make commercials and endorse products that might have brought him hundreds of thousands of dollars. The Knicks soon developed a reputation for their flashy style. Such teammates as Walt "Clyde" Frazier and Earl "the Pearl" Monroe spent thousands of dollars on clothes and jewelry. Yet Bradley continued to wear the same dull suits. His teammates nicknamed him "Dollar Bill," because they joked that he still had the first dollar he ever earned. Despite their teasing, Bradley's teammates liked him. Despite his college stardom, Bradley was no hotshot. Instead, he earned a reputation as a friendly team player.

The Knicks again won the Eastern Division title in 1971. But the team's hopes of repeating as NBA champions died when Bradley missed a last-second jump shot to eliminate the Knicks in the second round of playoffs. Though they made it to the NBA Finals in 1972, the Lakers beat them in five games. In a rematch in the 1973 finals, the Knicks captured their second NBA title by crushing the Lakers, four games to one.

Bradley played four more seasons for the Knicks. In 1976, he published an autobiographical book, *Life on the Run*. In it, he wrote about nearing the end of his career as an athlete: "There is a terror behind the dream of being a professional ballplayer. . . . When the playing is over, one can sense that one's youth has been spent playing a game and now both the game and youth are gone, along with the innocence that characterizes all games. . . . I have often wondered how I will handle the end of my playing days."

Bradley found out in 1977, when he retired from basketball. He took an unpaid job with the New Jersey Department of Energy. Then, in 1978, Bradley announced that he would run for the U.S. Senate. In his first bid for elected office, Bradley won 56 percent of the vote. Just 35 years old, he became the youngest member of the Senate. In his 18 years as a senator, Bradley became one of the Democratic Party's most respected leaders. In 1995, saying he had grown tired of politics, he announced that he would not seek re-election in 1996. Both moderate and liberal Democrats urged Bradley to run for president.

CAREER CAPSULE

A high school and college All-American and gold medalist in the 1964 Olympics. Player of the Year and NCAA Tournament MVP in 1965 with Princeton, All-America three times. Sullivan Award winner, 1965, and Rhodes Scholar. Helped New York Knicks win two NBA titles between 1967 and 1977. Served 18 years in the U.S. Senate.

Wilt Chamberlain

born August 21, 1936

"I WOULDN'T SAY it's always been the easiest thing being seven feet and black," Wilt Chamberlain once recalled, "but never once in my life did I ever feel like I was a misfit. Athletics probably had a lot to do with that." Yes, he was tall (7 feet, 1 inch) and strong. But he was also remarkably fast and agile for a big man. His mere presence on a basketball court intimidated nearly any opponent. He used these skills to become the greatest scorer ever to play basketball. Chamberlain holds more career, single season, and single game scoring records than any other player.

Wilt grew up with his eight brothers and sisters in a middle-class neighborhood in Philadelphia, Pennsylvania. His father worked as a porter for a local publisher, while his mother sometimes did domestic work outside their home. Wilt began playing basketball in junior high school—just about the same time he stopped sucking his thumb. By the time he played center for his high school team, Wilt was nearly seven feet tall. Since his long legs were so skinny, Wilt needed rubber bands to keep his socks up. Just in case he needed extras, he began wearing rubber bands around his wrists. He would continue this habit throughout his basketball career. In three years on the Overbrook High School team, he scored an amazing 2,252 points.

When Wilt graduated in 1955, more than 200 colleges offered him athletic scholarships. He chose the University of Kansas. In his first varsity game in 1956, Chamberlain scored 52 points. Kansas reached the finals of the National Collegiate Athletic Association (NCAA) tournament that year. In a thrilling game, the University of North Carolina edged Chamberlain's Jayhawks in double overtime. Chamberlain was named College Basketball Player of the Year. A two-time All-American, he averaged 30 points a game. In 1958, Chamberlain dropped out of college and joined the legendary Harlem Globetrotters. The Trotters were an all-black team that played exhibition games throughout the world. After his playing days had ended, he recalled his year with the Globetrotters as the happiest in his basketball career. All he had to do was play the game, have fun, and entertain the fans. No one expected him to break a record every game.

These expectations started in 1959. In his first season with the Philadelphia Warriors, Chamberlain shattered all scoring records. He set eight different NBA records, all of which remain rookie records. He scored 2,707 points (37.6 per game) and pulled down 1,941 rebounds. He scored 58 points in one game, then two weeks later grabbed 45 rebounds in another. Chamberlain became the first player to win both the Rookie of the Year and the Most Valuable Player (MVP) awards in the same season. He also won the MVP award in that year's All-Star Game.

Wilt spent a short time with the Harlem Globetrotters after college.

In the 1960–61 season, Chamberlain set new standards for himself, and the game. He shattered his own record by snatching 55 rebounds in one game. For the season, he averaged 27.2 rebounds per game, becoming the first person to collect more than 2,000 in a season. He also set a new mark of 38.4 points per game.

Chamberlain's third year was the most amazing in NBA history. He played every minute of every game to set an NBA record of 48.5 minutes per game. (Professional games last only 48 minutes unless they go into overtime.) He scored 4,029 points to become the only man ever to top 4,000. He *averaged* 50.4 points per game—more than 12 points higher than anyone else in NBA history!

He scored 30 or more points in 65 games—*in a row!* He scored 40 or more in 63 games, including 14 straight. He scored 60 or more in 16 games. And he achieved all these marks long before NBA rules allowed three-point shots.

On March 2, 1962, the Warriors hosted the New York Knicks in Hershey, Pennsylvania. (NBA teams in those days often scheduled games in other cities in order to build their following.) Chamberlain scored an incredible 100 points. No one else has ever come close to this record.

In the 1962–63 season, the Warriors moved to San Francisco, and Chamberlain averaged 44.8 points per game—second only to his own average the previous season. Despite his incredible scoring feats, however, his team had never finished higher than second place. Chamberlain, the big man fans loved to hate, was unfairly singled out for much of the blame.

Above, Chamberlain would often outmaneuver other players to rebound the ball. Left, Wilt Chamberlain vs. Bill Russell in one of their many on-court battles.

In 1963, coach Alex Hannum asked Chamberlain to imitate the Celtic's **Bill Russell** in his conventional style of play. Chamberlain focused more on passing to teammates, rebouding, and blocking shots. To his credit, he excelled at this new defensive style. Chamberlain—who always preferred the nickname "The Big Dipper," rather than "Wilt the Stilt"—led the Warriors to first place in the Western Division. Yet Russell and the Celtics crushed the Warriors in five games in the NBA Finals.

In 1966, back in Philadelphia with the 76ers, Chamberlain led the NBA in scoring for a record seventh straight year (a string later matched by **Michael Jordan**). He earned his second MVP award. In 1967, Chamberlain let his average sink to 24.1 points per game. Yet he led the league in rebounds and finished third in *assists!* The Sixers won a record 68 games—and the league MVP. Chamberlain won his first NBA Championship.

In 1968, Chamberlain led the league in assists with 702. His third straight MVP award tied Russell's NBA record. After a trade sent him to the Los Angeles Lakers, Chamberlain helped the team reach the NBA Finals in four of the next five seasons.

In 1972, the Lakers won a record 69 games (broken by the Chicago Bulls' 72 in 1996). At one point, the team won 33 straight games—the longest team winning streak in professional sports. Chamberlain averaged just 14.8 points, but led the league in rebounding and shooting percentage. The Lakers swept through the play-offs and won the NBA title in a five-game final against the New York Knicks. Chamberlain was named MVP of the series.

In his final season, Chamberlain set yet another record by shooting 73 percent from the field. When he retired, the seven-time All-Star had set new career marks in scoring and rebounding. His record of scoring 50 or more points in 118 games—and his single-game record of 100 points—will probably last as long as the game itself.

Career Capsule

All-time leader in rebounds (23,924) and rebounding average (22.9 per game). All-time season leader in points scored (4,029 in 1962), scoring average (50.4 in 1962), rebounding average (27.2 in 1961), and field goal percentage (.727 in 1973). All-time single-game most points scored (100 in 1962) and most rebounds (55 in 1960). Second all-time most points scored (31,419) and most field goals made (12,681). Won four MVP awards (1960, consecutively 1966–68), play-off MVP (1972), and Rookie of the Year (1960). Seven-time All Star with 30.1 points per game career scoring average. College Player of the Year in 1957, at the University of Kansas.

Ernie Davis

December 14, 1939–May 18, 1963

A three-time All-American running back, Ernie Davis was the first black player to win the Heisman Trophy as college football's best player. Tragically, leukemia ended his pro career before he ever played a game.

Born in New Salem, Pennsylvania, Ernie grew up in the Uniontown home of his mother's parents. Ernie's father had died before he was born and his mother found herself unable to care for him on her own. At age 12, Ernie moved to Elmira, New York, to rejoin his mother. At Elmira Free Academy, he starred in both basketball and football. In basketball, he scored 18.4 points per game and led his team to 52 straight wins over two years. In football, he averaged 7.4 yards per carry.

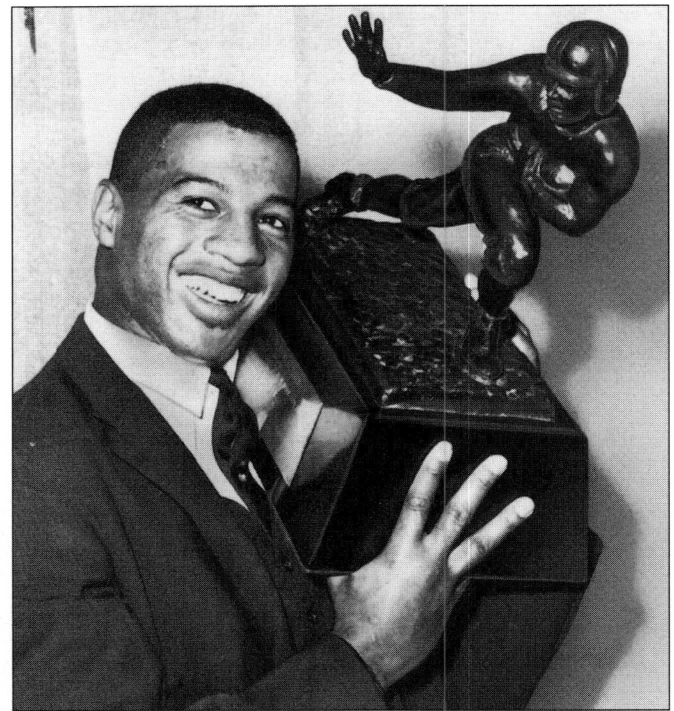

Davis was the first African-American football player to be awarded the Heisman Trophy.

At Syracuse University, Ernie was selected as an All-American in all three of his varsity seasons. During the 1959 season, he averaged seven yards per carry to lead the Syracuse Orangemen to an undefeated 11–0 season and the national championship. Despite a pulled hamstring, Ernie set a major college bowl record with an 87-yard pass reception in the Orangemen's 23–14 win over Texas in the Cotton Bowl. He scored two touchdowns and intercepted a pass to set up a third in that game.

Davis finished out his college career with 35 touchdowns and 2,386 yards, averaging 6.6 per carry. He broke nearly all of Jim Brown's rushing records at Syracuse. In 1961, he won the Heisman Trophy. The Cleveland Browns traded future Hall-of-Famer Bobby Mitchell to the Washington Redskins in return for the right to choose first in the NFL draft of college football stars. The Browns chose Ernie Davis in the hopes that he and Jim Brown could carry them to a championship. But Davis never played a game in the pros. While in the hospital to check on swelling in his neck, Davis learned through a blood test that he had leukemia, a deadly blood disorder. Less than a year later, the 23-year-old Davis had died.

Career Capsule

The first African American to win the Heisman Trophy (1961), All America three times at Syracuse University.
First selection in 1962 NFL draft, but died before he could play professionally.

Peggy Fleming

born July 27, 1948

COMBINING BALLETIC GRACE, style, glamour, and powerful technique, Peggy Fleming captured five consecutive national figure-skating titles, three consecutive world titles, and the Olympic gold medal in 1968.

Born in San Jose, California, Peggy did not begin skating until her family moved to Cleveland, Ohio, when she was nine. Though she later moved back to California, Peggy remained dedicated to figure skating. She spent long hours practicing both skating technique and dance moves. Peggy's parents encouraged her to pursue her dream. Her father took a second job to cover Peggy's training expenses (travel costs, renting rink time, hiring coaches, and buying material for costumes). Her mother designed and made most of her costumes. "There's something to be said for stage mothers," Fleming later recalled. "Kids need to be pushed. She was always at practice; she talked to the coach every single day."

Peggy won the Pacific Coast juvenile ladies' championship in 1960, and the novice ladies' title a year later. Yet Fleming—and the entire U.S. figure-skating community—suffered a devastating loss in 1961. An airplane crash killed Fleming's coach, Billy Kipp, and all 18 members of the U.S. figure-skating team on their way to the world championships in Prague, Czechoslovakia. Fleming, profoundly shaken by the tragedy, responded by focusing even more intently on improving her skating—in memory of her former coach.

Competing on a national level in 1962, Fleming finished second in the novice ladies' competition. The following year, she won the Pacific Coast ladies' championship and then became the youngest woman ever to win the women's senior title in the national championships. Fleming helped fill the void in the U.S. figure-skating team created by the 1961 plane crash, winning a spot on the U.S. Olympic team in 1964 at age 15. Yet she finished only sixth at the Winter Olympics in Innsbruck, Austria.

Fleming retained her national title in 1965, and won the bronze medal in the world championships

Fleming reestablished the United States as a power in figure skating with her Olympic gold medal at age 19.

in Colorado Springs, Colorado. Over the next year, she worked on building up her stamina, refining her technique, and improving her dancing skills. Fleming's hard work paid off, as she won the world figure-skating championship in Davos, Switzerland, in 1966. The following year, she retained her national figure-skating championship for a fifth straight year. She also successfully defended her world championship and won the North American title, too. Fleming became just the third woman (after **Tenley Albright** and **Carol Heiss**) to hold all three titles in the same year. Her considerable accomplishments helped reestablish the United States as an international power in figure skating.

At 19, Fleming competed in her second Winter Olympics in Grenoble, France. There she won the gold medal in figure skating, winning by 88.2 points. After building up a sizable lead in the compulsory figures, Fleming dazzled the judges with her grace and strength in the free-skate program. Fleming followed up her Olympic victory by winning the world championships for the third consecutive year.

Television made Fleming a star. The first live broadcast of the Winter Olympics had brought her skating into millions of American homes. Fleming, the only U.S. gold medalist in the 1968 Winter Olympics, helped make figure skating what it is today: the most popular event of the Winter Games.

Fleming retired from amateur skating after the world championships. She appeared in five television specials, toured the world as the star of the Ice Follies, and offered television sports commentary. Fleming has served on the President's Council on Physical Fitness and as goodwill ambassador for the United Nations Children's Fund (UNICEF). She is a member of the U.S. Figure Skating Association Hall of Fame, the Ice Skating Hall of Fame, and the Women's Sports Hall of Fame.

Career Capsule

Five-time U.S. figure-skating champion (1964–68) and three-time world champion (1966–68), Fleming won the 1968 Olympic gold medal. Member of three Halls of Fame: U.S. Figure Skating Association, Ice Skating, and Women's Sports.

Curt Flood

January 18, 1938—January 20, 1997

On the baseball field, Curt Flood was a good hitter and a smooth centerfielder. But Flood gained even greater fame off the field as an advocate for his fellow players. He helped baseball players win the freedom to change teams and sign the best contracts they could get.

Curt began playing baseball as a boy in Houston, Texas. In 1956, he signed a contract with the Cincinnati Reds. Life in the minor leagues was hard for the young black player. He had to live in a dorm room at an all-black college. After night games, he could seldom find an open restaurant that would serve him. Flood batted just four times with the Reds before being traded to the St. Louis Cardinals. From 1958 to 1969, Flood starred in center field for the Cardinals. A sparkling fielder, Flood was awarded the Gold Glove for fielding excellence seven straight years from 1963 to 1969. As a hitter, he led the National League in hits in 1964, and batted over .300 during six of his twelve years with the Cardinals. He finished with a career average of .293.

An accomplished oil painter, Flood often stayed up until dawn after a night game painting portraits. One portrait of Cardinal owner Gussie Busch increased the demand for his work. Another, of Martin Luther King, Jr., he donated for a charity drive.

After the 1969 season, the Cardinals traded Flood to the Philadelphia Phillies. Flood didn't want to play there, even after the Phillies offered him a $100,000 contract. Yet at that time, every player's contract had a "reserve clause." This clause gave his team ownership rights over the player. The player was viewed as the lifetime property of the club. The team had the right to keep the player, trade the player, sell the player, or fire the player. And players did not have the right to sign a contract to play for another team unless they were fired.

After the trade, Flood "belonged" to the Philadelphia Phillies. Flood thought this was unfair.

"There is no other profession in the history of mankind, except slavery, in which one man was tied to another for life," he complained.

No other business in the United States allowed companies to own their workers. In other businesses, employees could work for any company that they liked. But in professional sports, players could not play wherever they wanted to play. They could be traded without their permission to teams located in cities far from their homes. Baseball players did not have the freedom to negotiate for the best contract available. For some, the best contract might mean living and working in a particular city. For others, it might mean playing for a team that offered them more playing time. Still others might want a contract that offered them more money. But ballplayers had to accept the best offer from the team that "owned" them.

Baseball had become a big business by the 1960s and 1970s. Money paid by television stations for the right to broadcast games had added to baseball owners' fortunes. The number of major league teams had expanded from 16 in 1960 to 24 in 1969, and each new team had to pay the older owners to join the league. Baseball players wanted to share in this wealth. Like professional football and basketball players, they formed a strong labor union to try to reach this goal.

Flood's speed made him valuable on the bases as well as in the outfield.

Backed by the players' union, Flood sued baseball for his freedom. Hall-of-Famers **Jackie Robinson** and **Hank Greenberg**, among others, testified in support of his case. Flood contested that the reserve clause was illegal because it forced players to work only for the team that owned them. Flood argued that baseball's owners had formed a monopoly (a conspiracy to control the production and supply of an entire industry). This monopoly allowed them to keep players' salaries in check and to restrict the "free trade" of the players' skills. Since workers—the baseball players—were not free to seek employment elsewhere in baseball, the owners unfairly controlled their wages.

Despite this argument, Flood lost his case in court. In both 1922 and 1953, the U.S. Supreme Court had ruled that the Sherman antitrust law, which was designed to break up monopolies in the United States, did not apply to baseball. In ruling against Flood's case, the court, in 1970, pointed to these prior rulings as "precedents" (earlier court cases that helped to interpret the law and to determine future rulings). Flood appealed the decision all the way to the highest court in the nation. Yet the Supreme Court also ruled against him.

Flood's fight against baseball owners ended his career in the game he loved. He played in just thirteen more games for the Washington Senators in 1971, before quitting baseball. He had risked his career in order to fight for what he believed was right.

Flood wrote *The Way It Is*, a bitter account of his fight against the reserve clause, in 1971. He then left the country, living and painting for five years on the Spanish island of Majorca in the Mediterranean Sea. He later worked as a broadcaster for the Oakland Athletics and as commissioner of a sandlot baseball league for kids in Oakland.

Career Capsule

A career .293 hitter, Flood won seven consecutive Gold Gloves as a centerfielder from 1963 to 1969. His failed attempt to challenge baseball's reserve clause paved the way for free agency in all professional sports.

IN THE WAKE OF THE FLOOD

In 1975, two veteran pitchers, Dave McNally and Andy Messersmith, played the entire season without signing contracts. After the season ended, the pitchers declared themselves "free agents," arguing that the reserve clause bound them to their teams for only one year.

The players and their teams agreed to have the case decided by an arbitrator, an impartial listener who would hear each side of the dispute and issue a ruling that both sides promised to honor. The arbitrator ruled that McNally and Messersmith were free to sign a playing contract with any team that wanted to hire them.

This decision led to a new labor agreement between players and owners. All players with at least six years in the major leagues who completed their contracts now had the right to sign a new contract with any team. Although Flood lost his battle, he made it possible for the players to win the labor war.

CAROL HEISS 

born January 20, 1940

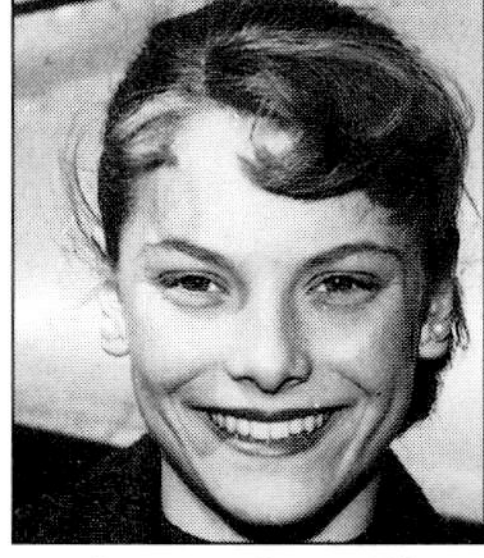

THE TOP WOMEN'S figure skater in the world during the second half of the 1950s, Carol Heiss won more world championships than any other North American skater. A petite blonde, Heiss was a daring skater: athletic, enthusiastic, and very fast. Her gold medal in the 1960 Olympics helped maintain U.S. women's figure-skating excellence and inspire young girls like **Peggy Fleming** and **Dorothy Hamill** to continue this tradition.

Born in New York City, Carol Heiss started roller skating at age four in the basement of her house in Queens. Her parents, impressed with her skill, took her to the Brooklyn Ice Palace to learn ice skating. A fast learner, she skated in an amateur ice show at age six. In 1948, she began taking lessons from 1932 Olympic ice-dancing gold medalists, Pierre and Andree Brunet. Carol's rigorous practice of five to eight hours a day for three years paid off. Only 13 years old, Heiss, the national junior champion, made the U.S. world figure-skating team. She finished fourth in the World Figure Skating Championships in Davos, Switzerland, in 1953.

Heiss' skating career almost ended in 1954, when her sister Nancy crashed into her during a practice session. (Nancy later placed second behind Carol at the 1959 nationals.) Nancy's skate severed a tendon on Carol's left leg. Yet Heiss allowed the injury to sideline her for only a few months.

From 1953 to 1955, the United States dominated women's figure skating. Heiss met U.S. teammate and rival **Tenley Albright** six times on the ice: three times at the nationals, twice at the North American championships, and once at the 1955 world championships in Vienna, Austria. Heiss finished second to Albright each time.

In 1956, Heiss qualified for the U.S. Olympic team by again finishing second to Albright in the nationals. Still just 16, Heiss was at that time the youngest girl ever to skate for the United States in the Olympics (though Fleming would break that record in 1964). Heiss won the silver medal at Cortina, Italy, as Albright edged her once again. (The pair made the United States the first country since Sweden, in 1908, to take both the gold and silver medals in women's figure skating.) Less than a month later, Heiss once again faced Albright in the World Championships held in West Germany. Outscoring Albright in the compulsories, Heiss finally won a senior figure-skating championship.

Heiss' mother died of cancer shortly after the World Championships. Shortly before she died, she asked Carol to promise not to turn pro until she had won an Olympic gold medal.

With Albright's retirement, no one was better on the ice than Carol Heiss. The new crown princess of figure skating, she kept the world title for five straight years. Only Norwegian Sonja Henie, who won ten consecutive world titles a generation earlier, surpassed this total. In addition to holding the world title, Heiss won four straight national championships from 1957 to 1960. Her North American championships in 1957 and 1959 made her only the second woman (after Albright) to hold all three titles in a single year.

Heiss honored her mother's dying wish that she win an Olympic gold medal before turning professional.

At the 1960 Winter Olympics in Squaw Valley, California, Heiss was heavily favored to win the gold. She skated brilliantly, earning the first-place votes from all nine judges. The gold medal was hers.

A few months after the Games, Heiss married Hayes Jenkins, the 1956 Olympic gold medalist and four-time men's world figure-skating champion. Heiss retired from amateur skating at the age of 20. A member of both the United States Figure Skating Association Hall of Fame and the Ice Skating Hall of Fame, Heiss remains active as a skating coach and television commentator.

Career Capsule

Gold medalist at 1960 Olympics and silver medalist in 1956 Olympics. Won five straight world championships (1956–60) and four straight U.S. championships (1957–60).

Billie Jean King

born November 22, 1943

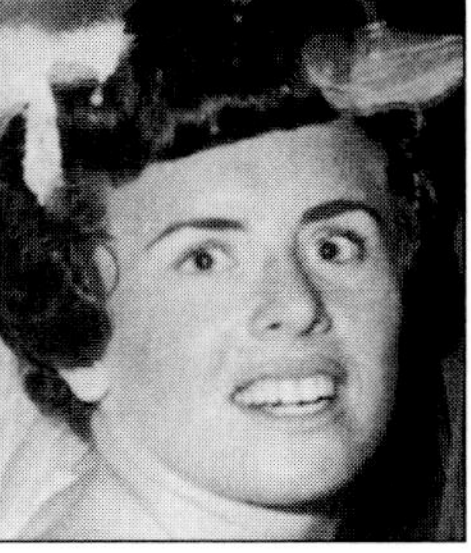

ONE OF THE BEST FEMALE players of all time, Billie Jean King brought women's tennis—and women's sports in general—into prime time. King won a record 20 Wimbledon championships in singles, doubles, and mixed doubles and 39 Grand Slam titles overall, a total exceeded only by Australian Margaret Smith Court in the 1960s and **Martina Navratilova** in the 1980s. A brilliant shot maker with lightning-quick reflexes, her skill at doubles was matched only by Navratilova's. King was aggressive and emotional on the court and outspoken off-court. In the 1970s, she helped establish both a players' union and the professional women's tour. King used her fame beyond the world of sports to promote the cause of equal rights for women.

Born in Long Beach, California, Billie Jean Moffitt played baseball as a child with her father and her

From serve to backhand, Billie Jean covered the court with power and agility. After taking lessons from Alice Marble, she moved up in the national rankings to number four in 1960, at age 17. By the time she was 22, she was the number one ranked player in the United States.

brother Randy (later a pitcher with the San Francisco Giants). In 1955, the 11-year-old Billie Jean began taking free tennis lessons on the city courts of Long Beach. From her first day on the court, she loved tennis. Billie Jean immediately announced to her mother her ambition to become the best player in the world. She practiced almost every day, first learning the basics and then focusing on consistent improvement. By age 14, she had won the Southern California Junior Championship.

Billie Jean improved dramatically after taking lessons from former champion and doubles great **Alice Marble** in 1960. Her ranking jumped from 19th to 4th in the nation. She would remain among the U.S. Top Ten for 18 of the next 23 years (a run later surpassed by **Chris Evert**'s 19 years). In 1961, Moffitt teamed up with another 17-year-old, Karen Hantze, to become the youngest winners of the all-England women's doubles championship at Wimbledon. The two successfully defended their Wimbledon crown in 1962. In Wimbledon singles play, Moffitt defeated the number one women's player, Margaret Smith, preventing Smith from winning a Grand Slam. (Smith had already won that year's Australian and French Open titles and would later win the U.S. Open.) At 18, Billie Jean had definitely arrived in the tennis world.

She won her next major championship, the U.S. doubles title, in 1964. After winning her third Wimbledon doubles title in 1965, Billie Jean King, now married, earned the number one ranking in the nation for the first time. A year later, she won the first of three straight singles titles at Wimbledon, where the fast grass courts best suited the aggressive serve-and-volley style King had mastered under Alice Marble's teaching. For the next three years, King was the world's top woman player.

After winning the 1967 French Open mixed doubles championship, King teamed with Rosie Casals to win the Wimbledon ladies' doubles title. Her victory in that year's mixed doubles championship with Owen Davidson gave her a Wimbledon "triple crown" (both doubles titles and the singles championship). King also won a triple in her next major tournament, the 1967 U.S. Open at Forest Hills, New York. The Associated Press named King Female Athlete of the Year. The following year, she won her first and only Australian titles, winning both the singles and mixed doubles championships, and later won her fifth doubles championship at Wimbledon. In 1970, King again won the Wimbledon women's doubles crown as well as her second French Open mixed doubles championship.

While playing some of her best tennis in the early 1970s, King struggled to establish the Virginia Slims circuit, the first professional tour for women tennis players. King had already joined an attempt to establish a professional tour in 1968. King, Casals, and three other women had given up their amateur status by signing a professional contract as the women's auxiliary of the National Tennis League (six top male players). But by 1970, the NTL was out of business, its male players absorbed by the rival World Championship Tennis and its female players abandoned. King and other top female players recognized that women would achieve greater recognition and significantly increased prize money only if they formed a tour entirely separate from the men's tour. King worked harder than anyone to drum up support for a women's tennis tour. Finally, Virginia Slims—a cigarette brand targeting female smokers—agreed to sponsor the tour. In 1971, the first full year of the women's professional tour, King appropriately reaped her reward.

As one of the most popular players, King played everywhere to make the tour a success. She earned a record 21 doubles titles that year in 26 tournaments (as well as 17 of 31 singles titles), winning a record 112 singles matches, 80 doubles matches, and 192 matches overall. She earned $117,000—the first time a woman in any sport had won more than $100,000 in a single year. That year, King also regained the top ranking in the world, winning the doubles and mixed doubles titles at Wimbledon and the singles and mixed doubles championships at the U.S. Open.

In 1972, King won her only French Open singles and women's doubles titles, her fourth singles and eighth doubles crowns at Wimbledon, and her third U.S. singles championship. *Sports Illustrated* named King Sports*man* of the Year. She was the first woman to receive this honor. The following year, she again completed a triple crown at Wimbledon. Her women's doubles title was her fourth straight, sixth in seven years, and ninth overall. She also won the mixed doubles championship at the U.S. Open.

King's success on the court during 1972 and 1973 made her the target of a challenge by Bobby Riggs, a former two-time U.S. men's champion and self-described "tennis hustler." Riggs claimed that no woman player could beat a male champion, even one who was now 55 years old. He challenged King to a five-set match. The heavily hyped match, dubbed the "Battle of the Sexes," drew more than 30,000 spectators to the Houston Astrodome. It was the largest audience for any event in the history of tennis. And millions more watched on television. King won in straight sets, 6–4, 6–3, 6–3. For many, the match came to symbolize women's right to compete equally with men, not just in athletics, but in all fields. The victory also helped lead to a boom of public interest not just in women's tennis, but in tennis in general.

King demonstrated a commitment to the advancement of women in sports throughout the 1970s. In 1973, she founded the Women's Tennis Association (WTA), the union for professional women players, and served as its first president. She also started *womenSports* (later called *Women's Sports and Fitness*), a magazine dedicated to women's achievements and issues in the sports world. In 1974, she helped found both the Women's Sports Foundation and the World Team Tennis (WTT) League. As player and coach for the Philadelphia Freedoms, she became the first woman to head any professional sports team that had male players.

King's success on the courts continued throughout the 1970s. In 1974, she won her fourth Wimbledon mixed doubles title and the U.S. Open singles and doubles championships. The following year, she won her sixth Wimbledon singles championship. In 1976, she won the U.S. mixed doubles title and led the New York Apples to the first of two straight WTT championships. Her last three Grand Slam triumphs came paired with Martina Navratilova in women's doubles. They won at the 1978 U.S. Open, at Wimbledon in 1979, and again at the U.S. Open in 1980. By 1978, King had also won 29 titles on the Virginia Slims tour.

In addition to her individual titles, King also helped the U.S. dominate team competition for both the Wightman Cup (against Britain and Ireland) and the Federation Cup (international team play). In her ten years on the U.S. Wightman Cup team (1961–67, 1970, and 1977–78), the United States won nine times. King took 14 of 16 singles and seven of ten doubles matches. In Federation Cup play, she won all 27 doubles matches and 25 of 29 singles matches. The U.S. made it to the finals in all of King's nine years (1963–67 and 1976–79) on the team and won the cup seven times.

Still ranked as high as 13th in the world in 1983, King at 39 became the oldest woman ever to win a professional tournament. The following year, King won her last doubles title in a Japanese tournament. She then retired from professional tennis. She had earned nearly $2 million in the professional tour she helped create. She had won 71 singles tournaments during her career.

King, in 1984, became the first female commissioner in professional sports history. She headed the Team Tennis league, which established professional teams in eleven cities and introduced such innovations as player substitutions during matches and on-the-court coaching. King was elected to the Women's Sports Hall of Fame in 1980 and the International Tennis Hall of Fame in 1987.

In 1990, *Life* magazine selected King as one of the 100 Most Important Americans of the Twentieth Century. King, **Muhammad Ali**, **Jackie Robinson**, and **Babe Ruth** were the only athletes on the magazine's list. King promoted the advancement of women's sports and increased opportunities for female athletes. She promoted the advancement of women off the court as well. Through both her words and her actions, King became a shining symbol of women's professionalism in sports—and of the entire women's rights movement.

Career Capsule

Wimbledon singles champion six times, U.S. champion four times. King was first woman athlete to earn $100,000 in one year (1971). Formed a professional women's tennis players' union, founded a league, and served as commissioner of the Team Tennis league. As a player, she won 39 Grand Slam tennis titles.

BILLY MILLS

born June 30, 1938

VERY FEW PEOPLE had heard of Billy Mills before the 1964 Olympics in Tokyo. Out of nowhere, Mills became the surprise winner of the 10,000-meter race as one of the most exciting finishes of a distance race came down to the wire.

Billy Mills, who is part Lakota Sioux, was born on the Pine Ridge reservation in South Dakota. By the time he was 12 years old, both his parents had died. Yet Billy later remembered his parents as a positive influence. "Before he died," Mills recalled, "my father taught me his philosophy. He told me, 'Find the positive desires in your life. With desire comes self-motivation, with motivation comes work, and with work comes success.' It made me a champion, and I try my best to pass it on to others."

After becoming an orphan, Billy was sent to Haskell Institute, a school for Native Americans in Lawrence, Kansas. His career as a runner began there almost by accident. He started running as part of his training program for boxing. After losing several amateur bouts, Billy gave up boxing. But he never stopped running. After graduating from the University of Kansas, Mills enlisted in the U.S. Marines.

Mills was given little chance of winning the 10,000-meter race in Tokyo. He had not placed first in the U.S. Olympic trials. In fact, he had never run the race in less than 29 minutes and 10 seconds. Ron Clarke of Australia, who was also running in the race, had set a world record almost one full minute faster (28:15.6). Yet Mills managed to stay among Clarke and the other leaders throughout the race. By the final lap, only three of the 38 runners remained in contention: Clarke, Mills, and Mohamed Gammoudi of Tunisia. In the backstretch (the first straightaway on the oval track), Clarke tried to pass Mills and several other runners whom the three leaders had lapped. When Clarke shoved Mills to the outside, Gammoudi squeezed between them and opened up a slight lead. Clarke caught up to Gammoudi at the beginning of the homestretch (the final straightaway). Yet Mills poured on the speed with a magnificent sprint that propelled him into the lead. In a thrilling upset victory, Mills won the gold medal by just three yards (less than half a second). He set an Olympic record with a time of 28:24.4—46 seconds faster than his previous personal best. Sadly, Mills, the sudden hero, was unable to take the traditional victory lap. So many runners had fallen so far behind the three leaders that a victory lap might have interfered with the others trying to finish the race. The disappointment at being robbed of his moment of glory gnawed at Mills for many years. He returned to Tokyo in 1984, to run his victory lap in an empty National Stadium.

The first American to win the 10,000-meter race at the Olympics was a Lakota Sioux from South Dakota.

The following year, Mills won another middle-distance race with a thrilling finish. The thrilling six-mile race at that year's Amateur Athletic Union (AAU) championships in San Diego ended in a photo finish. Mills won the race by one-twentieth (0.05) of a second. In the process, he sliced six seconds off the previous world record with a time of 27:11.6.

His Olympic and AAU victories made Mills a hero among the Sioux. The elders of the Oglala Sioux tribe made him a warrior—a status denied to him earlier because he was not a full-blooded Sioux. The tribe presented him with a ring made from Black Hills gold and gave him a new name: Loves His Country.

Mills became active in American Indian affairs after retiring from track competition. He founded a Hall of Fame for Indian athletes. He served as assistant to the commissioner of the U.S. Bureau of Indian Affairs. He also helped found Running Strong for American Indian Youth, an organization that improves living conditions and promotes leadership among Native American children.

Career Capsule

The only U.S. runner to win the Olympic 10,000-meter (6.2 miles) race when he set an Olympic record in 1964. Also set world record for six miles in 1965.

Joe Namath

born May 31, 1943

A brash and stylish crowd favorite, Joe Namath generated enough excitement to bring public acceptance to an entire football league. "Broadway Joe" boldly predicted victory in Super Bowl III—and then went out and led the New York Jets to their only championship. The win brought new respectability not only to the Jets but to the upstart American Football League (AFL) in which they played. In its ninth year, the AFL proved that its best could match the National Football League's best. The two leagues merged into one just four months after Namath's Super Bowl win.

Despite fragile knees, Broadway Joe was a strong passer.

The youngest of five children, Joe was born in Beaver Falls, Pennsylvania. His father, an emigrant from Hungary, worked in a steel mill. A natural athlete, Joe started playing football with his older brothers at age five. In high school, Joe was captain of the basketball team and also starred on the football and baseball teams. In his senior year, he completed 70 percent of his pass attempts (84 of 120). Joe generously credited his blockers for this success. He claimed that he hadn't been hit behind the line of scrimmage once all year.

His remarkable high school career brought Joe offers of athletic scholarships from 52 colleges and universities. He enrolled at the University of Alabama in 1961. As a sophomore, Joe became the starting quarterback. He led the Crimson Tide to a 10–1 record, including a 17–0 victory over Oklahoma in the Orange Bowl. The following year, Alabama won the Sugar Bowl—but without Namath. He had been kicked off the team three weeks earlier for drinking and breaking curfew.

Namath established himself as a top-notch scrambler. But his ability to get out of the pocket

In 1969, Namath demonstrated how to pass at a boys' camp the same year he led the New York Jets to a division title.

would cost him. In October 1964, the impact of a sudden stop caused his knee to buckle—the first of many knee injuries that would ultimately restrict his mobility and require surgery to replace them. Two more injuries to the same knee that season made it doubtful that he would play in the 1965 Orange Bowl. Yet with Alabama trailing Texas by 14 points, Namath limped onto the field to rally the Tide. Texas managed to hold on for an exciting 21–17 win. Despite the loss, Alabama was chosen as the national champion by the Associated Press. Namath was selected as an All-American.

Despite his ailing knee, several professional teams wanted to sign Namath. The AFL's New York Jets won a bidding war with the St. Louis Cardinals of the more established NFL. Namath's contract—three years for $400,000—made him the highest paid rookie of his day. "I just want to play football," Namath insisted. "I'm just lucky I got all that money, too."

The signing of Namath was important to the Jets. But it was critical for the new league. Handsome, charming, and confident, Namath brought star quality to the AFL. As Jet owner Sonny Werblin commented, "Some people are bigger than life. **Babe Ruth**. Clark Gable. Frank Sinatra. So is Joe Namath." Werblin knew that "Broadway Joe" would light up the AFL.

Namath started 1965 as a bench player. Yet in the second game of the season, Namath connected for a touchdown on his first pass as a pro. By midseason, he had won the job of starting quarterback. Ranked third in the league in passing, Namath won the league's Rookie of the Year award. He was also the only rookie named to that year's All-League team.

The Jets improved steadily with Namath as their quarterback. They won five games in 1965, six in 1966, and eight in 1967, the team's first winning season. Yet already, Namath's knees had begun to

Coach Weeb Eubank relied heavily upon Namath to lead the Jets as a first-year player.

betray him. By 1966, he needed to wear a bulky knee brace. Yet mobile or not, Namath could still throw passes with power and precision.

In 1968, Namath and the Jets went 11–3. In the AFL Championship game against the Oakland Raiders, a fourth-quarter interception led to a 23–20 Raider lead. But Namath quickly made up for his error, hitting Don Maynard for the game-winning touchdown. With a 27–23 win, the Jets were going to the Super Bowl.

Super Bowl III was perhaps the most important professional football game ever played. The first two Super Bowls had featured blowout victories by the NFL's Green Bay Packers. The NFL seemed vastly superior to the AFL and the future of the upstart AFL was in jeopardy. Oddsmakers favored the Baltimore Colts by nearly 20 points. Yet Namath not only predicted a Jet victory, he guaranteed it! Namath delivered on his promise. He threw for 206 yards in Miami as the Jets shocked the world with their upset victory, 16–7.

The bidding war for Namath's rookie contract four years earlier had scared team owners in both leagues. They feared that players' salaries would soon spin out of control if NFL teams had to bid against the AFL. The 1969 merger eliminated this extra level of competition. The owners kept salaries under control.

Namath led the Jets to their second straight Eastern Division title in 1969. But the Jets got no farther. Kansas City eliminated them in the playoffs, 13–6. Namath battled through injuries and remained with the Jets for seven more seasons. Yet neither he nor the team ever approached their success in Super Bowl III. The fortunes of Namath and the Jets fell swiftly. But his performance in a single game had already made him a legend, and didn't just give Namath a good shot at getting into the Pro Football Hall of Fame, it guaranteed it.

CAREER CAPSULE

Signed for record $400,000 with N.Y. Jets in 1965. Two-time All-AFL (1968–69) and All-NFL (1972). Led Jets to Super Bowl victory as MVP in 1969. Completed just 50.1% of his passes for 27,663 career yards.

ARNOLD PALMER

born September 10, 1929

GOLF'S FIRST TV STAR, Arnold Palmer is perhaps the most popular golfer in the history of the game. Palmer helped popularize golf in the late 1950s and early 1960s, creating a boom of interest in the sport. An exciting and aggressive player, Palmer came on the pro scene just as television began bringing golf into American homes. His warm personality and style won him a legion of fans who called themselves Arnie's Army.

Born in Youngstown, Pennsylvania, Arnold grew up on a golf course. "Ever since I was able to walk, I have been swinging a golf club," he later recalled,

Golf is a game of inches; this putt failed to fall in 1965. Arnie's face often told the story. Whether he was smiling or frowning, Arnie's friendly attitude toward the fans made him a favorite and helped him earn advertising dollars off the course.

"and ever since I was big enough to dream, I have wanted to be the best golfer that ever lived." Arnold's father worked as a golf pro, instructor, and greenskeeper at the Latrobe Country Club. Arnold began playing golf at age five. His father, his only golf tutor, stressed the importance of sportsmanship and tradition. After misplaying a ball, Arnold once angrily threw his club over some trees. His father scolded him for his temper tantrum and reminded him that golf was a "gentleman's game."

Palmer did not win an important amateur event until he was 23. He won the Ohio State Amateur tournament in both 1953 and 1954. After becoming U.S. Amateur champion in 1954, he turned pro. Palmer won only one event—the 1955 Canadian Open—and earned less than $10,000 in his first 18

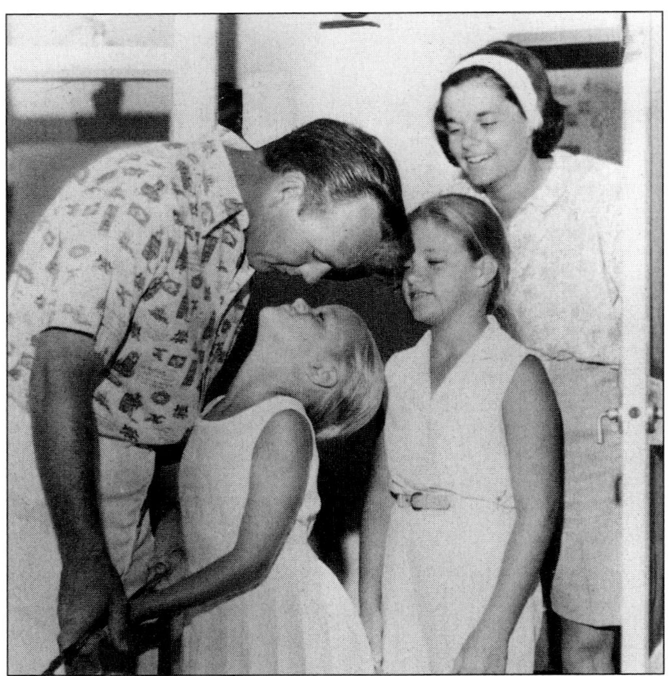

Palmer was often away from his wife and daughters when playing in tournaments.

months as a pro. But he won two events in 1956, and five tournaments the following year.

A strong driver and brilliant putter, Palmer came into his prime in 1958. He gained his first Masters title that year, winning by a single stroke. He earned more than $42,000 in prize money, tops on the tour. In 1959, Palmer led the Masters tournament after three rounds, but faded in the final round and finished third. At the 1960 Masters, Palmer approached the 16th tee two strokes behind the leader, Ken Venturi, with just three holes to go. Birdies on both the 16th and 17th holes tied the score. (A birdie is a score of one under par, the average number of strokes a first-class player would take to put the ball in the hole.) When he birdied the final hole, Palmer regained the Masters title. At that year's U.S. Open, Palmer began the final round of 18 holes seven strokes behind the leader. Yet he won the tournament by shooting the final round in just 65 strokes—the best final round at the Open (until Johnny Miller shot a 63 in 1973). Palmer wanted to match **Ben Hogan**'s feat of winning both major Opens and the Masters in the same year. But he placed second, one stroke behind Australian Kel Nagle, in his first appearance at the British Open. Palmer led all pros in prize winnings in 1960, earning more than $75,000. The U.S. Professional Golfers Association (PGA) named him Player of the Year.

Palmer almost won his third Masters championship in 1961. But on the final hole, he landed his ball in a sand bunker and finished one stroke behind Gary Player. At the British Open, however, Palmer took the title by a single stroke. The following year, he set a British Open record by completing the 72 holes in just 276 strokes—six strokes ahead of Nagle, the runner-up. (Tom Watson shattered this record with a 268 in 1977.) Palmer's victory made him the first American since Walter Hagen in 1928 and 1929 to win two straight British Open crowns. Palmer's play helped revitalize golf's oldest and most famous event. America's best golfers seldom traveled to Great Britain to play in the Open before 1960. But Palmer's success quickly inspired other American pros to cross the Atlantic.

Palmer also won his third Masters after a three-way play-off in 1962. At the U.S. Open, he finished three strokes behind in a play-off with **Jack Nicklaus**. The leading money winner for the third time, Palmer was again named U.S. PGA Player of the Year. For the second straight year, he won the Vardon Trophy, given to the pro who has the lowest scoring average for the year. In 1963, Palmer again led all pros in winnings, becoming the first golfer ever to earn more than $100,000 in a single year. The following year, he set a record by winning his fourth Masters title. (Nicklaus later broke this record with the fifth of his six victories in 1975.)

During Palmer's best years (1958 to 1964), he became the symbol of modern golf. His popularity led to offers from businesses all over the country. Manufacturers wanted to pay Palmer to endorse their products. A shrewd businessman, Palmer even introduced products with his name on them: clothes, clubs, and golf balls. He also invested in such businesses as insurance companies, dry cleaners, and power-tool manufacturers. Through his endorsements, investments, and golf winnings, Palmer became golf's first self-made millionaire.

Palmer placed second at the U.S. Open in both 1966 and 1967. He won the Vardon Trophy in 1967, for the fourth time in his career. In 1968,

Palmer became the first professional golfer to win more than $1 million in his career. Yet hip trouble and growing problems with putting made Palmer less competitive in the early 1970s. In 1971, he set a record (later tied by Nicklaus) by winning at least one pro event for the seventeenth consecutive year.

In the 1980s, Palmer showed he wasn't finished with golf yet. He helped establish and popularize the new U.S. Senior Tour, in which players must be at least 50 years old. As a senior player, Palmer has earned more than $1.5 million—almost as much as he did on the pro tour. Palmer has won 10 Senior events, including the U.S. PGA Seniors Championship in 1980 and the U.S. Senior Open in 1981.

Career Capsule

Winner of four Masters, two British Opens and a U.S. Open, and two-time PGA Player of the Year. With 60 professional wins in his career, including seven major titles, Palmer ranks fourth on the all-time list. First player to earn over $1,000,000 in career (1968). Annual PGA Tour money leader award named after him.

Wilma Rudolph

June 23, 1940–November 12, 1994

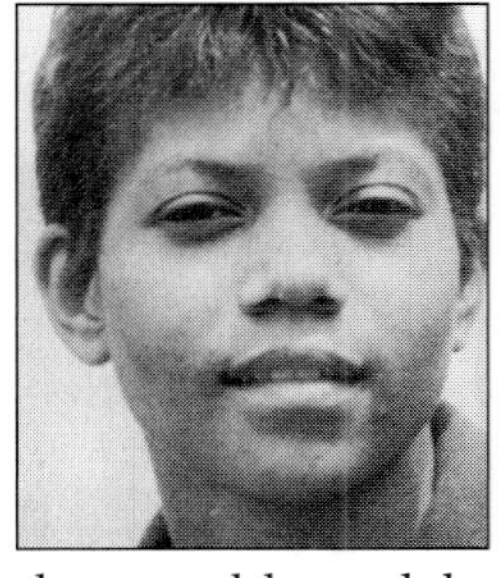

Wilma Rudolph could not walk without assistance until she was 11 years old. Yet incredibly, just nine years later, she earned the title, "World's Fastest Woman." Over tremendous odds, she became the first American woman ever to win three gold medals in track competition at a single Olympiad (1960).

Born prematurely, Wilma weighed just four-and-one-half pounds at birth. She was the fifth of eight children of a retired porter and a domestic worker.

Rudolph (left) and her Tennessee Tigerbelles teammates set a world record in the 4 × 100 meter.

(Her father had another 11 children by a previous marriage.) As a child in Clarksville, Tennessee, Wilma suffered from serious childhood illnesses of double pneumonia, scarlet fever, and polio. By age four, her left leg was partially paralyzed.

Wilma recovered from these illnesses through the efforts of her family. Her mother and three older children took turns massaging her leg four times daily. Once a week, her mother drove her 45 miles to Nashville, for heat treatments and hydrotherapy. Over the course of several years, Wilma progressed from not walking at all to walking with a brace to walking in a corrective shoe. At age 11, she threw away the shoe to join her brothers playing basketball.

Wilma attended the all-black Burt High School, where she was chosen for the All-State girls' basketball team all four years. As a sophomore, she set a state record, scoring 803 points in 25 games (more than 32 points per game). She also became the state high-school champion in sprints of 50, 75, and 100 yards. In three seasons on the track team, she never lost a race. Her coach, Clinton Gray, nicknamed her "Skeeter" because she was always buzzing around.

In 1955, Tennessee State University (TSU) track coach Ed Temple invited Rudolph to practice with the university's track team. The following year, she

Rudolf won this 50-yard sprint indoors at New York's Madison Square Garden in six seconds. She went on to win the gold medal in the 100-meter event with a time of 11.0 seconds in the 1960 Olympics held in Rome, Italy.

qualified for the U.S. Olympic Track and Field Team. As a member of the 4 × 100-meter relay team, Rudolph won her first Olympic medal—the bronze—in Melbourne, Australia.

After graduating from high school in 1957, Rudolph enrolled at TSU. Although an injury sidelined her for most of 1958, Rudolph won four Amateur Athletic Union titles in the 100-yard dash (1959 to 1962). After having her tonsils removed early in 1960, she underwent a period of severe post-operative illness. Yet Rudolph would not let illnesses and injuries stop her. Two months before the Olympic Games, she set a world record of 22.9 seconds in the 200-meter sprint in Corpus Christi, Texas. She won national AAU titles in both 100- and 200-meter sprints that year.

Rudolph and six of her TSU teammates—who would win a total of nine gold medals—made up a large part of the U.S. Women's Olympic Track and Field Team that went to Rome, Italy, in 1960. The day before her first race, Rudolph sprained her ankle. Yet in the semifinals of the 100-meter dash, she tied the world record of 11.3 seconds. She then won the final sprint in 11.0 seconds. (Since she had a favorable wind at her back, this was not regarded as a world record.) In a qualifying heat for the 200-meter sprint, Rudolph set a new Olympic record of 23.2 seconds. She went on to win the final sprint in 24 seconds flat, despite running in the rain against a strong wind. Finally, Rudolph anchored the 4 × 100-meter relay team, which set a world record of 44.4 seconds in the semifinals and went on to win the gold. No other runner would match her feat of three Olympic golds in a single year until Valerie Brisco-Hooks in 1984 (and later Florence Griffith Joyner in 1988). Both the Associated Press and United Press International named Rudolph the Female Athlete of the Year.

In 1961, Rudolph became the first woman in 30 years invited to take part in the most prestigious indoor track event, the Millrose Games at Madison Square Garden in New York. There, she tied her own world record of 6.9 seconds in winning the 60-yard dash. Two weeks later, she broke the record, shaving one-tenth of a second off her time. Rudolph also broke the 25-year-old world record in the 70-yard dash by nearly half a second in 1961. In yet another record-setting performance that year, she ran the 100-meter sprint in just 11.2 seconds, the best time ever. The Associated Press again named her Female Athlete of the Year. She was honored with the Sullivan Memorial Trophy, given annually to the nation's best amateur athlete.

Recognizing her dominance as a sprinter, the National Track and Field Hall of Fame inducted her as a member in 1974. She was also named to the International Women's Sports Hall of Fame, and the United States Olympic Hall of Fame.

After retiring from competitive athletics in 1962, Rudolph devoted herself to community service. As director of athletics for a youth foundation in Chicago, she developed sports programs for children. She served as U.S. Goodwill Ambassador to French West Africa. In 1982, she founded the Wilma Rudolph Foundation in Indianapolis. The foundation uses sports and education to help disabled children overcome obstacles, just as she did. It emphasizes the values of discipline, hard work, and dedication, not only in sports but in life.

After the Olympics triumph, Rudolph met President John F. Kennedy.

CAREER CAPSULE

Gold medalist in three events (100-, 200-, and 4 × 100 meter-relay) at the 1960 Olympics and a bronze medalist (4 × 100-meter relay) at the 1956 Olympics. Set world records at distances ranging from 60 yards to 200 meters. First woman invited to Millrose Games at Madison Square Garden in New York in 1961. Received Sullivan Award in 1961.

BILL RUSSELL

born February 12, 1934

CENTER BILL RUSSELL was the anchor of the Boston Celtics team that ruled pro basketball in the 1960s. Considered the best defensive player in basketball history, Russell controlled games with his shot blocking and rebounding skills.

William Felton Russell was born in Monroe, Louisiana, during the Depression. Seeking to escape both poverty and racism, his family moved to Oakland, California, when Bill was five. Bill first tried out for basketball in junior high school, but failed to make the team. He grew taller and stronger at McClymonds High School, however, and became a much better player.

Bill won an athletic scholarship to the University of San Francisco. Beginning in 1954, the 6 feet,

9 inch Russell led USF to 55 straight victories. The team won back-to-back national championships in 1955 and 1956. Russell won the Most Valuable Player award in the 1955 NCAA Tournament. In 1956, he scored 22 points in the final game to help the U.S. basketball team win the gold medal at the Olympic Games in Melbourne, Australia.

Though the Boston Celtics already had a high-scoring team, they had not yet won any National Basketball Association (NBA) titles. Adding Russell to the team transformed the Celtics into champions.

Early in his career, Russell displayed an unstoppable hook shot. Though defense was his strength, Russell scored over 10,000 points in the NBA.

Almost single-handedly, he led the Celtics to an incredible 11 NBA titles in 13 years with his defense alone!

Just as **Babe Ruth** totally changed the game of baseball with his power hitting, Russell transformed basketball. He changed the game from an uncontested challenge of two teams' offensive skills into one that stressed tough defense. Russell established the effectiveness of shot blocking as a defensive weapon. In fact, blocked shots did not become an official statistic until after Russell had left the game.

Russell's defense was the key to the Celtics' winning fast-break offense. He would guard the area under the basket. After blocking a shot or rebounding the ball, he seldom followed the ball upcourt. His blocked shots would end up in the hands of a teammate. Or he would quickly dish a rebounded ball off to Bob Cousy, who would pass upcourt to Tom Heinsohn or Frank Ramsey for the score.

Since Russell averaged *only* 15.1 points per game during his career, he did not get the recognition of his higher-scoring contemporaries like **Wilt Chamberlain**. But his controlled defensive game outmatched Chamberlain's—and that of everyone else in the league. Russell and Chamberlain, playing on several teams, met nine times for either the Eastern Division title or the NBA Championship. And though Chamberlain almost always scored more points, Russell achieved the ultimate goal: The Celtics won eight of those nine championship series.

From 1959 to 1966, Russell led the Celtics to eight straight NBA Championship titles—a streak that no team in any sport has ever matched. (No other NBA team has ever won more than three in a row.) Russell won the league's Most Valuable Player award five times, including a record-setting three in a row from 1961 to 1963.

While remaining the team's best player, Russell became the Celtics' coach in 1966. This made him the first black head coach or manager in any major professional sport. In his first season, the Celtics lost the Eastern Division title to Chamberlain's Philadelphia 76ers. Since this was the first time in Russell's career that his team had failed to reach the NBA finals, many critics questioned his coaching skills. But he silenced the doubters by winning the 1968 and 1969 championships.

Russell retired after the 1969 season. His total of 11 championships set a standard approached only by his Celtic teammates Heinsohn (8) and Cousy (6). (**Magic Johnson** is fourth all-time with five NBA titles.) As the heart and soul of the team, Russell made the Celtics nearly unbeatable for over a decade and brought new popularity to the NBA. For this reason, some regard Russell as the greatest player in basketball history.

Career Capsule

Won MVP award five times (1958, 1961–63, and 1965). Played on 11 championship teams with Boston (1957, 1959–66, and 1968–69). Player-coach 1968–69. Second all-time most rebounds (21,620), second highest rebounding average (22.5), and second most rebounds in a game (51 in 1960). Led league in rebounding four times. Played on two consecutive NCAA championship teams with University of San Francisco in 1955–56; tournament MVP in 1955. Member of Olympic gold medal team in 1956.

Kathrine Switzer

born February 21, 1947

UNTIL THE 1960s, women were barred from entering marathon races. Officials expressed concern—despite a lack of medical evidence—that distance running might injure women or endanger their ability to have children. Nonetheless, some women had sneaked onto the course of the Boston Marathon.

Then, in 1967, Kathrine Switzer, a 20-year-old student at Syracuse University, made an even bolder effort. A native of Falls Church, Virginia, Kathrine Switzer had been running since she was 13. She had wanted to be cheerleader, but her father had insisted that she participate in sports rather than stand on the sidelines. So she started running a mile a day to improve her chances of making the field hockey team. Kathrine soon discovered that running itself gave her confidence and a sense of accomplishment. She began running longer distances, pushing her limits progressively further.

In 1967, she submitted her application for the marathon under the name K.V. Switzer. Her

boyfriend took the pre-race physical exam for her. During the race, Switzer was noticed by Jock Semple, a marathon official, who ran after her and tried to strip away her number. Her boyfriend blocked for her, knocking the official to the curb and allowing Switzer to finish the race in 4:20. Photographs of the incident appeared in newspapers around the world.

The publicity turned women's running into a political issue. All across the country, women began running to make a point about their rights and abilities. Switzer was kicked out of the Amateur Athletic Union for running the race. But New York City's new marathon welcomed female runners in 1970, and Boston allowed women to run two years later.

After running more than 30 marathons, Switzer won the women's title in the New York Marathon in 1974, with a time of 3:07:29. Her winning margin—27 minutes and 14 seconds—was the largest ever for the race. She finished second (2:51:37) in Boston the following year. In 1977, Switzer headed the Avon International Running Circuit, which sponsored more than 300 women's distance races in 27 nations throughout the world. The women's marathon was added to the Olympic schedule in 1984. Switzer later became a sports commentator—mostly for running events—with ABC-TV.

In spite of the efforts of Jock Semple, Switzer finished the Boston marathon thanks to her companion who ran interference for her.

Career Capsule

The first woman to run the Boston Marathon with a registered number. Won the New York Marathon in 1974, and finished in second place the next year in the Boston Marathon.

Kathy Whitworth

born September 27, 1939

The first woman to earn more than $1 million on the Ladies Professional Golf Association (LPGA) tour, Kathy Whitworth won more pro tournaments (88) than any other female golfer. Athletic, dedicated, and intensely focused on the course, Whitworth was one of the game's best long-ball hitters, yet also excelled at the short game. Popular on and off the course, Whitworth helped legitimize the professional women's golf tour and gain acceptance among both sports writers and fans.

Born in Monahans, Texas, Kathrynne Ann Whitworth moved with her family to Jal, New Mexico, as a toddler. A natural athlete, Kathy found that sports such as football, softball, and basketball came easily to her. But in the 1950s, opportunities for young girls to play these sports were extremely limited. So at age 15, Kathy took up golf, which was regarded as a much more suitable sport for a young lady. She found golf harder to master than other sports, and the challenge hooked her. She practiced every day at the Jal Country Club.

In 1956, the local golf pro, who had been giving Whitworth lessons, referred her to Harvey Penick, a well-respected golf pro in Austin, Texas. Whitworth spent the next two summers with Penick, sharpening her game. In both 1957 and 1958, she won the New Mexico State Amateur Championship. After turning pro in 1958, at age 19, she struggled in her first few years on the tour. "In Jal, I was super," she later recalled. "But compared to what? When I got on the tour, I got a rude awakening."

Not until 1962 did Whitworth finally win her first event as a professional: Baltimore's Kelly Girl Open. She also won the Phoenix Thunderbird Open that year and was runner-up in eight other tournaments. The following year, she blossomed, winning eight tournaments. She would go on to win at least one title every year until 1978 (17 consecutive years).

After **Mickey Wright** retired from full-time touring in 1965, Whitworth achieved the consistency and confidence allowed her to dominate the women's pro tour. From 1965 to 1968, she won between eight and a career-high of ten tournaments a year. This gave her 35 titles—40 percent of her career total—in just four years. She led the professional women's tour in money earned eight times in nine years (1965–68 and 1970–73). She won the Vare Trophy, awarded to the golfer with the lowest scoring average for the year, seven times in eight years (1965–67 and 1969–72). The LPGA's first Player of the Year in 1966, she would win the award a record seven times in eight years (1966–69 and 1971–73). The Associated Press recognized Whitworth as Female Athlete of the Year in both 1965 and 1966. She won the LPGA Championship in both 1967 and 1971. Finally, in 1969, she won four scheduled tournaments in a row, matching the record set by Wright (twice). For nine years she was—no question about it—the best in the business. Her professionalism, consistency, and unprecedented success made Whitworth a role model for the next wave of women golfers, including **Nancy Lopez** and Patty Sheehan.

Whitworth was always all business on a golf course, never playing to the crowds. "I'm not colorful," she once acknowledged. "I can't divide my concentration by relating to the gallery. I owe it to myself and the game I love to score as well as I can." Her intense focus on the game allowed Whitworth to remain cool under pressure.

In 1975, Whitworth won her third LPGA championship, second only to Mickey Wright's four. (Lopez and Sheehan would also win three.) After her induction into the LPGA Hall of Fame in

In 1963 Whitworth won an incredible eight tournaments.

1975, Whitworth's game tailed off slightly. Yet she continued to win at least one tournament a year until 1979. At the 1981 U.S. Women's Open, Whitworth finished in third place to push her career earnings past $1 million, becoming the first woman to reach this milestone. (Curiously, though she won virtually everywhere else, Whitworth never took the title at the U.S. Women's Open.) By the decade's end, her career winnings would surpass $1,700,000.

In 1982, Whitworth won her 83rd LPGA tournament victory, surpassing the record established by Wright in 1973. Two years later, she claimed her 85th career victory at the Rochester International. With this triumph, Whitworth passed Sam Snead for the most professional golf tournaments won by any golfer, male or female. (**Jack Nicklaus** would later pass this, yet many of Nicklaus' wins came on the senior tour. He collected only 70 of his wins on the regular PGA tour. Whitworth gained all 88 of her victories on the LPGA tour.)

Whitworth was inducted into the World Golf Hall of Fame, the Texas Golf Hall of Fame, and the Texas Sports Hall of Fame in 1982. Two years later, she was named to the International Women's Sports Hall of Fame.

In addition to advancing women's golf through her outstanding play, Whitworth also promoted the sport off the course. She once was president of the LPGA and an officer for seven years. Whitworth helped to attract such sponsors as Colgate Palmolive, Suzuki, and Sears to expand the tour and to increase the purses for women's pro tournaments. In dominating professional women's golf, in tirelessly promoting her sport, and in surpassing the million-dollar milestone, Kathy Whitworth did as much as anyone to validate women's golf as a major professional sport.

Career Capsule

All time LPGA leader with 88 victories. Won LPGA Championship three times (1967, 1971, and 1975), Dinah Shore (1977), Titleholders Championship twice (1965–66), and Western Open (1967). Received Vare Trophy every year from 1965–72, except 1968. LPGA Player of the Year 1966–69 and 1971–73.

Mickey Wright

born February 14, 1935

PERHAPS THE GREATEST professional woman golfer ever, Mickey Wright dominated the women's tour in the late 1950s and early 1960s. A terrific all-around player, she used her flawless swing to launch powerful drives off the tee. Wright usually hit the ball around 230 yards and once sent it 272 yards under normal conditions—the longest drive ever hit by any woman.

Born in San Diego, California, Mary Kathryn Wright got her first set of clubs as a birthday present when she turned 11. Already 5 feet, 8 inches tall, shy, and somewhat withdrawn, she was subjected to a lot of teasing from her classmates. "The kids at school called me 'Moose,'" she later recalled. "I had

After ten tries, Wright won the Betsy Rawls Peach Blossom Open in 1964. This was one of 82 tournament victories she earned during her professional career.

a terrible inferiority complex. I needed something to show my prowess. Golf was it." In 1949, Mickey won the Southern California Girls' Championship. The following year, at age 15, she finished as the runner-up in the U.S. Junior Girls' Tournament.

Wright won her first national title at the U.S. Junior Girls' Tournament in 1952. After a year at Stanford University in California, she took second place in the U.S. Women's Amateur in 1954. Wright decided to leave college and join the profes-

In 1961, $1,247 was considered a good first prize for women.

sional tour. She won her first pro title in 1956, and went on to win at least one event a year for 14 straight years. In 1958, Wright won her first LPGA Championship and the first of two consecutive U.S. Women's Open championships. The most consistent woman in golf over the next decade, Wright averaged nearly eight professional titles a year from 1959 to 1968. In winning the Vare Trophy five straight years (1960–1964), Wright brought women's professional golf to a new level. In the mid-1950s, the Vare Trophy winners, the lowest scorers on the tour, averaged between 75 and 76 strokes per round; Wright brought that average down to between 72 and 73.

In 1961, she won an unprecedented ten tournaments. For the second time in her career, she won the LPGA and Open titles in the same year—a feat matched (but just once) in 1991, by Meg Mallon. Her victory in that year's Titleholders (Masters) gave her the Grand Slam of women's golf. A year later, she won a record four scheduled events in a row. Wright won another four in a row in 1963, on her way to 13 pro tour victories, a single-season record that may never be broken. Included among them was her fourth LPGA Championship, a record that still stands. She averaged less than 73 strokes per 18 holes and won $31,269—more than any other woman golfer had ever earned. In 1964, Wright won her fourth U.S. Women's Open, tying a record set the previous year by Betsy Rawls. She also established the record for the lowest recorded score (62) on an 18-hole course. The leading money winner for the fourth straight year, Wright was inducted into the LPGA Hall of Fame in 1964. The Associated Press named her Female Athlete of the Year in both 1963 and 1964.

Though wrist pain limited her tournament schedule in 1965, Wright rebounded with seven victories in 1966. She announced her retirement in 1970, but continued to compete in a few professional tournaments. In 1973, her final professional title gave her a record 82 for her career. (She had passed the previous record, Louise Suggs' 51, ten years earlier. **Kathy Whitworth** would later surpass Wright with 88 victories.) She was inducted into the World Golf Hall of Fame in 1976 and the International Women's Sports Hall of Fame in 1981.

Though uncomfortable in the limelight, Wright helped usher the women's professional golf tour into the television age. Her brilliant play and powerful drives drew larger and larger crowds of spectators to pro events. The heightened fan interest led to increased sponsorship, an expansion of the women's professional tour, and greater television coverage. Women's golf had secured a solid place in the American sports world.

Career Capsule

Second all-time in career wins (82) and major championships (13—tied with Louise Suggs). Won U.S. Open four times (1958–59, 1961, and 1964) and LPGA Championship four times (1958, 1960–61, and 1963), and Western Open three times (1962–63 and 1966). Holds the record for most tournaments won in a year (13).

CHAPTER 8

PRIME TIME

TELEVISION BRINGS BIG DOLLARS TO SPORTS

1971–1996

Barcelona '92

USA

Beginning in the 1970s, money poured into the sports world. Television offered contracts for hundreds of millions—and sometimes billions—of dollars to sports organizations for the right to broadcast their events. Athletes began earning their share of this new pot of money. The end of baseball's reserve clause in 1976 made baseball players free agents—able to sell their talents to the highest bidder. Within ten years, million-dollar salaries for athletes became common in all professional sports.

Many sports stars also became media stars. Superstars like basketball's **Magic Johnson** and **Michael Jordan**, football's **Joe Montana**, baseball's **Cal Ripken, Jr.**—and amateurs such as swimmer **Mark Spitz**, skater **Dorothy Hamill**, and hurdler **Edwin Moses**—received millions for commercials and other product endorsements. An athlete without a "sneaker contract" has not yet reached the highest level of stardom.

The vast amounts of money made available in the sports world have created new tensions. Athletes' labor unions have become more powerful. The clash between players who want to hold on to what they have gained and owners who want to win back some of their power has led to costly strikes in football, hockey, and especially baseball. One-third of the 1981 baseball season was lost. So was the final third of the 1994 season—including the World Series. Owners and players often seem greedy and uncaring to the fans.

Olympics Boycotted

In early 1980, President Jimmy Carter decided the United States would not send its team to the Summer Olympics in Moscow. The boycott was a protest against the Soviet Union's invasion of its neighbor, Afghanistan. Fifty-five other countries joined the boycott.

In all, 4,000 Olympic athletes and 200,000 anticipated visitors changed their plans to attend the first Olympics held in a communist nation. The Soviet Communist Party handbook proclaimed that "the selection of Moscow for the Olympics is a sign of world recognition of the correctness of Soviet foreign policy." But the boycott spoke the world's true feelings about Soviet aggression. Some felt the burden fell too heavily on the athletes, who sacrificed years of training. Others felt the athletes never stood taller.

As salaries rose, more athletes were motivated to extend their careers and earnings potential. Improved physical training programs made it possible for athletes to stay near-peak condition for many more years. World-class athletes such as pentathlete **Jackie Joyner-Kersee** and speed skater **Bonnie Blair** won medals at *three* different Olympiads. **Carl Lewis** competed in four Olympics and won nine gold medals. **Miki Gorman** won both the Boston and New York marathons at age 42. Pitcher **Nolan Ryan** tossed his sixth no-hitter at age 43—then pitched a seventh a year later.

For others, the lure of great wealth tempted them to use anabolic steroids—illegal drugs—to enhance their performances. Football defensive end Lyle Alzado, who used steroids for many years, paid the ultimate price. After retiring from the Oakland Raiders in 1984, his body quickly wasted away. Many believe that the drugs killed him.

Some young athletes who suddenly had lots of money used it to buy cocaine. Basketball's Michael Richardson and baseball's Darryl Strawberry, among others, damaged promising careers through cocaine use.

A fatal disease called Acquired Immune Deficiency Syndrome (AIDS) claimed thousands of lives in the 1980s and 1990s. Athletes were not spared. Those who contracted the virus that causes AIDS included **Magic Johnson**, diver Greg Louganis (a four-time Olympic gold medalist), and tennis champion **Arthur Ashe**. Yet despite their illnesses, these champions displayed grace and courage.

TRIUMPHANT WOMEN

Women surged stronger than ever. Swimmers **Tracy Caulkins** and **Janet Evans**, runners **Gail Devers** and **Mary Decker Slaney**, golfers **Jo Anne Carner** and **Nancy Lopez**, sled dog racer **Susan Butcher**, and auto racers **Shirley Muldowney** and **Janet Guthrie** became champions. Tennis became a popular women's sport, sparked by the 15-year rivalry between **Chris Evert** and **Martina Navratilova**. Title IX of the Education Amendments of 1972 forced schools to provide girls with educational facilities and programs—including those devoted to sports—equal to those offered to boys. The gains achieved through Title IX reached their peak in 1995, when **Rebecca Lobo** led the University of Connecticut women's basketball team to an undefeated record.

In 1996, Lobo and her teammates each received a $50,000 annual salary to train and play. In Atlanta, every U.S. Olympic team member received gifts worth $4,000 from corporate sponsors. A United States athlete could pocket as much as $65,000 for winning a gold medal. The ample supply of money from corporations, national sports federations, broadcasters, and ticket sales to the events, made this possible.

More than 12,000 athletes—3,800 of whom were women, an increase of 40 percent over the previous Olympics—from 197 nations competed in 271 events in 26 sports at the Atlanta, Georgia, Olympics in 1996.

Sports Pay Off

After the 1988 Olympics, professionals were allowed to compete. Nearly all of the 1996 Olympic athletes, including the 700 U.S. team members, were paid. In fact, some were millionaire superstars. The U.S. Olympic Men's Basketball Team—the Dream Team—was comprised entirely of National Basketball Association players. In tennis, professionals such as Andre Agassi and Monica Seles represented the United States. One hundred years after the ancient Greek games were revived, almost all of the best athletes were paid.

Like other major sports events near the end of the twentieth century, the 1996 Olympics demonstrated its power to gather and then spend vast sums of money. NBC sports paid $456 million in rights fees to televise the games to two billion viewers. Ten major sponsors invested $40 million each. The cost of staging the event for the two million visitors to Atlanta was $1.7 billion. The Atlanta Games installed more than $300 million worth of computer, telephone, and video technology.

Be Like Mike:

Unprecedented Money and Fame for Athletes

In 1976, an arbitrator decided that baseball's reserve clause was invalid. Baseball players, now free agents, could work for any team that made them an offer. Recognizing that teams spent a lot of money nurturing young athletic talent, the baseball players' union agreed to certain limits on who could become a free agent. Yet the resulting competition for those who did become free agents sent all player salaries skyrocketing. Other sports soon followed baseball's lead.

Television helped make high salaries possible. To win the right to air a league's games, TV networks began showering sports with billion-dollar deals. Sports leagues and television, each committed to building large audiences, began working together to promote players as celebrities and entertainers, rather than just athletes. Their success in these efforts further escalated the salaries of superstars.

By 1995, ten athletes made more than $3 million—off the field! Basketball star **Michael Jordan** topped them all. Estimates of his off-field earnings ranged as high as $35 million. Four others topped $10 million in endorsements: basketball center Shaquille O'Neal ($14.5 million), retired golfers **Jack Nicklaus** ($13 million) and **Arnold Palmer** ($12.6 million), and retired football quarterback **Joe Montana** ($12 million).

JIM ABBOTT

born September 19, 1967

JAMES ANTHONY ABBOTT was born without a right hand. His right arm ends in a rounded stub. At five, Jim had decided he no longer wanted to wear his prosthetic—a false hand made of steel and fiberglass. That same year, he started playing baseball with his father. Jim loved the game. He would spend hours throwing a ball against a brick wall. Through years of practice, Jim developed a remarkably fluid, graceful style of pitching and fielding. He would tuck his baseball glove onto the end of his right arm. Then he would fire the ball with his left hand and, in the same motion, slip the glove back onto his left hand to field the ball. By moving closer and closer to the wall, Jim steadily improved his quickness in fielding rebounds.

Jim joined the Little League at age 11. In his first game, he pitched a no-hitter. Other teams constantly tested him. In one game he pitched for his Flint, Michigan, high school team, the first eight batters bunted toward the mound, hoping to take advantage of the one-handed pitcher. The first bunter reached first base safely, but Jim threw out the next seven. In his senior year, Jim hit .427 with seven homers and 31 runs batted in (RBIs). As the starting quarterback and punter, Jim also led his school's football team to the Michigan state semifinals.

After high school, Jim received a baseball scholarship to the University of Michigan. In three years on the varsity team, Jim won 26 games, lost only eight, and sported a 3.03 earned run average (ERA). His Michigan Wolverine teams won two straight Big Ten titles in 1986 and 1987. Abbott next starred for the U.S. Team at the 1987 Pan-American Games in Indianapolis, Indiana. He won two games at the tournament and did not give up a single earned run. In 1988, Jim pitched the U.S. Baseball Team to a gold medal at the Olympic Games in Seoul, South Korea. He won the final game against Japan, 5–3.

At 6 feet, 3 inches and weighing 210 pounds, Abbott threw a fastball over 90 miles per hour. He skipped the minor leagues, going from college straight to the California Angels in 1989. In his rookie season, Abbott went 12–12 with a 3.92 ERA. He had a tough season the following year, going 10–14. The Angel hitters, however, offered little support, scoring only 15 runs in the 14 games he lost. He started poorly in 1991, with a record of 0–4 and a 6.00 ERA at the end of April. Yet he stormed through the rest of the season, finishing 18–11 with a terrific 2.89 ERA. Abbott was named to the American League All-Star team that year. In 1992, his 2.77 ERA was fifth best in the league. After a trade to the New York Yankees, Abbott pitched his best game as a major leaguer: a no-hitter against the Cleveland Indians on September 4, 1993.

Abbott was the winning pitcher in the final game of the 1988 Olympics.

Abbott's accomplishments as a pitcher have come through courage, hard work, perseverence, and a positive attitude. "I don't think I'm handicapped," he once explained. "My hand hasn't kept me from doing anything I wanted to do. I believe you can do anything you want if you put your mind to it."

Career Capsule

Pitched his teams to victories in the 1987 Pan-American Games and the 1988 Olympics. He later pitched a no-hitter for the New York Yankees in 1993. Awarded the Golden Spikes Award, presented every year to the best college baseball player in the United States, and became the first baseball player to win the Sullivan Award.

Bonnie Blair

born March 18, 1964

THE MOST SUCCESSFUL American woman athlete in the winter Olympic history, speed skater Bonnie Blair starred in three separate Winter Olympiads. A brilliant sprinter, Blair won five Olympic gold medals and one bronze medal.

Bonnie Kathleen Blair was born in Cornwall, New York, but moved to Champaign, Illinois, when she was two. The youngest of six children, her oldest sibling was 23 when she was born, while the next youngest was seven years older than Bonnie. The Blairs were a skating family. Four of Bonnie's five siblings won national speed-skating titles. They introduced the youngest Blair to skating when she was just two. Bonnie's feet were so small that they had to put her skates on over her shoes. But she took to the ice quickly. By age four, she had begun competing—and winning—in races. Three years later, she was competing in the state championships.

Blair and her teammates already looked like winners at the opening ceremonies of the 1994 Olympics.

Bonnie later credited much of her success to her family's closeness. "We were always a happy family," she explained. "There were very few times that I was angry or mad, and it's this outlook that I brought with me to sports. . . . If I put in the physical work and my competitor does the same kind of training, but doesn't have the strong positive mental outlook that I do, then she's going to be beaten."

In 1979, she began working with Cathy Priestner Faminow, the 1976 silver medalist from Canada, as her coach. That year, Bonnie ran her first Olympic-style race. Until then, all her races had been "pack-skating" sprints, in which several skaters compete on a 110-meter oval track. In Olympic-style sprints, just two skaters at a time race against the clock on a 400-meter track. At the U.S. Olympic trials, Bonnie just missed making the team at age 15.

Faminow advised Bonnie in 1982 to go to Europe to get more Olympic-style speed skating experience. The United States had only two Olympic-size speed skating rinks. Europe had many more. With the help of the Champaign police department, which sponsored raffles and bake sales, Bonnie raised the $7,000 she needed. Despite the extra experience, however, she finished a disappointing eighth in the 500-meter sprint at the Winter Olympic Games in Sarajevo, Yugoslavia, in 1984.

When she returned to Champaign, the police continued to raise money for her next Olympic attempt. The department sold bumper stickers that read, "Champaign Policemen's Favorite Speeder:

Olympian Bonnie Blair." In 1985, Blair moved to Butte, Montana, in order to work with U.S. national speed-skating coach Mike Crowe.

Although small for a speed skater, Blair has powerful calves and thighs. What made her a champion was her flawless technique: a crouching, streamlined, gliding style that brought her up to maximum speed.

In one of her last pack-skating events, Blair won the 1986 world championship in Chamonix, France. Pack-skating, she later said, taught her to get off to an explosive start—a skill that would help her in Olympic competition. "You don't collide with people if you're in front of them," Blair explained. At that year's World Sprint Championships, she finished in a second-place tie in the 500-meter race.

During the 1986–87 season, Blair raced in the United States, Canada, and Europe. She won the World Cup championship and lost only one 500-meter race all season. In the Netherlands, Blair set a new world record for the 500-meter sprint with a time of 39.43 seconds. The following season, however, she lost the World Cup—and the world record—to Krista Rothenburger, the 1984 Olympic gold medalist from East Germany.

Blair set a track record, qualifying for the Olympic 1,000-meter race.

In 1995, Blair skated competitively for the last time.

At the 1988 Olympic Games in Calgary, Canada, Rothenburger set a new world record of 39.12 seconds. Blair, racing two pairs later, broke from the starting line with a tremendous burst of speed. She finished in 39.10 seconds to win the gold in the 500-meter sprint. Her time remains an Olympic record. Blair also won the bronze medal in the 1,000-meter race and finished fourth in the 1,500-meter event. The only U.S. athlete to take two medals home from Calgary, she was given the honor of carrying the U.S. flag during the closing ceremonies.

After winning the overall title at the World Sprint Championships in 1989, Blair cut back her training schedule to attend the Montana College of Mineral Science and Technology. She finished second at the 1990 world championships and third in 1991. Looking toward the 1992 Olympics in Albertville, France, she then returned to full-time training.

Wholesome and unspoiled by success, Blair ate peanut butter-and-jelly sandwiches before races. She enjoyed TV soap operas so much that she had highlights faxed to her when she was skating overseas.

Blair won gold medals in both the 500- and 1,000-meter sprints at the 1992 Winter Olympics. Among American women, only **Andrea Mead Lawrence** had ever won two gold medals at the same Winter Olympiad. The Amateur Athletic Union chose Blair to receive the James E. Sullivan Award as the nation's best amateur athlete in 1992.

Blair was not done yet. In 1994, she recaptured the World Sprint Championship. She set a new world record, becoming the first woman ever to skate 500 meters in less than 39 seconds. At the Winter Olympiad in Lillehammer, Norway, Blair won her third straight gold medal in the 500-meter race. No other athlete in the history of the Olympics has won the same event in three separate Olympiads. Her fourth career gold medal tied the record held by diver **Pat McCormick**, swimmer **Janet Evans**, and sprinter Evelyn Ashford. She then won her second straight gold medal in the 1,000-meter race. Her fifth gold medal made her the U.S. recordholder among all women athletes.

CAREER CAPSULE

Won gold medal in 500 meters and bronze medal in 1,000 meters at 1988 Olympics and gold medals in both events in both 1992 and 1994 Olympics. Also 1989 World Sprint champion and winner of Sullivan Award in 1992.

SUSAN BUTCHER

born December 26, 1954

ONE OF THE WORLD'S BEST dog-sled racers, male or female, Susan Butcher won Alaska's legendary, 1,157-mile Iditarod Trail Sled Dog Race four times in five years. Only Rick Swenson has won the race more times. The Iditarod, run from Anchorage to Nome, covers a course of icy tundra, frozen rivers, burned-out forests, and two mountain ranges. Temperatures range from fifty below zero to forty degrees Fahrenheit, with violent snowstorms whipping winds up to 140 miles an hour. The treacherous course and harrowing conditions severely test the driver's physical and mental strength and tactical planning, as well as the stamina and endurance of both driver and dogs and their rapport with each other.

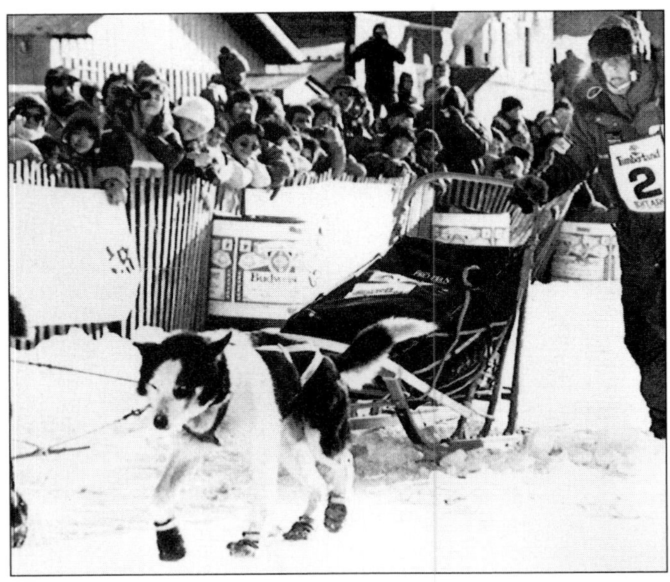

Butcher beat her winning Iditarod time by 13 hours in 1987.

Butcher finished 19th in her first race in 1978. Over the next six years, she showed steady improvement, placing second in both 1982 and 1984. In 1985, a moose attacked her sled, killing two dogs and injuring 13 others. Forced to withdraw, Butcher lost the opportunity to become the first woman to win the Iditarod when Libby Riddles won the race. But Butcher won the race in 1986, 1987, and 1988, setting a new speed record each year and becoming the first musher ever to win three years in a row. She won again in 1990, setting a speed record (broken in 1992 by Martin Buser) of 11 days, 1 hour, and 53 minutes. An inspiring athlete, Butcher never allowed gender to determine her goals. Her desire was not to be the first woman to win the Iditarod, or the best woman in the sport, but the best sled-dog racer ever.

CAREER CAPSULE

Won Iditarod dog-sled race four times, each time setting a new record. First person to win three years in a row (1986–88).

JOANNE CARNER

born April 21, 1939

JOANNE GUNDERSON CARNER was one of the two greatest women's amateur golfers of all time—and one of the best pros. Her accomplishments were rivaled only by the legendary **Babe Didrikson Zaharias**. Carner used her strong wrists and masterful physical training to drive the ball great distances. Carner never liked to practice much. She was always confident that everything would fall into place on the first tee. More often than not, she was right.

Born in Kirkland, Washington, JoAnne taught herself how to play golf by watching the golfers at the public nine-hole course where her brother watered the greens and her sisters ran the snack bar. She won the U.S. Girls' Junior Championship as a 17-year-old in 1956. Despite her youth, she finished second in the U.S. Golf Association Amateur championship that year. The following year, Gunderson won the U.S. Amateur title. At 18, she was the second youngest champion ever. She would go on to win the amateur championship a record five times (1957, 1960, 1962, 1966, 1968) as well as finishing second again in 1964. She played on the U.S. Curtis Cup teams from 1958 to 1964 that dominated matches with Britain.

Using her married name, JoAnne Gunderson Carner joined the Ladies' Professional Golf Association (LPGA) circuit at age 30. Carner won the nation's most prestigious tournament for women—the U.S. Women's Open—in 1971 and 1976, and finished second four times, most recently in 1983 at age 44. She was awarded the Vare Trophy, given to the golfer with the lowest scoring average for the year five times (1974–75 and 1981–83). The first woman to win as much as $300,000 in a single season (1982), Carner became one of the top money winners in women's golf, earning more than $2,840,000 in career prizes. The LPGA Player of the Year in 1974, 1981, and 1982, she won 42 professional tournaments in all. The recipient of the 1981 Bob Jones Award for distinguished sportsmanship, Carner was elected to the LPGA Hall of Fame in 1982.

Though she never practiced much, Carner earned over $2 million in prize money.

CAREER CAPSULE

Won 42 tournaments, including U.S. Women's Open (1971 and 1976) and du Maurier Classic (1975 and 1978). LPGA Player of the Year (1974 and 1981–82) and won five Vare Trophies (1974–75 and 1981–83).

TRACY CAULKINS

born January 11, 1963

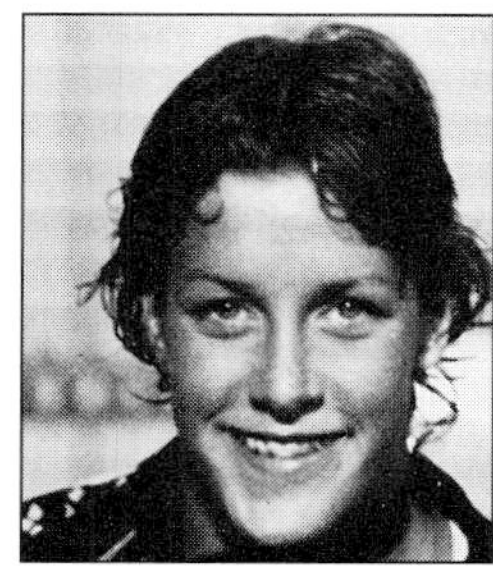

AN OUTSTANDING SWIMMER, Tracy Caulkins excelled in all four strokes—freestyle, breaststroke, the butterfly, and the backstroke.

Born in Nashville, Tennessee, Tracy won her first national title at age 14. She dominated the world championships in 1978, winning five gold medals and a silver medal. (Her older sister Amy was a member of the U.S. water polo team.) Just 15 years old, Tracy became the youngest winner of the Sullivan Award, given to honor the nation's outstanding amateur athlete. At the Pan American games in 1979, she won gold medals in both the 200- and 400-meter individual medley races, which

Caulkins swam to three gold medals in 1994.

feature all four strokes. Tracy also won silver medals in the 400-meter freestyle and the 100-meter breaststroke races. The next year, the U.S. boycott of the Olympic Games in Moscow forced Tracy to postpone her dreams of Olympic glory.

After a disappointing performance in the 1982 world championships, Caulkins tuned up for the 1984 Olympics by again winning the gold medals in both individual medley races in the 1983 Pan American games. As captain of the 1984 U.S. women's Olympic team, Caulkins took gold medals in both the 200- and 400-meter individual medleys and helped the American team win gold in the 4 × 100-meter medley relay. In the process, she set an Olympic record (2:12.64) in the 200-meter medley and a new U.S. record in the 400-meter race (4:39.24). After the Los Angeles Olympics, Caulkins retired from competitive swimming at age 21.

Career Capsule

Caulkins won 48 national titles from 1978 to 1984, more than any other U.S. swimmer. The winner of three Olympic gold medals, she set 61 American and 5 world records. Received Sullivan Award in 1978.

Peter Crowley

born May 31, 1957

PETER CROWLEY HAS WON wrestling matches and cross-country races and pitched his team to victory in softball games. He is a championship bowler, and he has scaled the summit of Mount Kilimanjaro. He has also earned a black belt in the Korean martial art of tae kwan do (pronounced "tie kwan doe"). Crowley achieved all of these goals despite being blind from birth.

Optic atrophy gave Peter just seven percent of normal vision at birth. By adulthood, he had only one percent vision. He could distinguish between light and darkness, but could see little more than that. Yet Peter refused to let his blindness limit him. In high school, he ran on the cross-country team, wrestled, and even played one season as a football lineman.

After high school, Crowley pitched against sighted athletes on a local softball team on Long Island, New York. Unable to see home plate, he used the pitching rubber to orient himself and demonstrated remarkable control. When he fielded a ball (by sound), the first baseman would call out

Guides helped Crowley and other blind climbers scale Mount Kilimanjaro.

his name so that Crowley could throw in the right direction.

In 1982, Crowley became the U.S. Blind Bowling Champion. Five years later, he won seven medals in power lifting, wrestling, and track and field in competition sponsored by the U.S. Association of Blind Athletes (USABA). That year, 1987, he also began taking lessons in tae kwan do. Wearing special eyeglasses that use ultrasound waves to locate objects, in 1992, Crowley attained a First Degree Black Belt, the highest level of achievement. He has won more than 20 awards in non-combative competition (exhibitions of form and feats such as board breaking) against sighted athletes.

In 1994, Crowley coordinated and made a difficult eight-day climb with three other blind climbers to the summit of Mount Kilimanjaro in Tanzania. The highest mountain on the African continent, Kilimanjaro is more than 19,300 feet high. Three of the four blind climbers, accompanied by nine sighted guides, made it all the way to the top. Crowley's achievements have inspired many blind and disabled people to refuse to listen when other people, however well-meaning, try to limit their goals.

Career Capsule

A black belt in tae kwan do in 1992, and one-time U.S. Blind Bowling Champion in 1982. Also won national medals in wrestling and track and field.

Gail Devers

born November 19, 1966

A world-class sprinter and hurdler, Gail Devers demonstrated strength and courage in overcoming Graves' disease to become known as the "World's Fastest Woman."

Yolanda Gail Devers, the daughter of a Baptist minister and an elementary schoolteacher's aide, grew up in San Diego, California. In high school, Gail won both the 100-meter sprint and the 100-meter hurdles at the California state championships. She also finished second in the long jump.

Devers claimed several championships in the 100-meter sprint through high school and college. Her real stardom, however, came when she suited up for the USA.

After graduation, Gail decided to attend the University of California at Los Angeles (UCLA). As a senior in 1988, she set a U.S. 100-meter hurdles record of 12.61 seconds. Devers also won the 100-meter dash at the NCAA Outdoor Championships. Surprisingly, Devers then performed poorly at that year's Olympic Games in Seoul, South Korea. She seemed a little sluggish and failed even to qualify for the hurdles final.

Devers felt washed up at age 21. She did not compete again for more than two years. Her weight fluctuated wildly. She lost 20 pounds, then gained 40. Her hair began to fall out. She suffered from hand tremors, migraine headaches, and almost constant menstrual bleeding. She lost vision in her left eye. She alternated between insomnia (inability to sleep) and deep, wakeless sleep. Her resting heart rate skyrocketed to 187.

Devers was the 100-meter gold medalist in the 1992 and 1996 Olympics.

In 1990, Devers was finally diagnosed with Graves' disease, a disease that affects the thyroid gland and its ability to regulate the body's metabolism. Graves' disease probably had begun to affect her as early as the 1988 Olympics. Unfortunately, the cure was almost as bad as the disease. Doctors used radiation in an attempt to destroy the diseased part of the thyroid. Devers' feet became so infected that she could not even walk, much less run. Her doctors warned that they might need to cut off both feet in order to save her legs. But when the radiation treatments stopped, Devers stabilized and improved. She will, however, have to take a metabolism-regulating drug for the rest of her life.

In 1991, Devers resumed training despite the continued soreness in her feet. At first, she just walked around the track in her socks. Gradually, she got stronger and added more rigor to her training program. In her first meet in nearly three years, Devers qualified for The Athletics Congress (TAC) nationals. She then finished first at TAC. Her time, 12.83 seconds, was the best recorded by an American so far that year. At the World Track and Field Championships in Tokyo, Japan, Devers finished second in the 100-meter hurdles. Two weeks later, in Berlin, Germany, she set a new American record of 12.48 in the 100-meter hurdles. Devers was back for good.

At the 1992 Olympic Games in Barcelona, Spain, Devers won the gold medal in the 100-meter sprint by inches. In just 17 months, she had progressed from crawling to become the World's Fastest Woman. In the Olympic 100-meter hurdles final, however, Devers had a significant lead when she tripped over the last hurdle. She stumbled across the finish line in fifth place.

The following year, at the World Championships in Stuttgart, Germany, Devers won both events. She ran the 100-meter dash in 10.82 seconds and lowered her American record in the hurdles to 12.46 seconds. Later that year in Toronto, Canada, Devers won the world indoor title in the 60-meter sprint (6.95 seconds). "The last three years of my life have definitely been a miracle," Devers later reflected. "I don't consider [my Olympic win] an upset. I consider it a blessing." Devers earned two more gold medals in the 1996 Olympics in Atlanta, Georgia, where she won at 100 meters and was a member of the victorious women's 4 × 100 meter team.

Career Capsule

Won 100 meters at 1992 Olympics and the 100 meters and 100 meter-hurdles (American record 12.46) at the 1993 World Championships. Also holds world indoor 60-meter record (6.95). Won 100 meters and women's 4 × 100 meters at 1996 Olympics.

JANET EVANS

born August 28, 1971

THE MOST SUCCESSFUL Olympic distance swimmer ever, Janet Evans won four gold medals and one silver medal at two Olympiads. In her best event, the 800-meter freestyle race, Evans went eight years (1987–1995) without a single loss. Beloved by the media, she combined joy, vivaciousness, and a winning smile with intense competitiveness.

As a teenager from Placentia, California, Janet set her first world record in freestyle swimming in 1987: racing 800 meters in 8 minutes, 22.44 seconds. During the next year, she also broke the freestyle record for 400 meters (4:05.45). Next, she became the first woman to swim 1,500 meters in less than 16 minutes. Her time, 15:52.10, remains a world record.

At the 1988 Olympic games in Seoul, South Korea, Janet—5 feet, 5 inches tall and just 101 pounds—won three gold medals. She won the 400-meter individual medley—100 meters each of freestyle, backstroke, breaststroke, and butterfly—in 4:37.76. In the 400-meter freestyle, Janet set another world record (4:03.85) that still stands today. Finally, she set an Olympic record for 800 meters (8:20.20), winning by a full ten feet.

After returning from Seoul a hero, Evans continued to set world records. In 1989, she swam 800 meters in 8:16.22—still the best time ever. That year, she won the Sullivan Award, given each year to the nation's best amateur athlete.

While a student in California and Texas, she continued to compete. She won both the 400- and 800-meter races at the 1991 World Championships in Perth, Australia. At the 1992 Olympic Games in Barcelona, Spain, she won gold for the 800-meter race. She also won a silver medal in the 400-meter freestyle race. Her four gold medals in individual events matched the record for swimmers—female or male. For the third time, Evans qualified for the Olympic U.S. swim team in 1996, in both the 400- and 800-meter freestyle events.

Evans was the first American to win a gold medal in the 1988 Olympics with her performance in the 400-meter individual medley of freestyle, backstroke, breaststroke, and butterfly (100 meters each).

Career Capsule

Four-time Olympic gold medalist (three in 1988 and one in 1992), Evans' world records in 400-meter freestyle (4:03.85 in 1988), 800-meter freestyle (8:16.22 in 1989), and 1500-meter freestyle (15:52.10 in 1988). Sullivan Award winner in 1989. Qualified for the 1996 Olympics in 400- and 800-meter freestyle.

Chris Evert

born December 21, 1954

One of the greatest women's tennis players ever, and probably the best ever on her favorite surface, clay, Chris Evert ranked among the top four players in the world for 17 consecutive years. The winner of 21 major titles in her career, she captured at least one Grand Slam tournament every year from 1974 to 1986, a record 13 straight years. Intensely focused, determined, and coolly professional, Evert was a base line specialist with sharp, powerful groundstrokes. Although she did not invent the stroke, she became best known for her overpowering two-handed backhand, a shot imitated by a generation of American girls.

Born in Fort Lauderdale, Florida, Chrissie (short for Christine) was the second of five children, all of whom began playing tennis at about the age of six. (Her younger sister Jeanne rose to number nine in the national rankings in 1974.) Her father, tennis pro Jimmy Evert, had won the Canadian singles championship in 1947. Encouraged and taught by her father, Chris practiced three to four hours a day. Though she originally developed the two-handed backhand to compensate for her small size as a child, the stroke became more and more powerful as she grew.

Evert's first impressive victory came as a 15-year-old, in the 1970 Carolinas Tournament. Chris reached the finals by defeating Margaret Court. Court, the number one player in the world, had just become the second woman to win tennis' Grand Slam (all four major singles titles). The following year, Chris became the youngest player to reach the semifinals at the U.S. Open. Though she lost in straight sets to **Billie Jean King**, the poised Evert became America's darling.

While still in her teens, Chris developed the cool, unflappable personality that would become her trademark. "I don't show a lot of emotion on the court because I don't want to waste my energy, and I don't want my opponents to see how I really feel," she later explained.

In 1972, Chris won the first of four straight U.S. clay court championships, a title she would capture six times in her career (1972–75, 1979, 1980). She also won the first of four championships (1972, 1973, 1975, 1977) sponsored by the Virginia Slims cigarette company.

Chris did not turn pro until 1973. (Her amateur status had prevented her from accepting nearly $50,000 in prize money in 1972 alone.) That year, the rivalry that made women's tennis more popular than ever began. King had helped bring long-overdue attention to the game of women's tennis. But when Evert and **Martina Navratilova** first stood across the net from each other in 1973, women's tennis soared to a new level. The two players

Even as a teenager, Evert was a celebrity in Florida.

Evert's father taught her to play the baseline game to perfection, and she popularized the two-hand backhand shot.

brought distinctly different styles to the game: Evert, the cool and relentless baseliner; Navratilova, the aggressive serve-and-volleyer. Their 15-year rivalry took place during the heart of an era when sports became more popular and profitable than ever before. Evert and Navratilova ignited both media and public interest in tennis. Though Evert dominated their matches in the early years, Navratilova would eventually win 43 of their 80 career matches.

Evert played the best tennis in the game, beginning in the 1970s. From 1973 to 1979, she won 125 consecutive clay-court matches. Her first major title appropriately came on the clay surface at the French Open in 1974, when she won both the singles championship and the women's doubles trophy. At the time, she was in the middle of a streak in which she won 55 consecutive matches on all surfaces. The streak also carried her through Wimbledon, where she captured her first All-England singles title.

From 1974 to 1978, Evert was the top-ranked woman player in the country. This made her the first woman to hold the number one ranking for five straight years since **Alice Marble** (1936–40). In 1975, she again took both the French Open singles and doubles championships. Later that year, she captured the first of four straight singles titles at the U.S. Open—a feat that had not been accomplished in more than 40 years. She now ranked number one in the world—and remained on top for three years.

Evert won her second Wimbledon and U.S. Open singles titles, as well as a Wimbledon doubles trophy, in 1976. The first woman to reach $1 million in career prize earnings, Evert became only the second woman named by *Sports Illustrated* as Sportsman of the Year. Although Navratilova took over as number one in 1978, Evert regained the world's top ranking in 1980. She won both her fourth French Open singles title and her fifth U.S. Open championship in six years. The Associated Press named her Female Athlete of the Year (1980) for the fourth time. (She had also won this honor in 1974, 1975, and 1977.) In 1982, she not only captured the U.S. Open crown but the one major title that had previously eluded her: the singles championship at the Australian Open.

After 1981, Evert remained the number two player in the world (after Navratilova) until 1986, by consistently reaching the semifinals of almost every major tournament. She won at least one Grand Slam event every year. Among the most memorable were her last two major titles. In 1985, she upset Navratilova in a three-set final to capture her sixth French Open title. A year later, she did it again against Navratilova, losing the first set before storming back to win the match. The victory gave her a record-tying seventh French Open singles title.

In 1989, Evert retired from tennis. In addition to her 157 tournament victories, she had reached the finals of 72 others. She had advanced to the semifinals 53 times in 57 Grand Slam tournaments. She had won seven French Open championships, six U.S. Open titles, three Wimbledon crowns, and two Australian Open titles. She earned almost $9 million in prize money.

The Women's Sports Foundation (WSF), in 1985, recognized Evert as the Greatest Woman Athlete of the previous 25 years. Five years later, she received the WSF's Flo Hyman Award in recognition of her "commitment to excellence in supporting women's advancement in sports." Chris Evert helped make the women's professional tennis tour a major drawing card in the prime-time world of sports today. She was inducted into the Tennis Hall of Fame in 1995.

Career Capsule

Second all-time in tournament victories (157) and third all-time in women's Grand Slam singles titles (18—tied with Martina Navratilova). Won French Open seven times (1974–75, 1979–80, 1983, 1985–86), won U.S. Open six times (1975–78, 1980, and 1982), and Australian Open two times (1982 and 1984). Won 90% of her 1,455 career matches, the highest success ratio ever. Reached semifinals in 52 of her last 56 Grand Slam tournaments.

Miki Gorman

born August 9, 1935

A two-time winner of both the Boston Marathon and the New York Marathon, Miki Gorman was the first woman to break the three-hour mark in Boston. She remains the only woman to win both marathons more than once.

Michiko Gorman, born in China to Japanese parents, immigrated to the United States in 1964. Two years later, at age 30, she took up running as part of a physical training program designed to help her put on some weight. Just 5 feet tall and 87 pounds, she won her first Boston Marathon in 1974. She became the first woman to complete the nation's most prestigious distance race in less than three hours—much less. She set a new record of 2 hours, 47 minutes, and 11 seconds—chopping nearly 19 minutes off the previous women's record. After finishing second to Kim Merritt's record-setting pace in New York, in 1975, Gorman set a new standard for the New York Marathon the following year. In a field of 88 women, she won the New York race in just 2:39:11, cutting more than seven minutes off Merritt's record time. At 41, she was older than any previous New York champion.

In the spring of 1977, Gorman won the Boston Marathon for the second time, finishing the race in 2:46:22. That fall, the number of women running the New York Marathon had grown to 250. Gorman won her second straight New York Marathon with a time of 2:43:10. With this victory,

Gorman was the first woman to finish the Boston Marathon in under three hours.

she broke her own record as the oldest New York Marathon winner. (Priscilla Welch of Great Britain, who won in 1987, was about nine months older.) She also became just the second woman to win America's two most famous marathons in the same year.

Career Capsule

Only woman to win both the New York and Boston marathons twice, Gorman also won both races in the same year (1977). She won her second New York Marathon at age 42. She was the first woman to break three hours in Boston and set a course record time with her first New York win.

JANET GUTHRIE

born March 7, 1938

SOME PEOPLE WOULD SAY that burning rubber at 190 miles per hour around an oval track is no sport for a lady. Janet Guthrie would disagree. "I'm not trying to establish the superiority of one sex over another," she once insisted. "I'm a good driver, but I'm no superwoman. What I'm trying to emphasize is that a driver is primarily a person, not a man or a woman."

The first woman to qualify for the Indianapolis 500 and the only woman ever to finish among the top ten drivers in the race, Guthrie broke the gender barrier in championship auto racing. The sport of auto racing did not welcome Guthrie with open arms. Yet Guthrie had the drive and determination needed to make her auto racing's first and best woman driver.

Guthrie, the daughter of a commercial pilot, was born in Iowa City, Iowa. Janet's first love was flying. By the time she turned 13, Janet had flown her first plane. A licensed pilot at 17, she logged 400 hours in the air and gained experience as a parachutist over the next four years.

Guthrie was the first woman to finish among the top ten drivers at the Indianapolis 500.

Guthrie obtained a degree in physics in 1960 from the University of Michigan. After accepting a job on Long Island as an aerospace engineer, she bought her first sports car: a used Jaguar XK 120. Guthrie then entered several local gymkhana races. Gymkhanas, held on winding or zigzag courses, demand precision driving at relatively low speeds. Guthrie was named the women's gymkhana champion of Long Island in 1962.

Guthrie bought her second Jaguar, an XK 140, in 1962. She taught herself auto mechanics, took the car apart, and rebuilt it for racing. By 1964, she had driven the Jaguar to two wins and three second-place finishes. In her first major event, the Watkins Glen (New York) 500, Guthrie placed second in her auto class and sixth overall. That year, Guthrie began competing in endurance events, which test how far drivers can take their cars in a specified time. One of the greatest challenges in endurance racing is simply finishing the race. Only half of the drivers who start these events finish them. Yet by 1971, Guthrie had completed nine straight endurance races.

In 1978, Guthrie qualified for the Indianapolis 500 race.

Despite her skill and track record, Guthrie had a difficult time convincing sponsors to back a woman driver. So she decided to pursue her dream on her own. She bought a Toyota Celica in 1971, and spent a year rebuilding it for racing. She had hoped to have it ready for the 1972 Toyota 2.5 Challenge. But the Sports Car Club of America, sports-car racing's governing body, cancelled the series.

Despite her disappointment, Guthrie never gave up on auto racing. She won the North Atlantic Road Racing Championship in 1973. Two years later, she won both the Vanderbilt Cup race and the Bridgehampton (New York) 400. In 1976, she passed the rookie driving test at Indianapolis Speedway, but was forced to withdraw from the race due to mechanical problems. While the Indy 500 got underway that Memorial Day, Guthrie competed in the Charlotte (North Carolina) World 600. This made her the first woman ever to race in a National Association for Stock Car Auto Racing (NASCAR) event.

In 1977, Guthrie averaged 188.4 mph for the four 2.5-mile laps in the Indianapolis 500 time trials. Her time made her the first woman ever to qualify for the race. Again, Guthrie met with disappointment. After 27 laps, an engine breakdown forced her to drop out. Still she raced on, finishing as the year's Top Rookie in the Daytona 500 and four other NASCAR races.

In 1978, Guthrie finally found a corporate sponsor: Texaco. Averaging 190.3 mph in the time trials, Guthrie again qualified for the Indianapolis 500. Though she fractured her wrist two days before the race, Guthrie became the first woman to complete the Indianapolis 500, finishing ninth. Her strong performance offered solid proof that the best female drivers could compete head-to-head with the world's best male drivers.

Career Capsule

First woman ever to qualify for the Indianapolis 500—and to complete the race; also first woman to race in a NASCAR event. Was Top Rookie in five NASCAR races in 1977.

Dorothy Hamill

born July 26, 1956

WARM, ENTHUSIASTIC, skilled, and graceful, Dorothy Hamill became the darling of the figure-skating world when she won the Olympic gold medal at the 1976 Winter Olympics in Innsbruck, Austria.

Born in Riverside, Connecticut, Dorothy received her first pair of ice skates in 1964, as a Christmas present. Frustrated because she could only skate forward, Dorothy asked her parents for lessons on how to skate backward. Her parents hired former U.S. figure-skating singles champion Sonya Dunfield as Dorothy's first coach.

With Dunfield's teaching, Dorothy quickly mastered fundamental figure-skating techniques. In 1969, she demonstrated athleticism, poise, and artistry in winning the U.S. national ladies novice singles championship. Encouraged by her victory,

Hamill's supportive parents played a big part in her success.

she quit school at age 14 in order to pursue more rigorous training. She completed her high school education through private tutors. During the 1970 Eastern junior ladies singles championships, Hamill first performed what came to be known as the "Hamill camel": a spiral spin to a sit spin. The innovative spin helped her win the Eastern title. In the national ladies singles championships that year, Hamill finished second.

Hamill's performance impressed figure-skating coach Carlo Fassi, who had helped **Peggy Fleming** win the Olympic gold medal in 1968. Fassi invited her to come to Colorado to train with him. By 1974, under Fassi's coaching, Hamill had begun to shine. After winning her first national ladies senior championships, Hamill won the silver medal in the world championships in Munich, West Germany. She repeated this showing in 1975, retaining her U.S. title but placing only second in the world championships.

Nineteen seventy-six was Dorothy Hamill's year. Though she successfully defended her national title to claim a spot on the U.S. Olympic Figure Skating Team, Hamill was not favored to win. Yet she took the lead in the first night's competition, the compulsory figures. In the two-minute short program, Hamill delighted the judges as well as the crowd. She scored perfect 6.0s for both technical merit and artistic expression. Her performance gave her a substantial lead going into the free skating competition. Hamill, considered the best women's free skater in the world, did not disappoint. She performed a nearly flawless long program, scoring 5.8s and 5.9s to win the gold.

Less than a month later, Hamill followed up her gold-medal performance at Innsbruck by finally capturing the world-figure skating title in Goteborg, Sweden. Hamill, extremely popular with both the media and the public, then turned professional. Signing a million-dollar contract with the Ice Capades, she performed in arenas and on television before millions of fans. Her warmth, strength, and style inspired thousands of girls across America to take skating lessons—and to copy the wedge-style haircut she had made so popular.

After leaving the Ice Capades in 1983, Hamill starred in an ice version of *Romeo and Juliet* for CBS-TV and joined Olympian John Curry's Skating Company. She won four straight women's World Professional Figure Skating titles from 1984 to 1987. In 1991, she was named to the U.S. Olympic Hall

Hamill's 1976 Olympic performance was almost perfect.

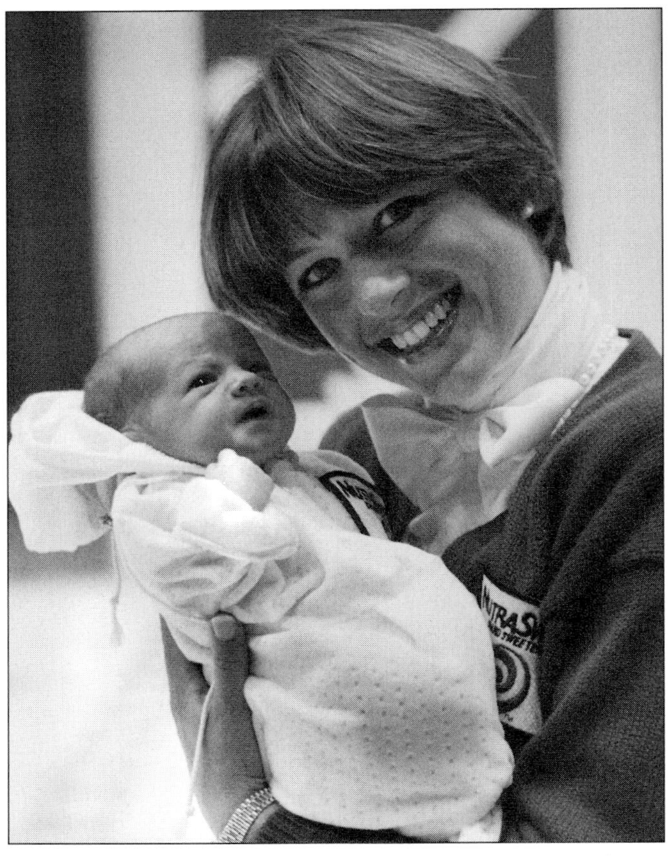

In 1988, Hamill introduced her daughter, Alexandra, to the world.

of Fame. Two years later, Hamill, her husband, and an Alaska businessman bought the Ice Capades, which had filed for bankruptcy in 1992. As part owner, she totally revamped the show, building the skating around a single story. Hamill returned to the ice in 1993, as the star of *Cinderella . . . Frozen in Time.* The show received critical acclaim and drew twice as many fans as the Ice Capades had drawn during previous seasons. In 1994, Hamill's group sold the Ice Capades. She and her husband, however, continue to produce the show.

Career Capsule

Three-time national figure-skating champion, Hamill won the Olympic gold medal and the world championship in 1976; also won four consecutive professional skating titles (1984–87). Eventually became part owner of the Ice Capades.

Sharon Hedrick

born April 26, 1956

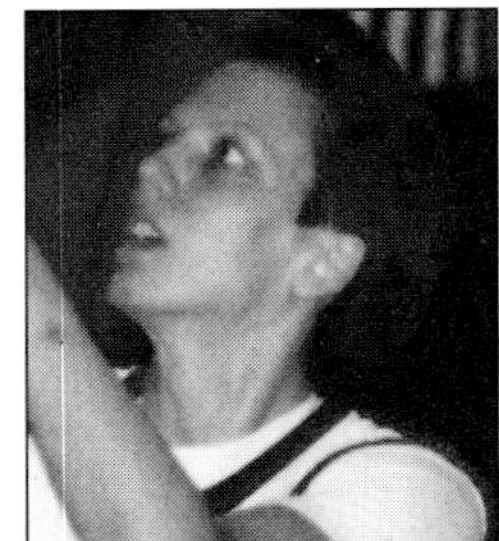

The most accomplished athlete in the history of wheelchair athletics, Sharon Hedrick has won international gold medals in both racing and basketball. Hedrick also won silver medals in national swimming competitions.

Sharon Rahn grew up in Willow Grove, Pennsylvania. When Sharon was nine, one of her two brothers accidentally shot her with their father's gun. The bullet lodged in her spinal column. Though Sharon still had sensation in her legs, she could no longer walk without braces or crutches.

Sharon focused on the things she could do, rather than the things she couldn't. She sang in the chorus, edited her school's yearbook, and trained show dogs. Sharon's high school class voted her Most Likely to Succeed.

She did not take up wheelchair athletics until 1975. A year later, at the Paralympics in Toronto, Canada, Rahn set a world record of 3:14.8 in the 800-meter race, winning the gold medal by 41 seconds! The national champion in the 60-yard dash,

Hedrick set a world record of 3:14.8 in the 800-meter race.

Rahn also won silver medals in the 50-yard freestyle and backstroke swimming races. In 1977, Rahn became the first woman in a wheelchair to complete the Boston Marathon. She finished in less than four hours.

In wheelchair basketball, Rahn led the Illinois MS Kids to their first national championship in 1978, taking the first of a record seven tournament MVP awards. Rahn married the team's assistant coach, Brad Hedrick, in 1980. Four years later, at the Los Angeles Olympic Games, Sharon Hedrick set a new world record of 2:15.50, winning the gold medal in the 800-meter race. It was the first wheelchair event ever held in the Olympics. She set another world record and won a second gold medal at the Olympics in Seoul, South Korea in 1988. By this time, Hedrick had not lost a single race in 12 years. At that year's Paralympics in Seoul, Hedrick averaged 13.5 points in leading the U.S. women to the gold medal. Through talent and determination, Sharon Hedrick has become a winner in every sport she's tried.

CAREER CAPSULE

Seven-time national MVP in wheelchair basketball. A two-time Olympic gold medalist in the 800-meter wheelchair race, she was the first woman to complete the Boston Marathon in a wheelchair in 1977.

EARVIN "MAGIC" JOHNSON

born August 14, 1959

PERHAPS THE MOST resourceful playmaker in basketball history, Magic Johnson brought new excitement to the game in the 1980s. With his friend and rival, Larry Bird of the Boston Celtics, he helped revive the professional game. An unselfish team player, Johnson set records for most assists and best assists-per-game average in a career (both broken by John Stockton in 1995). Most importantly, he always looked like he was having fun. And that made fans love to watch him play.

Johnson was a member of the 1992 Olympic Dream Team.

Earvin Johnson grew up in Lansing, Michigan, where his father worked in an auto factory and his mother managed a school cafeteria. The sixth of ten children, Earvin did not begin playing basketball until sixth grade. Earvin played with his brother or, when it rained, played inside with a pair of rolled-up socks and an imaginary hoop. Earvin made the All-State team during all three of his years on the Everett High School varsity team. The team reached the state quarterfinals in his sophomore year, the semifinals in his junior year, and won the state championship in his senior year. A local sportswriter who covered the team nicknamed Earvin "Magic."

After graduating from high school in 1977, Magic attended Michigan State University in nearby

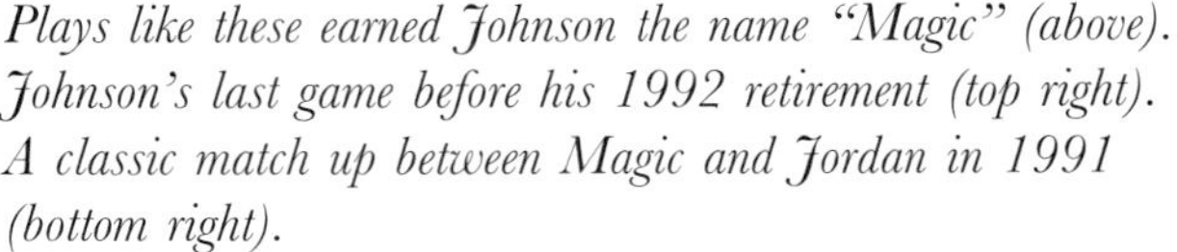

Plays like these earned Johnson the name "Magic" (above). Johnson's last game before his 1992 retirement (top right). A classic match up between Magic and Jordan in 1991 (bottom right).

East Lansing, where he studied communications. During his freshman year, he became the unofficial team leader. The Spartans, who had won just ten games in 1977, went 25–5 to win the Big Ten Conference title. In the NCAA tournament, Michigan State just missed the Final Four, losing to Kentucky in the Mideast regional final. As a sophomore, Magic played every position—guard, center, and forward—depending on what the team needed. The Spartans finished in a three-way tie for the conference title. Johnson then led his team to the 1979 NCAA Final. In the first of many meetings, Magic squared off against Larry Bird of Indiana State. Johnson scored 24 points while holding Bird to just 19. The Spartans won the game 75–64, and Magic was named the tournament's Most Valuable Player (MVP).

Magic and Jordan joined forces in 1992 at the Olympics as members of the Dream Team that won the gold in Barcelona, Spain. Even though Johnson had retired from professional basketball, he was able to play on the U.S. Olympic team.

Johnson left college to sign a pro contract with the Los Angeles Lakers. Size (6 feet, 9 inches) and quickness made him a star in Southern California. As a rookie in 1979, Johnson "was so enthusiastic, we couldn't believe he was for real," teammate Jamaal Wilkes later said. "But that's just the way he is." Despite his inexperience, Johnson quickly became the team leader on the floor. The Lakers improved by 13 games to finish with 60 wins. Even as a rookie, Magic showed his all-around ability: He averaged 18 points, 7.3 assists, and 7.7 rebounds per game. He also hit on 81 percent of his free throws. In the playoffs, Johnson staged a real Magic show. He averaged a "triple double" (10 or more points, rebounds, and assists) throughout the playoffs: 10 assists, 10 rebounds, and 18.3 points per game. With the Lakers' powerful center, Kareem Abdul-Jabbar, on the sidelines with an injury, Magic started at center for the sixth game of the NBA Finals against the Philadelphia 76ers. Johnson stole the show, scoring 42 points and grabbing 15 rebounds to lead the Lakers to the title. After the game, Magic became the only rookie ever to win the NBA Finals MVP award.

Johnson's 1980–81 season was cut in half by a knee injury. Back for the playoffs, Johnson played poorly and the Lakers were swept out in the first round. The Lakers were not disappointed with Johnson, however. They signed him to a 25-year contract worth $25 million—the longest and richest contract in sports history to that point. (The contract offered Johnson a job coaching or otherwise serving the team after he had retired as a player.)

The following year, when the Lakers fired head coach Paul Westhead, many in the news media suggested that Magic was responsible. Fans at the L.A.

Even after retiring in 1992, Johnson was a crowd favorite. Here he greeted fans at the Forum in Los Angeles, where the Lakers play.

Forum booed Johnson for the first—and only—time in his career. Yet when Magic and new coach Pat Riley led the Lakers to their second NBA title in three years, the boos turned to cheers. Johnson led the league in steals with 208 and was second in assists, averaging 9.5 per game. Once again, Johnson took home the MVP award in the NBA Finals.

Johnson and the Lakers lost the NBA Finals in 1983 to Julius Erving and the Philadelphia 76ers. Finally, in 1984, came the matchup basketball fans had waited five years to see: Johnson's Lakers and Bird's Celtics in the NBA Finals. The series went the full seven games, with the Celtics winning the title and Bird the playoff MVP award. Fans did not need to wait long for the rematch. The following year, the Lakers beat the Celtics, four games to two. In the final game, Magic scored a triple-double (14 points, 14 assists, and 10 rebounds) to lead the Lakers to the championship.

The two teams would meet once more in the NBA Finals in 1987. Johnson had led the Lakers in scoring for the first time that season, as the aging Kareem Abdul-Jabbar cut down on his playing time. Johnson was named the league's MVP. In the play-offs, Johnson averaged 26.2 points. The most important shot of his career came at the end of the fourth game of the NBA Finals showdown with the Celtics. At the buzzer, Johnson scored with a "junior skyhook": an arcing, one-handed, over-the-shoulder shot. It gave the Lakers the victory, 107–106, and a 3–1 lead in the series. When the Lakers won in six games, Magic won his record-setting third playoff MVP award (an achievement later matched by **Michael Jordan**).

In 1988, the Lakers became the first team in NBA history to win three seven-game playoff series in a single year. In the finals, the team came back to win the last two games after falling behind the Detroit Pistons, three to two. The victory made the Lakers the first team since the 1969 Celtics to win back-to-back championships. It was Magic's fifth NBA Championship in nine years. Only **Bill Russell** and his Celtic teammates Bob Cousy and Tom Heinsohn, in the 1960s, played for more championship teams. The following year, Johnson reached the NBA Finals for the eighth time in ten years—another streak surpassed only by Russell. Johnson, who led the Lakers in scoring, was the league's MVP.

Johnson won both the All-Star Game and the regular season MVP awards in 1990. The following season, the Lakers reached the NBA Finals for the ninth time in 12 years.

At the beginning of the 1991–92 season, Johnson shocked the world with the news that he had HIV, the virus that causes AIDS. His doctors had advised him to avoid the exertion of professional sports, and Johnson retired. With characteristic grace, he began a campaign to educate young people about AIDS, its prevention, and the dangers of unprotected sexual activity. Although retired, Johnson received more votes than any other player in that year's All-Star balloting. As a result, Johnson returned for the game in high style. He scored 25 points, grabbed five rebounds, and recorded nine assists to win the game's MVP award. That summer, he also joined Jordan, Bird, and other stars on the U.S. Dream Team to win the gold medal at the Olympic Games in Barcelona, Spain.

Johnson retired as the NBA record holder in career assists (9,921). Magic averaged 11.4 assists per game—a career mark matched only by John Stockton of the Utah Jazz. In addition, he holds records for most career assists (2,320) and steals (358) in the NBA play-offs. His assists record surprised no one who watched him play. No one ever passed more quickly, accurately, and stylishly than Magic Johnson. He could pass without looking, behind the back, over the shoulder, even between the legs. Sometimes, he even astonished himself. "When we're rolling and the break is going," he once admit-

MAGIC AND BIRD

The NBA faced a crisis at the end of the 1970s. Crowds were shrinking. Television audiences were changing the channel. Basketball had no electrifying heroes. Then, in 1979, two stars arrived to save the game: a sunny, smiling showman in the West and a serious, hard-working grinder in the East. Magic Johnson and Larry Bird began their rivalry in college before joining the NBA. Bird had won the College Player of the Year award in 1979. But Johnson's team had beaten Bird's for the ultimate prize: the NCAA Championship. Typically, Johnson excelled when the stakes reached their highest: No NCAA final before or since has drawn a larger TV audience. Their rookie years offered more of the same. Bird won the Rookie-of-the-Year award; Johnson led his team to the NBA title. The rivalry between the two, both excellent playmakers with style and personality, helped breathe new life into the game. The two drew new fans to the game—and won old fans back. The seventh game of the 1984 Finals between the Lakers and the Celtics attracted the largest television audience in NBA history. Basketball surged in popularity throughout the 1980s. And though the game grew even more popular with the entry of Michael Jordan in 1984, Bird and Johnson had already shown the way.

ted, "I guess it looks like I *am* performing magic out there. There are some nights I think I can do anything."

Johnson came back to coach the Lakers for part of the 1993–94 season and later became part owner of the team. He was forced to sell his share of the team, however, when he announced his return to the team as a player in January 1996. On his first night back on the floor, he dazzled a sellout crowd with 19 points and 10 assists. Turning in a solid season, he helped lead the Lakers back into the NBA playoffs in 1996, before retiring again after the Lakers were eliminated in the first round.

Career Capsule

Led Michigan State to NCAA title in 1979 and was tournament MVP. All NBA first team nine times, three-time MVP (1987, 1989–90). Led Lakers to five NBA titles, three-time playoff MVP (1980, 1982, 1987). Won Olympic gold medal as member of 1992 Dream Team. Named head coach of the Lakers in March 1994, but retired at end of season and later became a minority owner of the team. Returned to play part of the 1995–96 season with Lakers before retiring after team was eliminated in the first round.

This is how Jordan earned his nickname, His Airness.

Michael Jordan

born February 17, 1963

If not the greatest player ever, Michael Jordan is certainly the most celebrated player in basketball history. A talented showman, Jordan knows how to bring a crowd to its feet with dazzling displays of grace and athleticism. Apparently defying gravity, he leaps as high as 44 inches off the ground and then seems to hover in the air before jamming the ball into the hoop. Yet Jordan combines this flashy style with genuine skill. He has averaged more points per game than anyone else in basketball history.

Michael was born in Brooklyn, New York, and grew up in Wilmington, North Carolina. His mother was a customer-service supervisor at a bank, while his father, a mechanic, worked his way up to equipment supervisor for General Electric. His parents taught Michael and his four siblings to work hard and strive for excellence. One of his brothers nicknamed Michael "Rabbit" as a child because of the way he hustled on the basketball court.

Michael enjoyed all sports. As a Little Leaguer, he pitched two no-hitters. At Laney High School in Wilmington, he ran track, played baseball and football. But in basketball, he failed to make the varsity team until his junior year. By his senior year, however, the 6 feet, 6 inches tall forward had become good enough to earn an athletic scholarship to the University of North Carolina (UNC).

As a freshman, Jordan averaged 13.5 points per game. At the end of the year, with the national title on the line, Jordan sank a 16-foot jump shot with seconds left to give the Tar Heels a one-point lead over Georgetown University—and the NCAA Championship. He won the Rookie of the Year award in the Atlantic Coast Conference (ACC). In 1983, he averaged 20 points to lead the ACC in scoring. After his sophomore year, Jordan was named College Player of the Year by *The Sporting News.* In the 1983 Pan-American Games in Venezuela, Jordan topped all scorers on the U.S. team that won the gold medal.

In his junior year, Jordan was again selected as College Player of the Year. That summer, as co-captain of the U.S. Olympic Basketball Team, Jordan averaged 17.1 points per game. Team U.S.A. swept all eight games and the gold medal at the 1984 Olympic Games in Los Angeles. When the Chicago Bulls made Jordan the third pick in the nation in the NBA draft, he dropped out of college to turn pro.

In the 1984–85 season, Jordan averaged 28.2 points per game, one of the highest averages ever for an NBA rookie. He also had 6.5 rebounds and 5.9 assists per game. He was a starter in the All-Star Game—a rare opportunity for a rookie. He also won the Rookie of the Year Award.

Jordan improved the pitiful Bulls but did not instantly turn the team into a winner. During his first three years, the Bulls continued to finish under .500. The team never got past the first round of the playoffs. Though he had little initial impact on the team's success, Jordan had a dramatic effect on its popularity. The Bulls' attendance nearly doubled in his rookie year and the team, despite its mediocre record, led the league in attendance on the road.

When Jordan broke his left foot at the beginning of the 1985–86 season, his importance to the Bulls was underscored. With Jordan, the Bulls won nine and lost nine. Without him, they were 21–43. He returned in time for the NBA playoffs against the Boston Celtics, scoring 49 points in the first game and a play-off record of 63 points in the second game. But one great player seldom beats a great team. Despite Jordan's scoring, the Celtics swept the series.

In 1987, Jordan got into a groove. He scored 37.1 points per game and became the only player other than **Wilt Chamberlain** to score more than 3,000 points in a season. He also collected 236 steals and more blocked shots (125) than half of the league's centers. Jordan led all players in fan voting for the All-Star Game. He had become the NBA's star player. Yet some critics began to blame Jordan's showmanship for the Bulls' failure to win.

The 1987–88 season, however, silenced many of those who said that Jordan was not a team player. While leading the Bulls to 50 wins and a second-place finish, Jordan averaged 35 points per game to

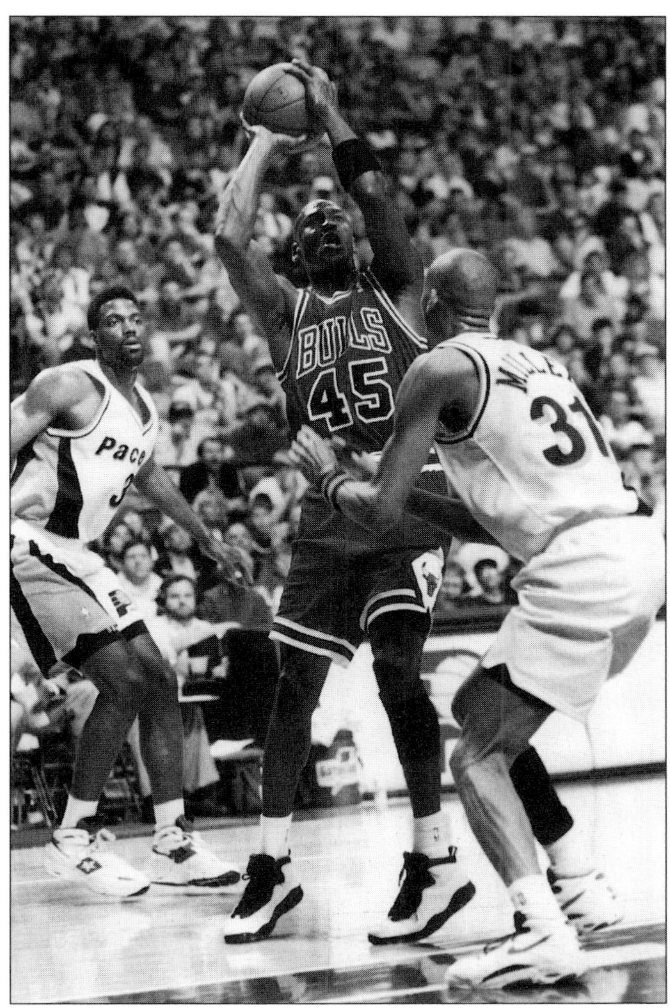

Jordan after his return to the NBA in 1995.

Jordan a split second after a slam dunk. Jordan's enthusiasm often spread to his teammates and brought out the best in them.

outscore everyone else in the league by at least four points. In one game, he stole the ball from the Nets ten times, just one shy of the single-game record. The Most Valuable Player (MVP) in the All-Star game, he scored 40 points. He became the first player to win the regular-season MVP award and be named the Defensive Player of the Year in the same season (a feat matched by Hakeem Olajuwon in 1994). Though the Bulls finally reached the second round of the play-offs and Jordan averaged 36.3 points to lead all play-off scorers, the Bulls were eliminated by the Detroit Pistons.

The following year, Jordan and the Bulls got one step closer to their goal. In the first round of play-offs, Jordan hit a 16-foot buzzer-beater in the fifth game to knock out the Cleveland Cavaliers. After beating the New York Knicks in six games, the Bulls headed for the Eastern Conference Finals—and another showdown with the Pistons. Yet Detroit beat them again.

In 1990, Jordan had a career-high 69 points in a game against the Golden State Warriors. During the play-offs, Jordan again topped all scorers with 36.7 points—the highest average in 15 years. Once again, the Bulls reached the conference finals only to be eliminated by the Pistons for the third year in a row. Critics again questioned whether Jordan could ever deliver a championship title.

In 1991, Jordan led the Bulls to 61 wins—a team record—and first place for only the second time in the team's history. Now surrounded by a strong supporting team of Scottie Pippen, John Paxson, Horace Grant, and B.J. Armstrong, Jordan did not always have to be the star of the game. The Bulls breezed through the play-offs, winning 11 of 12 games, beating the Knicks, the Philadelphia 76ers, and—finally—the Pistons. In the NBA Finals for the first time ever, the Bulls lost the first game to **Magic Johnson** and the Los Angeles Lakers but swept the next four. The Bulls had their first NBA

Championship, and Jordan took home both the regular-season and the play-off MVP Awards.

The Bulls repeated as NBA Champions in 1992—and Jordan again won both the regular-season and play-off MVP Awards. That summer, Jordan joined with Johnson, Larry Bird, and eight other NBA stars to form an Olympic Dream Team. A change in the rules now allowed professionals to compete in the Olympics. The U.S. Team dominated all competition, and Jordan won his second Olympic gold medal.

In 1993, Jordan won his seventh consecutive NBA scoring title to tie a record set by Chamberlain (1960–66). Yet the Bulls struggled all year. They won 57 games, ten less than they had in 1992. In the conference finals, they lost the first two games to the Knicks, but stormed back to win the next four. In the NBA Finals, they beat the Suns twice in Phoenix, but then lost two of three at home. In the sixth game, all eyes were on Jordan with the Bulls down by two points with four seconds to play. The focus on Jordan allowed Paxson to sink a surprise three-pointer to win the game. The Bulls became just the third team in NBA history to win three straight championships. For the sixth straight season (an NBA record), Jordan led all players in scoring average during the play-offs. He was also named play-off MVP for a record third straight year.

Jordan became America's top product endorser.

Not long after the Bulls' "three-peat," Jordan's father was murdered. Jordan was badly shaken by the death. That fall, he announced his retirement from basketball and his intention to pursue his dream of playing major-league baseball. Yet after less than two minor-league seasons in which he hit little over .200, Jordan gave up baseball.

When Jordan returned to the Bulls at the end of the 1994–1995 season, he seemed to have lost a step. In 17 games, he averaged just 26.9 points. In the playoffs, he could not stop the Orlando Magic from knocking out the Bulls in the second round. Yet in 1995–96, Jordan—and the Bulls—exceeded all expectations. Jordan led the league in scoring (30.4 ppg) for the eighth time, an NBA record. His performance propelled the Bulls to the best record in league history: an amazing 72–10 record—and a fourth NBA championship.

Career Capsule

Player of the Year with University of North Carolina in 1984, led NBA in scoring eight years (1987–93 and 1995–96), eight-time All NBA first team, four-time regular season MVP (1988, 1991–92, and 1995–96) and four-time MVP of NBA finals (1991–93 and 1996). Only three-time AP Male Athlete of the Year, led U.S. team to gold medals in the Olympics (1984 and 1992). Retired in 1993 to play baseball with Chicago White Sox minor league team in Birmingham, Alabama. Returned to Bulls in March of 1995. Played entire 1995–96 season leading the Bulls to NBA championship—MVP regular season, All Star game, and NBA finals.

SUPERSTAR FOR SALE

Michael Jordan earned millions of dollars as basketball's top drawing card. Yet he earned even more off the court. His estimated income from commercials and other endorsements exceeded $25 million a year—eight times more than his basketball salary.

Many sports heroes had been paid for endorsing products. **Arnold Palmer** had taken this to a new level in the 1960s, when he introduced a line of golf products with his name on them. By the 1980s, it seemed that every industry had a superstar to push their product.

Jordan's style and smile were seen everywhere: on billboards, in magazines, on cereal boxes, and of course, on TV. He sold soda, cars, fast food, shoes, and any other product whose manufacturer could meet his price. The Nike Shoe Company even named a shoe after him: "Air Jordan." The demand for these expensive sneakers was so great that they became the focus of many a schoolyard and neighborhood street fight, tragically cutting short the lives of young inner-city teenagers.

The NBA itself used Jordan to promote its product and increase ticket sales. Commercials for the NBA became fast-paced highlight films. And the flashy Jordan always made the highlights. Jordan's heroics and his winning smile made him not just the best celebrity to pitch burgers and sports drinks. He also became the best promoter of the game that basketball has ever seen.

JACKIE JOYNER-KERSEE

born March 3, 1962

A VERSATILE ATHLETE and fierce competitor, Jackie Joyner-Kersee holds the world record in the heptathlon, the most demanding event in women's track-and-field competition. In two physically draining days, heptathletes compete in seven different track-and-field events. The winner of the heptathlon gold at both the 1988 and the 1992 Olympics, Joyner-Kersee also won the gold medal in the 1988 long-jump competition.

Jackie was named after the First Lady at the time of her birth, Jacqueline Kennedy. Her grandmother always insisted that "someday this girl will be the first lady of something." When Jackie was born in a poor black neighborhood in East St. Louis, Illinois, her parents were both still teenagers themselves. Though both her parents worked, money was always tight. Jackie grew up in a dangerous neighborhood. By age 11, she had witnessed a murder in front of her house.

"I remember where I came from," Jackie later said. "If a young female sees the environment I grew up in and sees my dreams and goals come true, they will realize their dreams and goals might [also] come true."

Jackie honed her athletic skills at a city youth center. In her first track event, nine-year-old Jackie finished dead last. Yet she persisted and soon excelled at the long jump, making 17-foot jumps by age 12. Forbidden by her mother to date until she turned 18, Jackie poured her energies into sports and academics. While setting a state high school record in the long jump, she starred on her school's volleyball and basketball teams and graduated in the top ten percent of her class.

In 1976, her first year at Lincoln High School, Joyner began competing in the pentathlon. From

1978 to 1981, Joyner won four straight National Junior Pentathlon Championships. She also won the long-jump competition at the Pan-American Junior Games in 1979.

Joyner earned a basketball scholarship to the University of California at Los Angeles (UCLA) in 1980. At UCLA, she starred in both basketball and track. Her consistency on the basketball court placed her among the top ten in the school's history in scoring, rebounding, and assists. On the track, Joyner in 1982 set a new collegiate record in winning the NCAA heptathlon title and led the Lady Bruins to the NCAA Track and Field Championship. The following year, she received the Broderick Award, given to the nation's top female college track-and-field athlete.

Joyner-Kersee set an American record in the long jump with this leap in 1984.

In 1981, a year after the addition of the javelin throw and the 800-meter run transformed the pentathlon into the heptathlon, Joyner began training for both the heptathlon and long jump with coach Bob Kersee. By 1984, she had qualified for the U.S. Olympic team in both events. Hampered by a hamstring injury, Joyner finished a disappointing fifth in the Olympic long-jump competition in Los Angeles. Yet she won the silver medal in the heptathlon, finishing just four points behind Australian Glynis Nunn: 6,390 to 6,386. (Jackie's brother Al won an Olympic gold medal in the triple-jump competition that year.)

Joyner returned to UCLA, where she set college records in both the heptathlon (6,718 points) and the long jump (22 feet, 11¼ inches) in 1985. Recognized as the best collegiate sportswoman in the nation, Joyner won the Honda Broderick Cup that year. After marrying her coach in 1986, Joyner-Kersee became the first woman ever to score more than 7,000 points in the heptathlon at the Goodwill Games in Moscow, Russia. Breaking the world record by 200 points, she scored 7,148 points. Less than a month later, she broke her own record with 7,161 points, winning all seven events in competition at the U.S. Olympic Festival. That year, she won both the Sullivan Memorial Trophy (given to the nation's best amateur athlete) and the **Jesse Owens** Award (for the best track-and-field athlete).

At the U.S. Championships in 1987, Joyner-Kersee won the national heptathlon title and set a new U.S. record in long jump (23 feet, 4½ inches). She later tied the world record of 24 feet, 5½ inches at that year's Pan-American Games in Indianapolis, Indiana. At the World Track and Field Championships in Rome, Italy, Joyner-Kersee won both the heptathlon and the long jump. Her two gold medals made her the first athlete in more than 60 years to win both individual and multisport events at a single international competition. She again won the Jesse Owens Award and she was named Female Athlete of the Year by the Associated Press and Amateur Sportswoman of the Year by the Women's Sports Foundation.

At the 1988 Olympic Games in Seoul, South Korea, Joyner-Kersee was determined to capture the gold. She set personal bests in the 100-meter hurdles and the 800-meter run, and set a heptathlon record

Joyner-Kersee won the 1988 Olympic heptathlon with the help of this shot-put throw (top). Setting an Olympic record in the 100-meter hurdles during the heptathlon (above). Technique as well as strength enabled Joyner-Kersee to throw the javelin (at right).

in the long jump. Joyner-Kersee clearly outclassed the competition, beating the silver medalist by nearly 500 points, shattering the old Olympic record by more than 1,000 points, and establishing a new world record of 7,291 points. Before leaving Seoul, Joyner-Kersee had also won the gold medal in the long-jump competition.

Joyner-Kersee again won the gold medal in the long jump at the 1991 World Championships in Tokyo, but a hamstring injury forced her to drop out of the heptathlon. At the 1992 Olympic Games in Barcelona, Spain, Joyner-Kersee won only the bronze medal for third place in the long jump. However, she topped 7,000 points again to become the only woman to win two heptathlon gold medals.

At the 1993 World Championships in Stuttgart, Germany, Joyner-Kersee struggled to overcome asthma and a high fever. Trailing the host country's Sabine Braun by seven points going into the last event, Joyner-Kersee easily outraced Braun in the 800-meter run. Her closest heptathlon since 1984 ended with Joyner-Kersee edging Braun by just 40 points. In May 1994, she set a new American record in the long jump (24 feet, 7 inches) at the New York Games.

In her fourth Olympics in 1996, Joyner-Kersee was forced to drop out of the heptathlon because of an injury, but she won a bronze medal in the long jump.

CAREER CAPSULE

Two-time world champion in both the long jump (1987–91) and heptathlon (1987 and 1993). Won Olympic gold medals in heptathlon (1988 and 1992) and long jump (1988), silver in heptathlon (1984), and bronze in long jump (1992 and 1996). Received Sullivan Award (1986) and was only woman to receive Man of the Year award. Holds the world record in the heptathlon: 7,291 points.

CARL LEWIS

born July 1, 1961

THE GREATEST PERFORMER in U.S. Olympic history, Carl Lewis collected nine Olympic gold medals and one silver medal at four separate Olympiads. Lewis has also won eight gold medals in the World Track and Field Championships. Remarkably durable, he has remained a world champion sprinter and long jumper for 15 years—longer than anyone else in history.

The son of two athletes, Frederick Carlton Lewis was born in Birmingham, Alabama. Carl's mother had represented the U.S. as a hurdler at the 1951 Pan-American Games. His father had starred in track and football at Alabama's Tuskegee Institute. The Lewises were an athletic family. Carl's sister Carol became a top-ranked U.S. long jumper as well as an excellent sprinter, hurdler, and high jumper.

In the long jump, Lewis won his ninth Olympic gold medal in 1996—his fourth in this event.

One of his two brothers played professional soccer; the other was a high-school sprinter.

Carl grew up in Willingboro, New Jersey, where his parents taught high school and founded the Willingboro Track Club. Carl began running for the club at age eight. Four years later, he won his first long jump competition. At the national junior championships in 1978, Carl set a new high-school record with a jump of 25 feet, 9 inches. The following year, he was named an All-American in the long jump and the 200-meter race. The top high-school track and field athlete in the nation, Carl won an athletic scholarship to the University of Houston, in Texas.

Lewis won at 100 meters in the 1984 Olympics and was eventually declared the winner in this event at the 1988 Olympics.

At the Pan-American Junior Games in 1980, Lewis won the 100-meter sprint and qualified for the Olympic team. But the U.S. boycotted that year's Olympics in Moscow to protest the Soviet Union's invasion of Afghanistan. At the 1981 National Collegiate Athletic Association (NCAA) indoor championships, Lewis won both the 100 meters and the long jump (27 feet, 3/4 inches). No one else had ever won NCAA events in both track *and* field. Two weeks later, he won the same events at the U.S. outdoor track and field championships. The Amateur Athletic Union (AAU) recognized Lewis as the nation's outstanding amateur athlete, presenting him with that year's Sullivan Award.

Lewis held on to both the long jump and 100-meter titles at the 1982 outdoor championships. He did even better at the 1983 outdoor championships sponsored by The Athletics Congress (TAC). He won three events at a single meet for the first time: the long jump (28 feet, 10 1/4 inches), the 100 meters (10.27), and the 200 meters (19.75). This marked the first time in 97 years that any athlete had won three events in national championship competition. Lewis next won three gold medals at the World Track and Field Championships in Helsinki, Finland. On his own, he won the long jump and the 100 meters. He also helped the U.S. team set a new world record of 37.86 seconds in the 4 × 100-meter relay. Both United Press International (UPI) and the Associated Press (AP) selected Lewis Male Athlete of 1983.

Lewis started 1984 with a world indoor long jump record of 28 feet, 10 1/4 inches at the Millrose Games in New York's Madison Square Garden. At that year's Olympic Games in Los Angeles, Lewis won four gold medals to match the record performance of **Jesse Owens** in the 1936 Olympics. In the 100-meter sprint, Lewis won by eight feet—the widest lead in Olympic history. In the long jump, he won by almost a foot despite taking only two of the six jumps allowed (to save his strength for the races still to come). He then set an Olympic record of 19.80 in the 200-meter sprint. As anchor (last runner) of the 4 × 100-meter relay team, his split time of 8.94 seconds helped set a new world record of

37.83 seconds. Both AP and UPI again chose Lewis as Male Athlete of the Year.

In 1987, Lewis lost the 100-meter race at the World Championships to Canada's Ben Johnson, who set a new world record of 9.83 seconds. When his father died later that year, Lewis buried his 100-meter Olympic gold medal with him. (The event had been his father's favorite.)

At the 1988 Olympic Games in Seoul, South Korea, Lewis again lost the 100-meter sprint to Johnson. He suspected Johnson of using illegal steroids (drugs) to enhance his strength. Yet he chose to say nothing. "I didn't have the medal to replace the one I had given [my father], and that hurt," he later wrote. "But I could still give something to my father by acting the way he had always wanted me to act, with class and dignity." When a drug test proved that Johnson had used steroids, he was disqualified. Lewis was awarded the gold medal. Lewis also won gold in the long jump and silver in the 200-meter race won by his teammate Joe DeLoach.

At the World Championships in Tokyo, Japan, in 1991, Lewis set a new world record of 9.86 seconds in the 100 meters. Then, after 10 years and 65 long-jump competitions without a single loss, Lewis was finally beaten. Teammate Mike Powell broke Bob Beamon's 23-year-old record in the event. Lewis rebounded to help the U.S. 4 × 100 relay team set a new world record of 37.5 seconds.

Lewis (number 1136) set a world record at 100 meters—9.86 seconds at Tokyo in 1991.

A virus during the 1992 Olympic Trials kept Lewis from qualifying for either the 100- or 200-meter race. In Barcelona, he beat Powell to become the first athlete ever to win the Olympic long jump three times. He then helped the U.S. relay team set another world record (37.4). He had now won eight Olympic gold medals—more than anyone except Finnish distance runner Paavo Nurmi, who won nine in the 1920s. At the 1996 Olympics he won his fourth gold medal in the long jump.

Career Capsule

Held world record for 100 meters (9.86) set in 1991. Won four gold medals in 1984 Olympics (100 meters, 200 meters, 4 × 100-meter, and long jump). Also won two gold medals (100 meters and long jump) and silver medal (200 meters) in 1988 Olympics and two gold medals (4 × 100-meter relay and long jump) in the 1992 Olympics. Won gold medal in the long jump at the 1996 Olympics. Received Sullivan Award in 1981. Also won eight gold medals in the World Track and Field Championships.

Rebecca Lobo

born October 6, 1973

A college basketball sensation, Rebecca Lobo led the University of Connecticut Huskies to a national championship and an unprecedented 35–0 record in 1995. This success, and Lobo's outstanding talent, brought wide media attention to the blossoming of a new era for women's sports, the seeds of which had been planted the year before Lobo was born. In 1972, Title IX of the federal Education Amendments forced all schools to provide girls and women with athletic opportunities equal to those offered to boys and men.

The youngest of three children, Rebecca grew up in Southwick, Massachusetts. Both her parents were educators in nearby Granby, Connecticut. Rebecca learned how to play basketball in her own backyard, where she and her brother and sister also played wiffle ball, volleyball, and soccer together. Her brother Jason even arranged boxing matches between Rebecca and her sister Rachel, both wearing mittens. (Rachel grew up to become a college basketball coach. Jason played basketball at Dartmouth College before becoming a lawyer.) Since there was no local girls' team, Rebecca began playing basketball on a boys' team in fourth grade. That year, she wrote legendary Boston Celtic coach Red Auerbach a letter vowing to become "the first girl to play for the Celtics."

In her first high school game, Rebecca scored 32 points. She went on to score a high of 62 points in a single game and finished high school with 2,710 points. This was a Massachusetts record—for either girls or boys. When not on the basketball court, she starred in field hockey, track, and softball. She spent summers working in the local tobacco fields.

Rebecca received scholarship offers from more than 100 colleges. She chose nearby University of Connecticut (UConn) in Storrs. Her college coach, Geno Auriemma, was at first disappointed with Lobo's performance. During her sophomore year, he almost cut her from the team. Instead, he encouraged her to be tougher, more aggressive, and even selfish on the court—an attitude that went against Lobo's modest, friendly nature. By her junior year, the 6 feet, 4 inch Lobo had become an intimidating presence. She was the one person on the Huskies team who could be counted on to make the big play.

In 1993, just after Rebecca had led UConn to upset wins over high-ranked Auburn and Virginia, her mother developed breast cancer. She had to undergo a mastectomy and three months of chemotherapy. Yet she still managed to make it to nearly all of Rebecca's games. Her mother's strength and unwavering support despite her illness inspired Rebecca to work even harder to achieve her highest potential both on the court and in the classroom.

Lobo led her UConn team to an undefeated 1994–95 season.

During the 1994–95 season, Lobo helped UConn make history. She played only 28 minutes per game. Yet she averaged 17.3 points, 10.3 rebounds, 3.4 blocked shots, and 3.8 assists per game. Halfway through the season, UConn met the top-ranked Tennessee Lady Vols in perhaps the biggest non-tournament game in women's basketball history. The Huskies took over the number one spot with a convincing 77–66 victory. UConn went on to an undefeated regular season (29–0).

That year's NCAA women's tournament stirred up nearly as much March Madness as the men's tournament. After going 5–0 in the early rounds, UConn met Tennessee again in the title game. UConn trailed 38–32 at the half, but Lobo scored 14 of her 17 points in the second half to rally the Huskies over the Lady Vols, 70–64. The game drew the largest TV audience ever for a women's basketball game.

In leading the Huskies to a perfect 35–0 season and a national title, Lobo was named the most valuable player in the Final Four. She also won the Women's Sports Foundation's Team Sportswoman of the Year award. Lobo also lived up to the ideal of student-athlete. Named an Academic All-American, she achieved a 3.65 grade point average. Lobo was a member of the U.S. women's basketball team that won the gold medal at the 1996 Olympics.

Shots like this helped Lobo become a 1996 Olympian.

CAREER CAPSULE

Averaged 17.3 points, 10.3 rebounds, 3.8 assists, and 3.4 blocked shots to lead the UConn Huskies to undefeated season in 1994–95; member 1996 Olympic basketball team. College Player of the Year 1995.

NANCY LOPEZ

born January 6, 1957

"I'M VERY CONFIDENT in myself, and I love what I'm doing," Nancy Lopez once confessed. "I'm very relaxed when I'm playing because it's not a job. It's a game." That relaxed attitude and sense of perspective have helped make Lopez a champion golfer.

A favorite of both the news media and sports fans, Lopez revived women's professional golf when she burst onto the tour in 1978. Lopez combined power and precision on the golf course. She drove the ball long distances and was a flawless putter. Her grace and skill has made Lopez a hero and role model among fellow Mexican Americans and other Spanish-speaking Americans.

Born in Torrance, California, Nancy Lopez moved with her family to Roswell, New Mexico, at age three. She was active in many sports, including basketball, volleyball, swimming, track, touch football, and gymnastics, as well as dance. But golf, which both her parents loved, soon became her passion, too. As a young girl, she used to follow her parents as they played on Roswell's public golf course. When she was eight, her father—the only person who ever gave Nancy lessons—gave her a sawed-off wood and asked her to join them.

The Lopez family quickly recognized Nancy's talent and did everything they could to nurture it. Since the family was not rich, Nancy's mother gave

The youngest golfer to win $1 million.

up golf to allow her two daughters to play. Nancy was not allowed to wash dishes or do other chores that might damage her hands. For five years, Nancy wore braces on her teeth though the family could scarcely afford to pay for them. Yet her parents wanted to give their daughter a beautiful smile because one day, they knew, she would be a star.

By age 12, Nancy had outshot adult golfers to win the New Mexico state amateur tournament. From 1972 to 1974, she won three straight Western Junior championships. In both 1972 and 1974, she won the national girls' title, too. At 16, she already ranked number one in the world among amateur women golfers. She led her otherwise all-boys golf team at Godard High School to a state championship. Playing as an amateur, Nancy tied for second in the U.S. Women's Open in 1975. Her talent helped her win an athletic scholarship to Tulsa University (Oklahoma). There, she won the national collegiate title in 1976.

The following year, Lopez dropped out of school and turned pro at just 20 years old. She finished as runner-up in her first two tournaments, both major events: the U.S. Women's Open and the Colgate European Open. In 1978, her first full season as a professional, Lopez stunned the golf world with her success. Lopez won 9 of 25 pro tournaments that year. In a six-week period in May and June, she won a record-setting five events in a row! One of these five wins came in the Ladies Professional Golf Association (LPGA) Championship, a tournament rivaled in prestige only by the U.S. Women's Open. Lopez earned more than $189,000 in 1978, breaking the LPGA record for prize winnings by almost $40,000. She averaged 71.76 strokes per 18 holes for the year, an LPGA record. This earned her the Vare Trophy, given annually to the golfer who has the lowest scoring average on the women's tour. The LPGA honored her with both its Rookie of the Year and Player of the Year awards. (Lopez remains

Lopez turned professional when she was only 20 and within two years had broken the LPGA record for prize money.

the only golfer ever to win both awards in the same year.) *Golf Magazine* also named her Player of the Year and the Associated Press (AP) selected her as the Female Athlete of the Year. No woman or man ever had a better rookie year as a professional golfer.

The smiling, delightful Lopez breathed new life into the LPGA tour. At the time, the public, newspapers, and television were focused on women's tennis—the sport of such stars as **Martina Navratilova**, **Chris Evert**, and **Billie Jean King**. Women's golf hadn't had any exciting star players since **Mickey Wright** in the 1960s. Lopez brought the fans back to golf. In her first year as a pro, attendance at events on the LPGA tour tripled! TV increased its coverage of women's golf to take advantage of the game's new star. For the first time in history, two different women's sports (golf and tennis) commanded significant public and media attention.

In 1979, Lopez entered 19 events, finished among the top ten 16 times, and won 8 tournaments. She earned her second consecutive Vare Trophy by breaking her own scoring record with an average of 71.20. She again led the women's tour in winnings ($197,000) and was honored with her second straight LPGA Player of the Year award.

Though at the height of her career, Lopez limited her touring schedule throughout the 1980s and 1990s. She wanted to have as much time as possible to devote to her marriage, pregnancies, and child rearing. She married major-league baseball player (and later manager) Ray Knight in 1982. They have had three daughters: Ashley (1983), Erinn (1986), and Torri (1991).

Despite curtailing her tournament play, Lopez achieved one milestone after another. From 1978 to 1993, Lopez won at least one LPGA tournament every year except 1986. In 1983, just 26 years old, she became the youngest golfer, male or female, ever to win more than one million dollars in prize money. She won her second and third LPGA Championships in 1985 and 1989. (Only Wright has more.) In 1985, Lopez set a still-standing LPGA record by completing all four rounds (72 holes) of the Henredon Classic in North Carolina, in just 268 strokes. She won two more Vare Trophies (1985 and 1993). In 1985, Lopez was again named AP Female Athlete of the Year. Her third and fourth LPGA Player of the Year awards (1985 and 1988) placed her second behind only **Kathy Whitworth** in receiving that honor. In 1987, her 35th victory as a pro earned Lopez a place in the LPGA Hall of Fame. Yet though her record is spectacular, her influence on the game—and on women's sports—has been even more enduring.

CAREER CAPSULE

Four-time LPGA Player of the year (1978–79, 1985, and 1988), Rookie of the Year (1977), three-time LPGA champion. Reached Hall of Fame at age 30 with 35 victories.

JOE MONTANA

born June 11, 1956

QUARTERBACK Joe Montana never had the strongest arm in football. He was never the best at scrambling away from onrushing linemen. Several others could get the ball away quicker than he could. Yet Montana had one talent that made him the best quarterback in NFL history: He knew how to win. He led Notre Dame to a national championship and the San Francisco 49ers to four Super Bowl wins.

Joe Montana, the only child of a secretary and a finance company manager, was born in Monongahela, Pennsylvania. His father, a sports fan, gave Joe a baseball and bat before he was one. He also put up a basketball hoop and hung up a tire for Joe to throw footballs through. A standout athlete at an early age, Joe pitched three perfect games as a Little Leaguer. In high school, he starred in basketball, baseball, and football.

After high school, Joe accepted a football scholarship to the University of Notre Dame. Joe remained the third-string quarterback for more than two seasons. Yet whenever he got into a game, he seemed unbeatable. He engineered six "miraculous" comebacks in three seasons, half of them after coming off the bench late in the game. In 1975, he overcame a 14–6 deficit to North Carolina with just over a minute left to play. Down 30–10 to Air Force, Joe came in and threw three touchdown passes in eight minutes to win. Two years later, he left the bench to throw three touchdowns for a 31–24 victory over Purdue. With this comeback, Montana finally was made starting quarterback. In the 1978 Cotton Bowl, fifth-ranked Notre Dame upset top-ranked Texas, 38–10. Montana had quarterbacked the Fighting Irish to a national championship.

Montana's string of impossible comebacks continued in 1978. In just eight minutes, he turned a 17–7 deficit into a 26–17 Irish win over the University of Pittsburgh. In Montana's final college game, the 1979 Cotton Bowl, sixth-ranked Notre Dame trailed Houston 34–12, with just over 7½ minutes left. Despite an ice storm and frigid winds, Montana led Notre Dame to a 23-point comeback. His touchdown pass with no time left brought the Irish within one point. Then he threw another quick pass for a two-point conversion and the victory.

Despite his college heroics, Montana was not chosen by the 49ers until the third round of the NFL college draft. He did not start a game until mid-season in 1980. Against the New Orleans Saints, the 49ers fell behind 35–7 before Montana piloted four touchdown drives in the second half to tie the score. It was the greatest single-game comeback in NFL history. A field goal in overtime capped Montana's final 55-yard drive. His pass completion rate (64.5%) led the league at season's end.

In 1981, his first full season as the 49ers starting quarterback, he threw 90 straight passes without a single interception. The 49ers, who had the worst record in football (2–14) just two years earlier, went 13–3 to win the NFC West. A thrilling come-from-behind 28–27 win over Dallas in the NFC Final sent the 49ers to their first Super Bowl. Montana hit on 12 of 18 passes to build up a 20–0 lead over the Cincinnati Bengals at halftime. The 49ers held on to win 26–21, and Montana was named the Super Bowl's Most Valuable Player (MVP).

As the 49ers developed a strong offensive line to protect him, Montana gained more time to throw. His remarkable downfield vision allowed him to spot the open receiver. Montana became a leader through his personal qualities as much as his talent. No matter what the situation, he kept his poise and focus. He refused to give up, confident that his resourcefulness would ultimately lead to victory. "He is one of the coolest competitors, one of the greatest instinctive players this game has ever seen," 49er Coach Bill Walsh once explained.

In 1985, Montana and the Niners returned to the Super Bowl after a nearly perfect 15–1 season. The 49ers dominated the Miami Dolphins in Super Bowl XIX, 38–16. Montana was again named the game's MVP.

Montana led the 49ers to a win in the 1985 Super Bowl.

Although Montana didn't start until his senior year at Notre Dame, he played in four winning Super Bowls for San Francisco.

Four years later, the 49ers and Cincinnati Bengals met for the second time in the Super Bowl. With just 3:20 remaining, the Bengals took a 16–13 lead. Demonstrating his typical poise under pressure, Montana then completed eight of nine passes for 87 yards, culminating the drive with a surprise ten-yard touchdown pass to unheralded receiver John Taylor. The 49ers won Super Bowl XXIII, 20–16. Montana had passed for a record 357 yards. Yet the MVP award went to wide receiver Jerry Rice, who caught 11 Montana passes for 215 yards—both Super Bowl records.

"If every game was a Super Bowl," 49er center Randy Cross commented, "Joe Montana would be undefeated."

The following season, Montana led the Niners to a 14–2 record. In the play-offs, the 49ers crushed both the Vikings (41–12) and the Rams (30–3). They then embarrassed the Denver Broncos, 55–10, in the most lopsided game in Super Bowl history. In three post-season games, the Niners had outscored the rest of the NFL's best by 100 points! Montana took home his record third Super Bowl MVP award. Montana, who was never intercepted in four Super Bowl victories, now held virtually all career marks among quarterbacks in the Super Bowl.

An elbow injury caused Montana to miss most of the 1991 and 1992 seasons. His career seemed over. Yet in 1993, now with the Kansas City Chiefs, Montana returned almost as strong as ever to lead the Chiefs to an 11–5 record. Montana then engineered two fourth-quarter comeback wins in the play-offs before losing to the Buffalo Bills in the AFC Final. Montana played one more solid season before announcing his retirement in 1995.

Though he achieved greatness on the field, Montana was quiet, calm, and modest off the field. He always felt uncomfortable being called a legend. "I go to the store, buy milk, and forget the bread," Montana once said. "I try to hammer a nail and I hit my thumb. Do legends do that?"

Career Capsule

Led Notre Dame to a national title in 1977; led San Francisco to four Super Bowl victories. Three-time Super Bowl MVP, two-time NFL MVP, and led the NFL in passing five times. Second in all-time passing efficiency (.92.3), fourth in TD passes (273) and in yards passing (40,551). Threw just 139 interceptions in 5,391 attempted passes.

EDWIN MOSES 

born August 31, 1955

NO ONE HAS EVER dominated a track event the way that Edwin Moses dominated the 400-meter hurdles for more than a decade. "I'm a professional," he once commented. "This one event is what I do." He did it very, very well. A two-time Olympic gold medalist, Moses went ten years without losing a single race. He set new world records four different times.

Edwin Moses grew up in Dayton, Ohio. He was not particularly athletic as a child. Instead, he loved to read, especially about science. A National Merit Scholar, he won an academic scholarship to Morehouse College in Atlanta, Georgia. Morehouse did not even have a track. Moses achieved a grade-point average of 3.57 and graduated with a degree in physics. He learned how to hurdle through a Boy Scout handbook. Self-taught and self-coached, Moses represented a new breed of athlete. He used computers and his scientific knowledge to analyze and improve his performance.

"It's becoming increasingly difficult to be a great athlete and not be smart," he once explained. "People think running is just physical. But I try to keep up with research on physiology . . . , and I've studied physics and biomechanics. . . . Preparation is hard work; running is the easy part."

The Olympic Games in Montreal, Canada, in 1976 was his first international meet ever. Yet he won the gold medal with a world record time of 47.64 seconds. His eight-meter lead at the finish line was the longest in the history of the event.

In August 1977, Moses lost a race to Harald Schmid of West Germany. He would not lose again for almost ten years. In 1980, Moses lowered his world record time to 47.13 seconds. Yet he lost the chance to defend his title when the United States boycotted the Olympics in Moscow. *Track & Field News* still named Moses Athlete of the Year.

Moses set his final record (47.02 seconds) in the 400-meter hurdles in 1983. This would remain the record until the 1992 Olympics, when Kevin Young ran the hurdles in 46.78 seconds. Moses also won the event at the 1983 World Track and Field Championships. The nation's best amateur athlete, he received that year's Sullivan Award.

At age 33, Moses qualified again for the Olympics.

Moses so thoroughly dominated the 400-meter hurdles that by 1984, he had the nine best times ever in the event. Only three other hurdlers had broken 48 seconds in the event—none more than three times. Moses had broken 48 seconds 27 times! A heavy favorite at the Olympic Games in Los Angeles, Moses ran away with the gold medal in 47.75 seconds.

Moses was making nearly half a million dollars a year from running. Yet he managed to retain his amateur status by putting his earnings into a trust fund. He kept only enough to cover his expenses.

By 1987, Moses had won 122 consecutive 400-meter hurdle races—the longest winning streak in the history of track events. He finally lost in June

1987—to U.S. teammate Danny Harris in Madrid, Spain. However, he bounced back to win at the World Championships that year.

In 1988, Moses just barely won the event at the Olympic trials. For the first time ever, five different hurdlers finished under 48 seconds. At the Olympic Games in Seoul, South Korea, Moses came in third to win a bronze medal. Curiously, he ran faster (47.56 seconds) in winning the bronze than he had in either of his gold medal races. Yet the rest of the field had caught up to—and finally passed—him. It was only the fourth race he had lost since 1976.

Moses then dropped out of competition to pursue a master's degree in business administration at Pepperdine University in California.

Career Capsule

Two-time Olympic gold medalist (1976 and 1984); won bronze in 1988. Won 122 consecutive 400-meter hurdles races between 1977 and 1987.

Shirley Muldowney

born June 19, 1940

Shirley Muldowney overcame the prejudice of sponsors, other drivers, and fans to break down the gender barrier in the male-dominated sport of drag racing. Driving a pink dragster, Muldowney showed that women could not only compete with men, but excel.

Shirley Roques was born in Schenectady, New York. At 16, she dropped out of school to marry Jack Muldowney. Jack, a mechanic, introduced Shirley to the world of late-night drag races on dark suburban streets. Though the couple divorced in 1972, a year after her first win in a major race, Shirley had by then developed a passion for racing.

Muldowney's 2,000 horsepower dragster cost $40,000 to build in 1980.

Muldowney had her first successes racing "Funny Cars," dragsters that have the engine mounted in the front. However, three fiery crashes convinced her to switch in 1974, to the faster but safer Top Fuel dragsters, which keep the engine in the rear. A year later, she became the first woman in the nation licensed to drive Top Fuel dragsters.

In 1976, she became the first woman ever to win a National Hot Rod Association (NHRA) event: the Springnationals in Columbus, Ohio. By winning three straight national races the following year, she won the NHRA Top Fuel World Championship crown, again the first woman ever to do so. Despite her success though, she had difficulty finding a sponsor willing to back a woman driver.

When she won 11 races in 1980, she became the first drag racer, female or male, to win the NHRA Top Fuel World Champion title twice. Two years later, she won the U.S. Nationals in Indianapolis, for the first time, setting a new drag racing record of 5.57 seconds down the quarter-mile track. In doing so, she was crowned World Champion for the third time. She had proved her skill beyond a doubt: not just as a woman driver, but as the best drag racer in the world.

Career Capsule

First woman to win an NHRA event and to win the NHRA Top Fuel World Championship, which she won three times. She also set a drag racing record for the quarter mile (5.57 seconds).

MARTINA NAVRATILOVA

born October 18, 1956

PERHAPS THE GREATEST TENNIS player of all time, Martina Navratilova won more Open-era tournaments than any other player. She won 18 Grand Slam singles championships, the third highest career total behind Margaret Smith Court of Australia and **Helen Wills Moody**. She was the singles champion at Wimbledon nine times, a record for women or men. An awesome doubles player, Navratilova won 37 Grand Slam doubles titles, giving her 55 Grand Slam championships in all (second only to Court's 62). Navratilova had a wide array of tools. Her powerful lefthanded serve was clocked at more than 90 miles per hour. She had quick reflexes and brilliant volleying skills. Her overhead shot was devastating. Her superb physical conditioning and an unyielding will to win made her formidable.

Navratilova was born Martina Subertova in Prague, Czechoslovakia. When her mother—a gymnast, tennis player, and ski instructor—divorced and remarried a tennis instructor, Mirek Navratil, Martina took the feminine form (Navratilova) of her stepfather's name. Martina began taking lessons from Navratil at age six. In 1965, just eight years old, she reached the semifinals of a 12-and-under tournament. She then studied with the national Federation Coach George Parma for two years. Parma, however, defected from Czechoslovakia in 1968, when the Soviet Union sent troops to suppress the nation's democratic movement.

After winning the national girls' title in 1971, Navratilova won the national women's title the following year at age 15. She would remain the highest ranked Czech player until 1975, when she left the country. In 1973, Navratilova reached the quarterfinals of the French Open. In her first trip to the grass courts of Wimbledon, she won the All-England junior tournament. Navratilova shared her first major title, the French mixed doubles championship, with partner Ivan Molina in 1974. She then joined the new pro tour, winning her first Virginia Slims event in Orlando, Florida. *Tennis* magazine selected Navratilova, who won 13 of 22 pro matches, as Rookie of the Year.

Navratilova led the Czech team to its first victory in the Federation Cup in 1975. Paired with **Chris Evert**, she captured the first of a record seven French women's doubles titles. (She would also win with Anne Smith in 1982, and a record-tying five in a row from 1984 to 1988. In four of those years, she played with long-time partner Pam Shriver.) At the 1975 U.S. Open, following her semifinal loss to Evert, Navratilova announced her intention to defect from Czechoslovakia and become a U.S. citizen.

Navratilova's passion for playing at the net made her a devastating doubles player. In 1976, again with Evert, she won the first of seven women's doubles crowns at Wimbledon (in 1979 with **Billie Jean King**, and 1981–84 and 1986 with Pam Shriver). Although she did not win in women's doubles at the Australian Open until 1980 (with Betsy Nagelsen), Navratilova then added a record-setting seven in a row from 1983 to 1989, all with Shriver.

Navratilova and Billie Jean King won the doubles at Wimbledon in 1979.

However, her greatest success in doubles was achieved at the U.S. Open. There she won nine titles: 1977 with Betty Stove; 1978 and 1980 with King; 1983–84 and 1986–87 with Shriver; 1989 with Hana Mandlikova; and 1990 with Gigi Fernandez.

By 1977, Navratilova ranked third in the world—yet she had still never won a Grand Slam singles tournament. That would soon change. After losing the first set to Evert, she came back to win the 1978 singles final at Wimbledon. Navratilova would beat Evert again in the following year's final. The two Wimbledon victories helped Navratilova earn the number one ranking in the world in 1978 and 1979.

In 1982, Navratilova won 160 matches.

Navratilova's 16-year rivalry with Evert added a new dimension of drama and excitement to the game. Evert won their first match in 1973, and dominated the early years of their competition, winning 21 of their first 25 matches. Yet Navratilova reigned supreme in the 1980s. She steadily caught up to Evert and finished with a record of 43–37 in their 80 matches.

In the early 1980s, Navratilova revolutionized physical training in women's tennis. She adopted a rigorous daily program of weight lifting, running, basketball playing, and nutrition. In her teens, she had been somewhat overweight. Five feet, eight inches tall, she weighed as much as 167 pounds following her defection in 1975. Yet when she lost more than 20 pounds through diet and exercise, what remained was all muscle. Navratilova then set the standard for physical conditioning in women's sports. Few could keep up with her as she became the strongest woman on the court.

Navratilova finally became a U.S. citizen in 1981. To her, being an American has meant speaking her mind honestly and openly. "I've always had this outrage against being told how to live, what to say, how to act, what to do, when to do it," she explained. Always outspoken, she promoted various social causes from animal rights to environmental protection, from women's equality to lesbian and gay rights. Nine days after gaining her citizenship, Navratilova became one of the first star athletes to go public with her homosexuality. Her honesty came at a price. Some players refused to share a locker room with her. Sponsors who sought stars to endorse their products rejected Navratilova. "I've always stayed the same," she once said. "But people accept me now because attitudes have changed." Courageous enough to be herself, Navratilova eventually won the hearts of almost all tennis fans.

Navratilova was the best in the game in the early 1980s. In 1981, she won the first of three Aus-

Strength and physical fitness were an important part of success. Martina's serve was clocked at 90 miles per hour. In her prime, she stood at 5 feet, 8 inches and 150 pounds—all muscle.

tralian Open singles titles (1981, 1983, 1985). From 1982 to 1986, she overpowered women's tennis, compiling a match record of 427–14 in singles. In 1982, she set career highs with 160 matches won (90 in singles, 70 in doubles) and 29 titles (15 in singles, 14 in doubles). She lost only seven matches (3 in singles, 4 in doubles) all year. She won her first of two French Open singles championships (the second was in 1984). She won the first of a record six straight Wimbledon singles titles. In 1983, she lost only one singles match (to Kathy Horvath at the French Open) all year. She won 86 of 87 matches and 16 of 17 singles tournaments. She again won 29 titles overall (13 in doubles). For the first time, Navratilova also won the U.S. Open Championship in a straight-set final over Evert. Navratilova would go on to win three more in the next four years (1984 and 1986–1987).

Navratilova continued her dominance in 1984, winning 78 of 80 singles matches and 13 of 15 tournaments. From January to December, she won 74 straight matches to break Evert's record for consecutive victories. Her winning streak was broken in the semifinals of the Australian Open, which also ended Navratilova's quest for a Grand Slam. She had won the final three Grand Slam titles in 1983, and the first three in 1984. This tied Margaret Court's record of six major championships in a row. Yet she never achieved the Grand Slam within a single calendar year.

With Pam Shriver, Navratilova did win the Grand Slam in 1984, in doubles. Perhaps the best women's doubles pair ever, Navratilova and Shriver won 109 consecutive matches from April 1983 to July 1985. Together, they won 79 tournaments, including a record-tying 20 Grand Slam victories.

After her streak-ending loss in the Australian Open, she started another streak, winning her first 54 matches in 1985. With Heinz Gunthardt, she won three Grand Slam mixed doubles titles that year: the French Open, Wimbledon, and the U.S. Open.

The following year, she returned to Czechoslovakia for the first time. She led the U.S. team to a Federation Cup victory by continuing her unbeaten record in Federation play (going 36–0 in her career). In adding the mixed doubles title (with Emilio Sanchez) to her singles and women's doubles championships in 1987, Navratilova captured the triple crown at the U.S. Open.

For a while, her U.S. Open victory in 1987 looked like it would be the last major singles title of her career. Germany's Steffi Graf tied Navratilova's and Court's record of six straight Grand Slam victories in 1988 and 1989. Navratilova lost the Wimbledon final to Graf in both years. But in 1990, Navratilova faced Zina Garrison in her record ninth straight Wimbledon final. Navratilova's ninth Wimbledon victory broke the record set by Helen Wills Moody in 1938. Navratilova had one more terrific run at Wimbledon before ending her singles career. After announcing her intention to retire from singles play at the end of 1994, she reached the finals at Wimbledon for the 12th time. The fans' favorite at last, Navratilova lost in three sets to Spain's Conchita Martinez.

Navratilova retired as a singles player in November 1994. However, she continued to play doubles—well enough to have captured (with Jonathan Stark) the 1995 mixed doubles crown at Wimbledon. Over two decades (1975–94), she had never ranked lower than fifth in the world. She was the number one U.S. player for a record 13 straight years (1982–94). And she had earned more than $20 million as a pro, more than any other tennis player except Ivan Lendl. She received numerous honors, including election to the Women's Sports Hall of Fame (1984) and selection as Female Athlete of the Decade (1980s) by three different organizations. But Navratilova was more than the athlete of the decade. Her professionalism, courage, and integrity on and off the court made her an athlete for the ages, one of the all-time greats.

Career Capsule

Third all-time most women's Grand Slam singles titles (18—tied with Chris Evert). Won a record nine Wimbledon titles, won four U.S. Open titles (1983–84, 1986–87), three Australian Open titles (1981, 1983, and 1985), and two French Open titles (1982 and 1984). Reached Grand Slam final 13 other times and won 36 Grand Slam doubles titles. Set mark for longest winning streak with 74 matches in 1984. Ranked as the best player in the world seven times (1978–1979 and 1982–1986). Won 167 singles tournaments—more than any other player, male or female.

Jack Nicklaus

born January 21, 1940

The most successful pro golfer of all time, Jack Nicklaus won 18 major professional tournaments. A powerful and accurate driver, Nicklaus could send the ball farther than anyone else on the professional tour. Known as the Golden Bear because of his blond hair and fierce competitiveness, Nicklaus won six Masters titles, two more than any other golfer in history. He also shares the record for most U.S. PGA titles (5) and U.S. Open championships (4). Including his two U.S. Amateur titles, Nicklaus won 20 major events—seven more than the great **Bobby Jones**.

Born in Columbus, Ohio, Jack started playing golf at the local country club by age ten. At Upper Arlington High School in Columbus, Jack played football, basketball, and baseball. But he shone on the golf course. When he was 16, he won the Ohio state amateur championship. In 1959, Nicklaus was chosen for the U.S. Walker Cup team and won both his matches to help defeat Great Britain, 9–3.

Despite making this shot, Jack was unable to beat Arnold Palmer in the 1964 Masters.

"Simply being selected for it gave me a new confidence in myself," he later explained. "Then I began to demand much more of myself, and I began to play better than I ever had. The way it seems to me, in golf you're always breaking a barrier. When you bust it, you set yourself a little higher barrier and try to break that one."

At age 19, Nicklaus became the second youngest golfer ever to win the National Amateur title. He lost only one match that year. In 1960, he scored the lowest total (282) ever by an amateur at the U.S. Open. He finished as runner-up to **Arnold Palmer**, who shot a 280 to win the title. Nicklaus closed out his amateur career by winning the National Amateur title a second time in 1961.

In his first tournament as a professional in 1961, Nicklaus won just $33.33. Yet Nicklaus stormed onto the pro tour during his first full year. He finished the 72 holes of the U.S. Open tied with Palmer for the lead. In an 18-hole play off, Nicklaus won by three strokes. His putting was flawless over the five-day tournament. Only once in 90 holes did he need three putts to sink a ball once he had reached the green. (By contrast, Palmer three-putted ten times.) He later tied for third at the U.S. Professional Golfers Association (PGA) Championship. His impressive first year led the PGA to name him Rookie of the Year.

The popular Palmer was the star of the tour when Nicklaus turned pro. His rivalry with Palmer made Nicklaus very unpopular during his early years. Unlike the sleek Palmer, Nicklaus was so pudgy (until 1967 when he took off 15 pounds) that his nicknames included Ohio Fats and Fat Jack. Nicklaus also lacked Palmer's magnetic personality. While Palmer always seemed to enjoy himself on the course, Nicklaus was all business. His total focus on the game gave the impression of detachment—in sharp contrast to Palmer's emotional intensity. Palmer's many fans would boo Nicklaus—and even worse, shout, "Miss it, Jack!" or cheer on the rare occasions when he flubbed a shot. Yet the players' rivalry helped the professional game become more popular than ever. The 1962 U.S. Open, their first major showdown as professionals, set an attendance record of 62,000 fans—14,000 more than the previous record!

In 1963, Nicklaus won two more of golf's four major titles and just missed tying for a third. At 23, he was the youngest Masters winner until Severino Ballesteros won the title in 1980. At the British Open, Nicklaus misfired into a sand bunker on the final hole and finished third, just one stroke behind the leaders. He then won the year's final major event, the PGA Championship.

Nicklaus tied for second at both the Masters and the PGA Championship in 1964. He also finished second at the British Open, where he shot the last 36 holes in a record 134 strokes. Nicklaus earned more than $113,000 (about $100 more than Palmer) to become golf's leading money winner—the first of eight times he topped the tour in earnings.

In 1965, Nicklaus set a new record of 271 shots in winning his second Masters title. This record, though matched in 1976 by Raymond Floyd, remains the best score ever at the event. In 1966, Nicklaus held on to the winner's green jacket by winning a three-way play-off by two strokes to claim his third Masters championship in four years. He then won his first British Open crown by a single stroke. This victory made Nicklaus, just 26 years old, the fourth golfer to capture the "Grand Slam": winning all four of golf's major events (the Masters, the U.S. and British Opens, and the PGA Championship) at least once. (Only Gene Sarazen, **Ben Hogan**, and Gary Player had accomplished this feat.)

In 1967, Nicklaus won his second U.S. Open with a record score of 275 (matched the following year by **Lee Trevino**). His second-place finish at the British Open and tie for third at the PGA Championship earned him his first PGA Player of the Year award.

After his 1967 U.S. Open victory, Nicklaus failed to win a major event until 1970. He found his way back to the top at the 1970 British Open. In a play-off, he birdied (shot one under par) on the final hole to win by a stroke. His second PGA title in 1971 made him the only golfer ever to win all four Grand Slam tournaments more than once. That year, he also finished as runner-up in the Masters and the U.S. Open.

Though very serious about golf, Nicklaus showed a carefree attitude at times.

Nicklaus was named the PGA Player of the Year in both 1972 and 1973. In 1972, he captured his third U.S. Open title and his record-tying fourth Masters championship. He also finished just one stroke behind Trevino at the British Open. He collected his third PGA title the following year. He became the first golfer to earn more than $300,000 in a single year (1972). A year later, he became the first golfer to top $2 million in career earnings.

With his renewed success (and with Palmer's withdrawal from the tour), Nicklaus achieved a new popularity in the early 1970s. He was inducted into the World Golf Hall of Fame in 1974. Yet he kept winning. He won his fifth Masters in 1975, to break the record he had shared with Palmer. He also won his fourth PGA Championship. He again won the PGA Player of the Year award in both 1975 and 1976. His fifth award broke the record previously held by Hogan. (Tom Watson would later break this record with six Player of the Year awards between 1977 and 1984.)

With his victory in the 1978 British Open, Nicklaus collected his third set of Grand Slam trophies—a feat no other golfer has accomplished more than once. *Sports Illustrated* named him Sportsman of the Year.

Nicklaus placed second at the 1979 British Open for the seventh time, but finished the year winless for the first time. The next year, at age 40, when most golfers near the end of their careers, Nicklaus won two major titles—the U.S. Open and the PGA championship. At the 1980 U.S. Open, he set or tied record scores for 18 holes (63 strokes), 36 holes (134 strokes), and 54 holes (204 strokes). This 272 score for the tournament, though eventually matched by Lee Janzen in 1993, has never been beaten. His fourth U.S. Open title tied the record held by Hogan, Jones, and Willie Anderson. He then won his fifth U.S. PGA Championship and tied Walter Hagen's record for PGA titles.

Nicklaus finished as runner-up at the 1981 Masters and the 1982 U.S. Open (both for the fourth time). He also tied for second at the 1983 PGA Championship. Yet his career on the pro tour seemed to be winding down. These were his only

top three finishes in major events from 1981 to 1985. Incredibly, however, Nicklaus won his sixth Masters title in 1986. At age 46, he was the oldest player ever to win the event.

In 1990, though still active on the pro tour, Nicklaus turned 50 and became eligible to join the U.S. Senior Tour. He won his first senior event in 1990 and later captured the Seniors Championship. He won the U.S. Senior Open tournament in both 1991 and 1993.

A devoted father, Nicklaus often found time to be with his sons. Nicklaus has always been a study in concentration on the course. He loosened up his back muscles before tournament play in 1965. Professional golfers play practice rounds to get familiar with the course.

Though Nicklaus has made his mark on the Senior Tour, he shattered all marks on the PGA pro tour. In the 25 years from 1962 to 1986, 100 major golf tournaments were played. Nicklaus won 18 of them, placed second in 19 others and third in nine more. He won 70 PGA tournaments in his career, second only to Sam Snead's 81. Eight times the leading money winner in professional golf, he made more than $5 million during his career. No one ever has challenged his total of 18 major pro titles.

Career Capsule

All-time leader in major championships (20), second all-time career in wins (70). Winner of six Masters (1963, 1965–66, 1972, 1975, and 1986), five PGA Championships (1963, 1971, 1973, 1975, and 1980), U.S. Open four times (1962, 1967, 1972, and 1980), British Open three times (1966, 1970, and 1978), and U.S. Amateur two times (1959 and 1961). PGA Player of the Year five times (1967, 1972–73, 1975–76). Also NCAA champion with Ohio State in 1961.

THE PROS VS. THE PGA

Nicklaus, Palmer, Player, and Trevino helped make golf a game of superstars. More and more companies lined up to sponsor major tournaments. TV networks outbid one another to broadcast the major events. As a result, prize money for golf's professional events skyrocketed. Yet the PGA held down the player's share of prize money, much to the surprise of the pros. Nicklaus and other star players wanted a larger share of the money pouring in from TV and advertisers. So in 1968, the top pros banded together to break away from the PGA and form American Professional Golfers (APG). APG scheduled its own tour (28 events and $3.5 million in prize money) to compete with the PGA. Nearly all of the tour's stars defected to the APG. To win the top players back, the PGA accepted all of their conditions: The pros on tour received a larger share of PGA money and gained more control over the tour itself.

WALTER PAYTON

born July 25, 1954

PERHAPS THE BEST all-around running back in football history, Walter Payton gained more yards rushing (16,726) than anyone else who has ever played the game. Payton, whose nickname was "Sweetness," may not have been the most graceful runner in football. But he was the most intense and persistent. He always gave a second effort, going for any extra yardage he could get.

Walter was born in Columbia, Mississippi. His older brother Eddie was the family's first football star. (Eddie later played for the Minnesota Vikings.) Walter, a drummer in the Columbia High School band, did not even play football until his junior year, after Eddie graduated. Yet on his first carry, Walter ran 60 yards for a touchdown.

At Jackson State University in Mississippi, Walter starred as a rusher, passer, and punter. He scored 464 points, an NCAA Division II record. He also excelled academically, earning a B.A. in special education in just three and a half years. He returned to Jackson State between the 1976 and 1977 football seasons to work toward a masters degree in education of the deaf.

Drafted by the Chicago Bears in 1975, Payton as a rookie returned fourteen kickoffs for 444 yards—a league-leading 31.7 yards per return. By 1977, Payton was the best running back in the league. In one game against the Vikings, he rushed for 275 yards, breaking O.J. Simpson's single-game record of 273. For the season, Payton led the league with 1,852 yards in 339 attempts (5.5 yards per carry, his career high). He also caught 27 passes for 269 yards. At age 23, he became the youngest player ever named the NFL Player of the Year. Payton also led the Bears to a 9–5 record—and the play-offs for the first time since winning the NFL championship in 1963.

Though very shy and protective of his privacy, Payton was a terrific team player, modest, well-liked, and gracious. He developed a habit of handing the ball to one of his linemen after he scored a touchdown. Letting the blocker spike the ball was his way of saying thanks. Payton could not only rush and catch but also served as an extremely effective blocker when he didn't have the ball.

In 1978, he collected the longest rush of his career: 76 yards against Denver. He also caught 50 passes for 480 yards—including 119 receiving yards in one game against Detroit. A year later, he threw 54 yards for his first career touchdown pass. Payton could block, catch, and throw, but most of all, he could run. By 1980, Payton had led the National Football Conference in rushing for a record five straight years. Yet the Bears had reached the play-offs just twice and had lost both games.

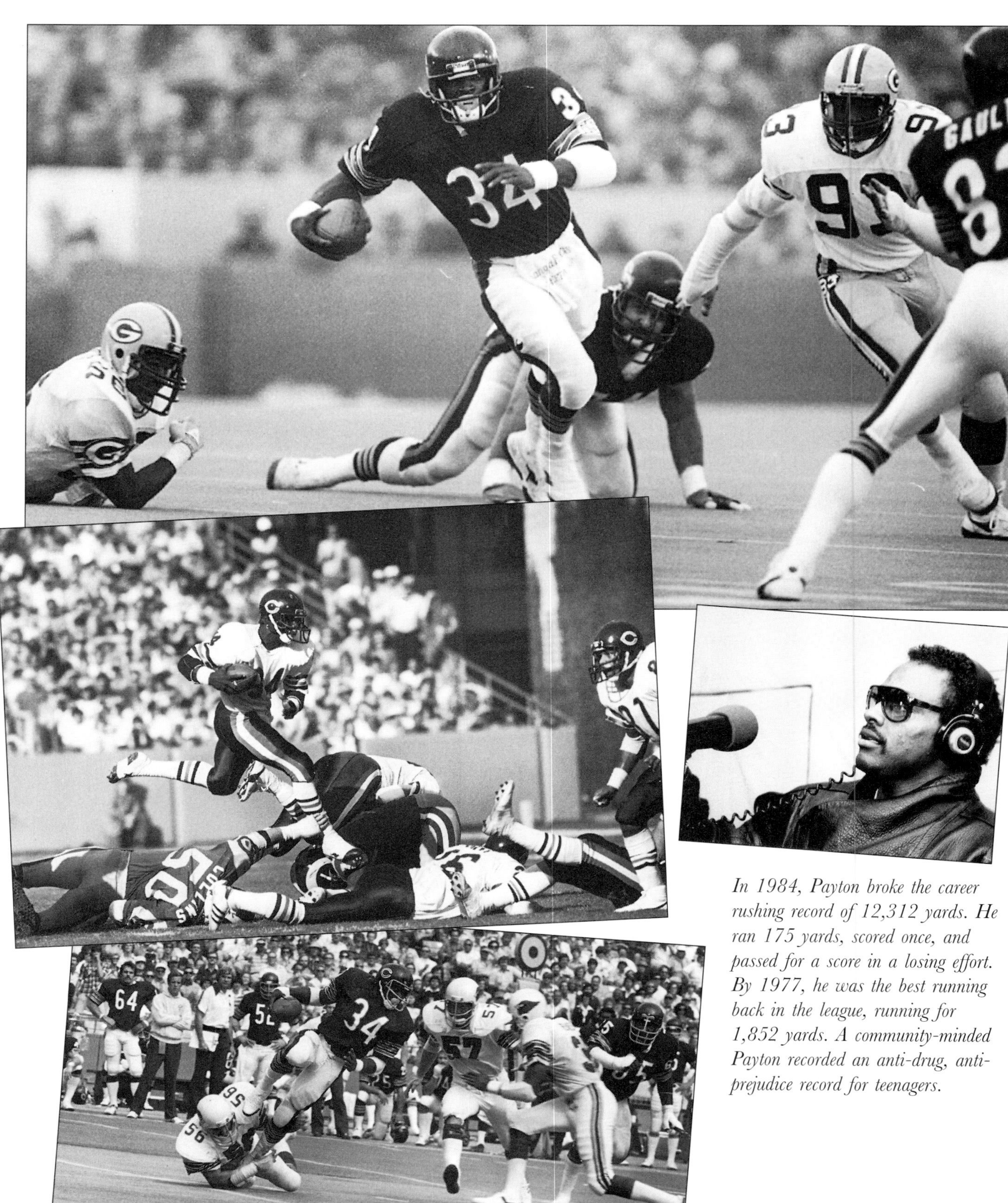

In 1984, Payton broke the career rushing record of 12,312 yards. He ran 175 yards, scored once, and passed for a score in a losing effort. By 1977, he was the best running back in the league, running for 1,852 yards. A community-minded Payton recorded an anti-drug, anti-prejudice record for teenagers.

In 1984, Payton made history by breaking Jim Brown's career rushing record of 12,312 yards.

Payton and the Bears had an almost perfect year in 1985. For the third straight year and fourth time in his career, he gained more than 2,000 yards through rushes and pass receptions combined. He rushed for 1,551 yards (4.8 yards per carry). For the sixth time in eight years, he also led the team in *receptions* (49 for 483 yards). For his efforts, Payton was named the NFL Player of the Year for the second time in his career. After going 15–1 in the regular season, the Bears crushed the Giants and the Rams in the play-offs by a combined score of 45–0. In Super Bowl XX, Payton rushed for only 61 yards as the Bears won, 46–10.

Career Capsule

All-time leader in yards rushing (16,726), rushing attempts (3.38), games gaining 100 yards or more (77), seasons gaining 1,000 yards or more (10), and rushing touchdowns (110). Selected for the Pro Bowl nine times, Player of the Year two times (1977 and 1985), and led the league in rushing five consecutive seasons. Career span 1975–87 with Chicago.

Richard Petty

born July 2, 1937

"I KNOW I'M NOT going to win every race," admitted Richard Petty, the undisputed king of stock car racing, "but I expect to win going into every race." Petty won an incredible 200 races—nearly twice as many as any other driver in the history of stock car racing. Extremely well-liked, he won the Most Popular Driver award a record nine times. Stock car fans, especially in the Deep South, worshipped Petty. A self-described "good ol' boy," Petty did more than anyone else to make stock car racing one of America's biggest spectator sports. He also revolutionized the sport. He introduced such innovations as the roll bar to protect drivers in overturned cars, helmet coolers, and the use of two-way radios to talk directly to the pit crew.

Richard Petty was born in the tobacco country of Level Cross, North Carolina. His father, Lee, ran a small trucking business, but also rebuilt second-hand cars for racing. Richard and his brother took after their father. They raced toy cars, wagons, and bicycles. In the late 1940s, Richard's father began entering stock car races. Richard went along as an apprentice mechanic and later a member of the pit crew. By the time Richard was 17, Lee Petty had won the 1954 National Association for Stock Car Auto Racing (NASCAR) championship. Richard's father also won the NASCAR title in 1958 and 1959, and retired with a record 54 wins in NASCAR Grand National events.

"From the time I was 12 years old until I was 21," Richard Petty later recalled, "I did everything there is to do to a race car except drive it—built it, worked on it, pitted it, tore it down, whatever." That changed in 1958, when he began racing one of his father's old cars. He entered eight races and won a total of $76. Petty did better in his second year, winning NASCAR's Rookie of the Year award. He finished among the top ten in 9 of 21 races and earned $8,000 in prize money—not enough to cover his expenses.

Petty won his first race in Charlotte, North Carolina in 1960. He placed among the top five in 16 of 40 races to finish second in that year's NASCAR point standings. His father's retirement from racing in 1962 jump-started Petty's own career. He won 14 races and finished runner-up in NASCAR standings in 1963. A year later, he won the Daytona 500—NASCAR's most prestigious race—for the first time. He also won eight other races and won his first Winston Cup Grand National Championship. The crown of stock car racing, the Winston Cup is awarded to the driver who compiles the most points during the racing season. (Points are awarded based on the driver's standing and the number of miles in each race.)

In 1965, NASCAR introduced a new limit on the size of a car's engine. The Chrysler Petty had

When driving 147 mph, you have to be cautious because accidents and injuries are part of race car driving. Petty won the Daytona 500 seven times. Petty wore a neck brace two days before his last race in 1992.

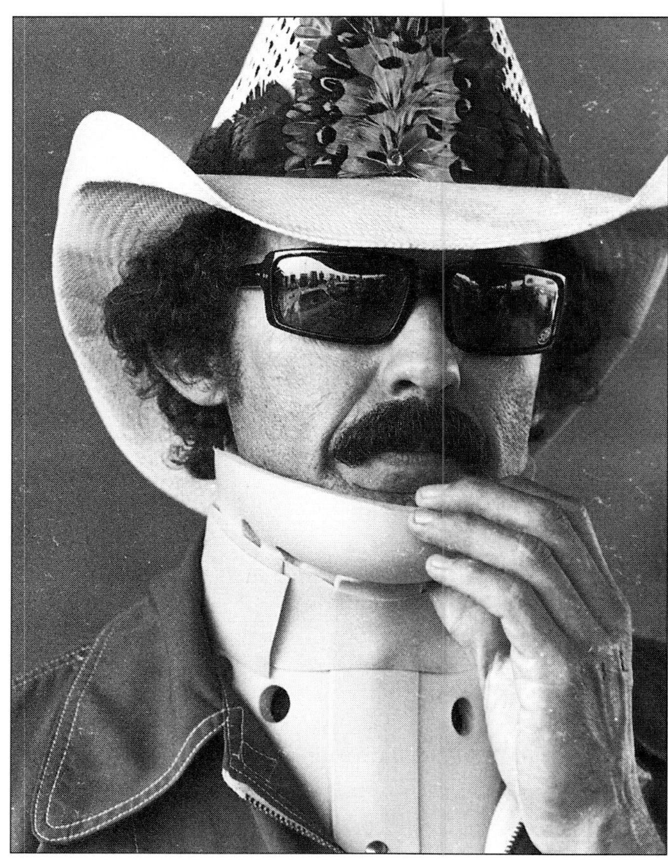

driven to the 1964 Winston Cup fell over that limit. Outraged, both Petty and Chrysler quit stock car racing for a year. Petty tried his hand at drag racing in which drivers try to reach the highest speed on a quarter-mile straightaway. But after a break in the suspension caused his car to crash into a group of spectators and kill a young boy, Petty quit drag racing.

Returning to stock car racing in 1966, Petty became the first driver to win the Daytona 500 twice. In 1967, Petty entered 48 races and won 27 of them, setting a new NASCAR record for a single season. He earned more than $130,000 and easily captured his second national title. Already he had broken his father's record for most career victories.

At South Carolina's Darlington Speedway in 1970, Petty's car bumped off a wall, flipped several times, and landed upside down. Petty escaped the worst crash of his career with a dislocated shoulder. Despite missing six weeks due to the injury, he won 18 of 40 events. Petty won 21 of 46 races—including his third Daytona 500—in 1971. By winning his third Winston Cup Championship, he tied his father and David Pearson for most in a career. His record earnings of $309,225 for the year made him the first stock car driver ever to reach $1 million in career earnings.

Petty won his second straight NASCAR title—and the record-breaking fourth of his career—in 1972. He would win the cup again in 1974 and 1975. When the six-time NASCAR champion was asked to name his greatest accomplishment, he said, "I guess still being alive." By 1977, his career earnings approached $2.5 million.

In 1978, Petty failed to win a single race. "As long as I enjoy racing and do it well enough to make some money, I'll keep going," he commented at the time. By the 1979 Daytona 500, he had not won in 18 months. Going into the last lap at Daytona, Cale Yarborough and Donnie Allison were well ahead of Petty. But when the two leaders collided, Petty cruised to his sixth Daytona win. He went on to win five races and finish among the top five in 23 of 31 races that year. This gave him his seventh and last Winston Cup Championship. (Dale Earnhardt would tie this record in 1994.)

On the Fourth of July, 1984, Petty won the Firecracker 400 in Daytona Beach, Florida. It was his 200th career NASCAR victory. Though he continued to race for eight more years, Petty would never win another race. Having earned close to $8 million in prizes, Petty retired as NASCAR's most successful driver in 1992.

Career Capsule

Seven-time winner of Daytona 500, seven-time NASCAR national champion (1964, 1967, 1971–72, 1974–75, and 1979). First stock car driver to win $1 million in career, all time NASCAR leader in races won (200) and wins in a single season (27 in 1967).

Mary Lou Retton

born January 24, 1968

At age 16, Retton was the first American female to win Olympic gold in an individual gymnastic event. She won the gold medal in the women's all-around event and earned two silver and two bronze medals in individual events.

A native of Fairmont, West Virginia, Mary Lou took her first gymnastics lessons at age seven. Her father was a two-sport star at West Virginia University, where he played basketball and baseball. Mary Lou's brother Ronnie played baseball, and her sister Sheri was an All-American gymnast at West Virginia where they were both scholarship athletes.

Had it not been for the injury of another gymnast the day before an important competition, we might have never even heard of Mary Lou Retton. At age 15, she was to be only an alternate in the International 1983 McDonald's American Cup. Retton was more than ready to fill in. She took top honors and burst into the national spotlight.

Retton won the national all-around title in preparation for the 1984 Olympics. She was so determined that she dreamt about gymnastics. "I'll be lying there . . . dreaming about my routines. Suddenly, my whole body will give a great jump and practically throw me out of bed."

In the Olympics, Retton won the all-around competition on vault, uneven bars, balance beam, and floor exercise. In the vaulting portion of her program, she scored a perfect 10. She also won silver medals in team competition and in the individual vault, and bronze medals in the individual uneven bars and floor exercises.

Retton filled in by taking top honors in 1983.

Mary Lou's athletic achievements were matched by her success following the Olympics. She had offers for many product endorsements. She was the first female athlete to have her picture on the front of the Wheaties box. Retton also gave motivational speeches to business groups and developed a fitness video for children. She was named to the Presidents' Council on Physical Fitness and Sports. She is also a spokeswoman for nationally known companies.

Career Capsule

Won an Olympic medal in an individual women's gymnastics event. Won five medals: gold in the all-around event, silver in the vault, bronze medals in the uneven bars and floor exercises, and silver in team competition. Won the national all-around title in 1984, and was named Sportswoman of the Year by *Sports Illustrated.*

Cal Ripken, Jr.

born August 24, 1960

In 1994, baseball's owners and players failed to reach a labor agreement. This resulted in a players' strike that cancelled the World Series for the first time in 90 years. Baseball's fans were angry. Attendance at major-league games dropped 20% in 1995. Baseball needed a hero.

Enter the longtime shortstop for the Baltimore Orioles, Cal Ripken, Jr. Ripken won back the fans' hearts simply by showing up for work, day after day after day. In doing so, in 1995, Ripken broke **Lou Gehrig**'s streak for consecutive games played (2,130), a record that for decades had been considered unbreakable. Named Sportsman of the Year by *Sports Illustrated*, Ripken earned the respect of fellow players and the nation's fans through his endurance and devotion to duty.

Ripken did more than play every day, though. A good fielder and solid power hitter, Ripken has won two American League (AL) Most Valuable Player (MVP) awards. He hit 20 or more home runs in 11 straight seasons. With well over 300 career home runs, he has blasted more balls over outfield walls than any other shortstop in baseball history. Baseball fans throughout the country rewarded him for his excellence by voting him the starting shortstop in 13 straight All-Star Games.

A shortstop has to be able to complete the double play as well as field ground balls.

Ripken began his streak in May 1982, and has not missed a game since then. Named the league's Rookie of the Year, Ripken followed up that season with an MVP year in 1983. Playing in every inning of every game, he led the Orioles to a world championship. He hit .318 with a league-leading 211 hits and 121 runs, while slugging 27 homers and knocking in 102 runs. In 1990, he set a shortstop record by not committing an error in 95 straight games and fielding .996 for the season. In one of the greatest seasons ever for a shortstop, Ripken hit .323 with 34 homers and 114 RBIs in 1991. His performance earned him his second MVP award.

Despite his achievements on the field, Ripken will be best remembered for playing the game day in and day out. Asked to explain his endurance, Ripken revealed his love for the game. "If you could play baseball every day," he asked, "wouldn't you?"

CAREER CAPSULE

Broke Lou Gehrig's record of playing in 2,130 straight games. Two-time American league MVP (1983 and 1991), Rookie of the Year (1982), starting shortstop in All-Star game 1984–96.

Midway through the 1985 season, Ryan had struck out 4,000 batters.

NOLAN RYAN 

born January 31, 1947

FROM FIREBALLING KID to ageless wonder, Nolan Ryan threw a baseball harder and longer than anyone else in the history of the game. He pitched an incredible seven no-hitters—nearly twice as many as anyone else. Rigorous training and incredible fitness kept Ryan pitching—and pitching well—into his mid-forties. Easy-going and rarely ruffled, he showed remarkable longevity, playing more seasons (27) than any other player.

The youngest of six children, Lynn Nolan Ryan was born in Refugio, Texas, and grew up in the small town of Alvin. His father worked for an oil company and delivered Sunday newspapers. "Dad worked two jobs to put four girls through college," Ryan later recalled. "I know he didn't want to get up at one in the morning, but that's what he had to do, so he did it. I think that's the way I am." Nolan developed his throwing arm hurling rocks at snakes and turtles. At age 11, in Little League, Nolan pitched his first no-hitter. In high school, Nolan won 20 games and lost only four in his senior year. In one seven-inning game, he struck out 19 batters!

In 1965, Nolan signed a contract with the New York Mets. Placed in a rookie league, he struck out 115 in just 78 innings. The following year, he led the Western Carolina League in wins (17) and strikeouts (272). Named the league's Pitcher of the Year, Ryan earned a brief trip to the major leagues. He struck out six in just three innings, but he gave up five runs.

Ryan returned to the big leagues to stay in 1968. He had a decent 3.09 Earned Run Average (ERA) and struck out 134 batters in 133 innings as a rookie. Ryan's second season, in 1969, was the Mets' Miracle season. He helped the Mets get to the World Series by winning the third game of the National League Championship Series against the Atlanta Braves. Ryan relieved starter Gary Gentry with two runners on base and nobody out in the third inning. In seven innings, he allowed just three hits and two runs while striking out seven. Ryan then saved the third game of the World Series against the Baltimore Orioles by pitching 2⅓ innings of one-hit ball and striking out three. Incredibly, although he would pitch for 24 more years, Ryan would never again play in the World Series.

In four full seasons with the Mets, Ryan never reached his full potential. Though he struck out nearly a batter per inning, he had little sense of the strike zone. He walked more than six batters every nine innings with the Mets. After the 1971 season, the Mets gave up on Ryan, trading him to the California Angels.

Ryan's career took off with the Angels. In 1972, he won 19 games with a league-leading 329 strikeouts. He tossed nine shutouts, best in the league, and had an ERA of 2.28. The next season, Ryan started throwing no-hitters. He pitched two of them in 1973. He won 21 games with a 2.87 ERA and an all-time record of 383 strikeouts.

Ryan pitched his third no-hitter in 1974. He went 22–16, winning more than 20 games for the second—and last—time in his career. His 367 strikeouts gave him 1,079 in just three seasons with the Angels. Ryan's fourth no-hitter in 1975 tied the record set by Sandy Koufax ten years earlier.

Ryan led the American League in strikeouts seven times in his eight seasons with the Angels. Yet he also led the league in walks six times, still averaging more than

A great pitcher and an excellent fielder, Ryan was still pitching in the major leagues at age 46. By the time he retired, Ryan had struck out 5,714 batters.

five every nine innings. So when his ERA climbed over 3.50, and his combined record for 1978 and 1979 was just 26–27, the Angels probably thought his career was just about over.

As a free agent, Ryan moved to the Houston Astros in 1980. The small-town Texas boy had finally come home. Ryan, who had married his high-school sweetheart in 1967, had never stopped calling Alvin his home. Even when pitching in New York and California, he had never lost his soft-spoken Texas twang. Now he could live on his 200-acre ranch all year long.

Ryan did not impress the home crowds right away. Although he was baseball's first million-dollar pitcher, he started off with an 11–10 season. But in 1981, he tossed his record-breaking fifth no-hitter. He went 11–5 in a strike-shortened season and, for the first time in his career, led the league with an astonishing 1.69 ERA. By 1983, Ryan had broken Walter Johnson's 56-year old record for career strikeouts (3,508). Though he led the league in ERA (2.76) again in 1987, and in strikeouts in both 1987 and 1988, the Astros let him go after the 1988 season.

The 42-year-old Ryan signed a $2 million deal with the Texas Rangers in 1989. That year, he won 16 games and became the oldest pitcher ever to win an All-Star Game. In 1990, nine years after his fifth no-hitter, he pitched a sixth. Already the oldest man to pitch a no-hitter, he tossed another a year later at age 44. Typically, Ryan celebrated his triumph by going back to work. He rode his exercise bike for an hour after the game. His work ethic and devotion to fitness only grew stronger as his career stretched out longer and longer.

Career Capsule

Pitched a record seven no hitters plus 12 one hitters. All-time leader in strikeouts (5,714), league leader in strikeouts 11 times, shutouts three times, and ERA two times. Struck out 300 batters a season six times, including season record of 383 in 1973. Won 324 games over a career which spanned 1966–93. Opposing hitters batted just .204 against him, a record low.

Alberto Salazar

born August 7, 1958

An intensely focused, determined runner, Alberto Salazar performed the unprecedented feat of winning the first four marathons he entered—all with times under 2:10! Already the world record holder for five miles, he established a new world marathon mark in 1981.

The fourth of five children, Salazar was born in Havana, Cuba. His mother was a portrait painter. His father, who directed construction projects aimed at increasing the tourist trade after the Cuban revolution, fled the country in 1960. (He feared arrest after arguing with the new communist leaders that a community housing development needed a church at its center.) He escaped to Miami, where his wife and children soon followed. There, his father trained for, but did not take part in, the failed invasion of Cuba at the Bay of Pigs in 1961.

In 1982, Salazar won both the Boston and the New York Marathons.

In Boston, police protect the first and second place finishers.

After ten years in Manchester, Connecticut, Alberto's family moved to Wayland, Massachusetts. While growing up, Alberto discovered that despite being four years younger, he could often challenge his brother in races. During high school, he developed his running skills by training with the Greater Boston Track Club. *Track & Field News* ranked him number one among high school 5,000-meter runners in both 1975 and 1976.

Salazar enrolled at the University of Oregon in 1976, to take advantage of its excellent track program headed by Bill Dellinger, a 5,000-meter bronze medalist at the 1964 Tokyo Olympics. He won the NCAA cross-country title in 1978, and finished as the runner-up as a senior. Later that year, he set a new world record (22:13) for a five-mile race. He was the Amateur Athletic Union's national cross-country champion in 1979.

Salazar trained long and hard for the 1980 Olympic marathon trials. When the United States boycotted that year's Moscow Olympics, Salazar turned his attention to the world's largest marathon race: the New York Marathon. Supremely self-confident, Salazar wrote on his entry form that he estimated that he would finish the race in two hours and ten minutes. (The world record was then 2:08:34 and the best time in New York had been 2:10:09.) Yet he was true to his word. In his first marathon ever, he set a new course record of 2:09:41—the fastest first marathon ever run.

In 1981, Salazar broke his own world record for five miles (22:04). When it came time to register for New York's marathon, Salazar estimated that he would finish the race that year in 2:08—which would set a new world record. He did just that, averaging 4:53 per mile to finish at 2:08:13 and break the world record set in 1969, by 21 seconds. Salazar's gutsy prediction, his endurance, and his record-breaking performance literally captivated millions of people. In addition to the two million spectators lining the course, 12 million more were at home watching the first non-Olympic marathon broadcast live on network television.

Macho and self-confident, Salazar always dictated the pace of his races. As he admitted years

Salazar won this Boston Marathon by only two seconds.

later, "I was an arrogant, antagonistic athlete who was never satisfied with any race, any victory. I was always so obsessed with the next race or workout that I could never relax or enjoy life. People thought I was a jerk, and I probably was."

In 1982, Salazar achieved something accomplished by just one other male runner (Bill Rodgers) before: He won both the Boston and the New York marathons in the same year. Both races featured extremely close finishes for such a long course. In hot and humid Boston, Salazar set a new course record of 2:08:52, beating Dick Beardsley by just two seconds. It was the first time two runners in the same marathon had finished in under 2:09. In blustery New York, powerful winds slowed the runners for the first seven miles. Yet Salazar still finished in 2:09:29, holding off Rodolfo Gomez to win by just four seconds. In between his two marathon victories, Salazar set American indoor records for both 5,000 meters (13:11) and 10,000 meters (27:25).

Due to injuries, operations, and chronic fatigue, Salazar stopped competing after finishing 15th in the 1984 Olympic marathon in Los Angeles. He worked for several years as a restaurateur and later an executive with the Nike shoe company. In 1993, he began coaching middle-distance champion **Mary Decker Slaney** in a comeback attempt.

A year later, a more relaxed, comfortable Salazar competed in his first major race in ten years. At age 35, he ran South Africa's Comrades Marathon—a gruelling, uphill, 53.75-mile ultramarathon—in 5:38:39. In a field of more than 12,700 runners, Salazar endured and won the race.

Career Capsule

Won the first four marathons he entered: the New York Marathon three times (1980–82) and the Boston Marathon once (1982). Twelve years later, he won his first ultramarathon in South Africa. Set a world record in the marathon (2:08:13) in 1981, also set American indoor records at 5,000 meters (13:11) and 10,000 meters (27:25).

Joan Benoit Samuelson

born May 16, 1957

The best female long-distance runner in American history, Joan Benoit Samuelson won the gold medal in the first Olympic women's marathon in 1984. A two-time winner of the world's most prestigious race, the Boston Marathon, Samuelson set a new record with each victory. During her career as a distance runner, she established U.S. or world records in the marathon, the half marathon, and races of 10 miles, 10 kilometers, and 25 kilome-

Benoit won at many long distances, such as this 10-kilometer race.

1979 Boston Marathon winners, Bill Rodgers and Joan Benoit.

ters. Her performances consistently demonstrated determination, strength, and endurance.

Born in Cape Elizabeth, Maine, Joan Benoit was an all-around athlete as a child. She began skiing while still a toddler and long regarded it as her favorite sport. But she also enjoyed playing tennis, basketball, lacrosse, and field hockey. Joan did not begin running until her senior year in high school. After breaking her leg in a skiing accident, Benoit started running to help her get back in shape. She soon found that she liked running as much as any other sport. In less than a year, she improved her running so much that she qualified for the Junior Olympics track competition in North Carolina.

By her sophomore year at Bowdoin College in Maine, Benoit had decided to focus all of her athletic efforts on running. She spent three of her eight semesters as a visiting student at North Carolina State University. This transfer allowed her to take advantage of NC State's first-rate running program.

Just before receiving her degree from Bowdoin in 1979, Benoit entered the Boston Marathon, only the second time she had ever run the race. She not only won, but set a new American record. She completed the 26 miles and 385 yards in just 2 hours, 35 minutes, and 15 seconds. Winning the Boston Marathon gave Benoit many opportunities for commercial endorsements and other publicity. Turning her back on these offers, she instead retreated to Maine, where she continued to train alone.

Marathon running puts an enormous stress on the body. By 1981, Benoit needed an operation on her Achilles tendon. Yet by lifting weights and riding a stationary bicycle throughout the ten weeks of recovery following her surgery, she was able to return to competition stronger than she had ever been. For the next two years, Benoit coached—and trained with—the Boston University track and field and cross-country teams. In 1983, however, she left BU to pursue her own running career.

In the 1983 Boston Marathon, Benoit once again finished first while setting an incredible women's world marathon record of 2:22:43. In just four years, she had chopped 12½ minutes off her record-setting marathon time! Benoit's time would remain the Boston Marathon record until 1994, when Germany's Uta Pippig ran the race in 2:21:45,

Benoit won the first woman's Olympic marathon in 1984.

shaving about a minute off the record. Later that year, Benoit also established a record time of 31 minutes and 36 seconds in a 10-kilometer race (about 6.2 miles).

Benoit spent much of 1983 training for the Olympic debut of the women's marathon the following summer. Every week for six months, she ran 100 miles, including at least one 20-mile run. Concerned that she might be overtraining, Benoit cut back on her running schedule early in 1984. However, the damage had already been done. Her right knee required arthroscopic surgery in April—just 17 days before the U.S. Olympic marathon trials. Less than a week after surgery, Benoit began training again. Her determination paid off. Despite pulling her left hamstring in the rush to train, Benoit's time (2:31:04) at the trials in Olympia, Washington, was good enough to win the race—and assure her a spot on the Olympic team.

Starting and ending at the Los Angeles Coliseum, the Olympic marathon posed a difficult challenge for Benoit. She would compete head to head against the world record holder, Norwegian marathoner Grete Waitz. Waitz and Benoit had competed in 11 marathons prior to the Olympics, and Waitz had won 10 times. In Los Angeles, Benoit took the lead before the three-mile mark, just 14 minutes into the race. She held on to it for the rest of the race. She won the gold medal in the first Olympic women's marathon ever with a time of 2:24:52. Waitz, the silver medalist, finished almost a minute and a half behind her, completing the race in 2:26:18. "This win is a triumph for women's athletics," Benoit proclaimed. "We have proved that we can stand the conditions of the marathon."

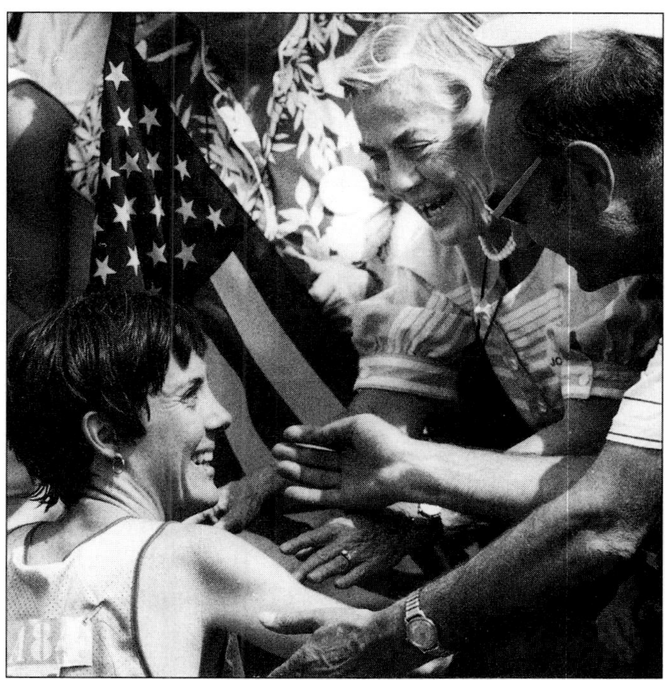

Benoit was congratulated by her parents after her Olympic win.

Six weeks after the Olympics, Benoit set a world record in the Philadelphia Distance Run, running the half marathon (13.1 miles) in just 1:08:34. In recognition of her Olympic performance, the Women's Sports Foundation honored her as a co-recipient (with Olympic gymnast **Mary Lou Retton**) of its Sportswoman of the Year award.

Shortly after getting married, Joan Benoit Samuelson completed the 1985 America's Marathon, in Chicago, in just 2:21:21. This established a U.S. women's record that still stands. She was awarded that year's Sullivan Memorial Trophy, presented annually to the nation's outstanding amateur athlete.

After becoming pregnant with her first child, Samuelson took a hiatus from running for the next six years. Following the birth of her second child, Samuelson returned to marathon running on an occasional basis in 1991. She finished fourth in that year's Boston Marathon. She also ran in the 1994 Chicago Marathon and finished sixth. At the 1996 U.S. Olympic trials, Samuelson ran a 2:36:54 marathon. Finishing in 13th place, she failed to qualify for the U.S. team. Yet this loss did not diminish her place as the nation's best long-distance runner.

Career Capsule

Gold medalist in first women's Olympic marathon (1984). Won Boston Marathon twice (1979 and 1983). Sullivan Award winner in 1985.

MARY DECKER SLANEY 

born August 4, 1958

AMERICA'S BEST FEMALE middle-distance runner, Mary Decker Slaney combined strength, stamina, and nearly perfect running form. Slaney was the only American woman ever to hold a world record at a distance longer than 200 meters—and she held them at every distance from 800 to 10,000 meters. Yet all her records have been overshadowed by a single image: a tangle of legs that knocked Slaney out of the 1984 Olympic 3,000-meter race, robbing her of her best chance for gold.

Born in Bunnvale, New Jersey, Mary Decker began running in 1968, when her family moved to California and settled in Garden Grove, a Los Angeles suburb. She won her first cross-country race at age 11. Just four years later, Mary set world records in the outdoor 800 meters, indoor 880 yards, and indoor 1,000 yards. In a USA vs. USSR meet in Moscow, she won the 800-meter race. In a relay race, a Russian runner bumped her off the track. Mary, enraged, twice threw her baton at the runner, but missed both times.

Injuries and painful shin splints kept Mary—already regarded as the best middle-distance runner in the country—out of the 1976 Olympics. Though she continued to set records when she could race, her injuries and operations kept her from training rigorously until the end of the decade.

From 1980 to 1984, Decker was unquestionably the best middle-distance runner in the world. She did not lose a single race during that time. In 1980, she set world records for distances of 880 yards (1:59.7), 1,500 meters (4:00.8), the outdoor mile (4:21.7), and the indoor mile (4:17.55). But when the U.S. boycotted the Olympiad in Moscow, Decker again missed her chance for Olympic gold. "I would love to win an Olympic gold medal," she said. "But if it isn't possible, it isn't possible. Maybe I can prove I'm the best in other ways."

In 1982, Decker set seven world records, including distance races of 5,000 and 10,000 meters. She became the first woman to win the Jesse Owens Award, given annually to the nation's best track-and-field athlete. Decker also won the Sullivan Memorial Trophy, awarded to the nation's best amateur athlete, and was named Sportswoman of the Year by *Sports Illustrated.* The following year, she won gold medals in the 1,500- and 3,000-meter races at the first World Track and Field Championships in Helsinki, Finland. For the third time in four years, she was named WTF's Sportswoman of the Year.

Youth, injuries, and the U.S. boycott had denied her the opportunity to compete in the previous three Olympiads. When she finally made it to the Los Angeles Olympics in 1984, Mary Decker owned every

Disaster—Slaney tripped in the 1984 Olympics finals of the 3,000-meter race. Unfortunately, she never won an Olympic medal even though she won gold medals at the World Track and Field Championships.

Slaney held seven U.S. records at distances from 800 to 10,000 meters.

U.S. distance record from 800 to 10,000 meters. Since she had won a record ten straight 3,000-meter runs since 1982, Decker entered the race as the favorite. With three laps to go, she was among the leaders when her legs became entangled with South African Zola Budd's. Decker tripped and collapsed into the infield with an injured hip and agony on her face.

After marrying British discus thrower Richard Slaney in 1985, Decker continued to set new U.S. and world records. (Her 1981 marriage to marathoner Ron Tabb had ended in divorce two years later.) Pregnancy, childbirth, and injuries limited her running during the next three years. In 1988, she competed again in the Olympics in Seoul, South Korea, but finished out of the medal standings for the 3,000-meter race. Although fate conspired to deny her Olympic gold, Mary Decker Slaney is nonetheless the greatest middle-distance runner America has ever seen. In the Olympic trials she earned a spot on the U.S. Olympic team by qualifying in the 5,000-meter race.

Career Capsule

A champion middle-distance runner, Slaney set 36 American records and 17 world records. Her times of 1:56.90 for 800 meters, 2:34.8 for 1,000 meters, 3:57.12 for 1,500 meters, 4:16.71 for the mile, and 5:32.7 for 2,000 meters—all run between 1983 and 1985—remain American records today. She also holds four national indoor records: 800, 1,000, and 1,500 meters and the mile. Qualified at 5,000 meters in 1996 Olympic trials.

Mark Spitz

born February 10, 1950

In the best performance in Olympic history, swimmer Mark Spitz brought home seven Olympic gold medals in 1972. No athlete in any sport had ever won more than five at a single Olympiad. In all, Spitz set 27 world records in individual freestyle and butterfly races between 1967 and 1972.

Born in Modesto, California, Mark Spitz grew up in Honolulu, Sacramento, and Walnut Creek, California. He began swimming off the beaches of Waikiki when he was two. His father, a steel company executive, was committed to molding Mark into a champion athlete. Arguing that "even God likes a winner," he convinced his rabbi to excuse

Spitz won the 100-meter butterfly in world-record time.

Mark from Hebrew lessons so that he could increase his hours in the pool. He moved the family around the country to allow his son to train with the best coaches. Mark's father always stressed the importance of winning above all else. He was never satisfied with his son's best effort—unless he had won the race.

Mark made his first splash at the 1967 Pan-American Games in Winnipeg, Canada, where he won five gold medals. He captured both the 100- and 200-meter butterfly races and swam on three winning U.S. relay teams.

By the time he left for the Olympic Games in Mexico City in 1968, Spitz had already set ten world and 28 U.S. swimming records. The cocky swimmer boasted that he would win six gold medals. He did win gold medals with the 4 × 100- and 4 × 200-meter freestyle relay teams. Yet in individual events, the best he could do was a silver medal in the 100-meter butterfly race and a bronze medal in the 100-meter freestyle. Though he held the world record in the 200-meter butterfly, Spitz finished a shattering eighth (last) in the Olympic final. Spitz took home four Olympic medals, but he regarded his outstanding performance as a complete failure. "I had the worst meet of my life," he said.

As captain of the swim team at Indiana University in Bloomington, from 1968 to 1972, Spitz continued to set records. He earned the Sullivan Award as the best amateur athlete in the country in 1971 when he set seven world marks and won four national and two collegiate championships.

At the 1972 Olympic Games in Munich, Germany, Mark Spitz outshone all other athletes. With each of his seven gold-medal performances, he set a new world record. (The four records that he broke in individual events were his own.) He swam the 200-meter butterfly race in just two minutes, 0.70 seconds. Later that same evening he helped the U.S. set a new world record of 3:26.42 in the 4 × 100-meter freestyle relay. In the 200-meter freestyle race, he set a new world mark of 1:52.78. Spitz completed the 100-meter butterfly in just 54.27 seconds. An hour later, he swam with the U.S. relay team that broke the 4 × 200-meter freestyle record by an incredible 7.5 seconds. In his closest race, the 100-meter freestyle event, his time of 51.22 seconds beat U.S. teammate Jerry Heidenreich's time by less than a half second. Finally, Spitz swam the butterfly leg with the 4 × 100-meter medley relay team that set a new standard of 3:48.16. His eleven Olympic medals (nine gold, one silver, and one bronze) in 1968 and 1972 set a record later matched by U.S. swimmer Matt Biondi, who collected eight gold, two silver, and one bronze medal between 1984 and 1992. Named World Swimmer of the Year for the third

After winning big in 1972, Spitz was a television commentator for swimming events at the 1976 Olympics.

time, Spitz was also selected by the Associated Press as Male Athlete of the Year.

Back home, the American Olympic hero earned millions through public appearances and endorsements of such products as razors, hair dryers, goggles, swimsuits, and milk. A poster of Spitz, wearing just swim trunks and his gold medals, sold 300,000 copies.

Career Capsule

Won a record seven gold medals (two in freestyle, two in butterfly, three in relays) at 1972 Olympics, setting a world record in each event. Also won two gold medals and a silver and a bronze medal at 1968 Olympics. Received Sullivan Award in 1971.

Lee Trevino

born December 1, 1939

As well known for his wit and good humor as for his golf, Lee Trevino delighted crowds with his enthusiasm and his wisecracks. Yet he is also one of the greatest golfers of the modern era. A brilliant shotmaker, Trevino won six Grand Slam events. He had even greater success as the star of the U.S. Senior Tour.

Lee's grandfather, who had emigrated from Mexico to Dallas, Texas, worked as a gravedigger. Lee, who never knew his father, lived with his two sisters and his mother in his grandfather's house—a small shack with no electricity or hot water, standing in a hayfield next to the Glen Lakes Country Club. Lee spent a lot of time on the country club's golf course. By the time he was eight, he had begun to work as a caddie. At 14, Lee dropped out of school and found work at a driving range. Lying about his age, he joined the Marines at age 17. Sergeant Lee Trevino began playing golf seriously when stationed in the Pacific. While playing matches with other Marines for money, he found out how good he really was. Once he shot a round of 18 holes in just 66 strokes. His success in these pick-up matches convinced Trevino to turn pro in 1960.

Unlike most new professional golfers, Trevino did not join the pro tour. Instead, he returned to Texas, where he became a golf "hustler." He challenged locals to money matches and lived off his winnings. Trevino tried a number of different stunts to entice his opponents to play with him—or to increase their bets. Sometimes he would "handicap"

This putt earned Trevino $35,000 in a tournament in 1971.

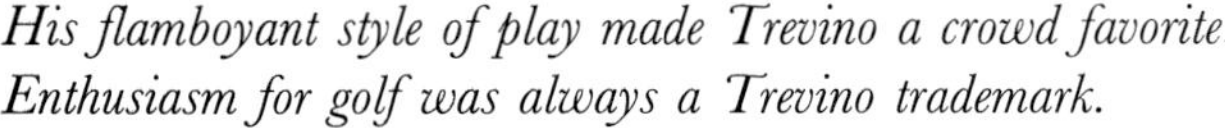

His flamboyant style of play made Trevino a crowd favorite. Enthusiasm for golf was always a Trevino trademark.

himself, adding extra strokes to his score. At other times, he would play using a soda bottle wrapped in adhesive tape as a club. His opponents would play with real golf clubs. Yet Trevino usually won. He made about $200 a week playing with his bottle club. In later years, he would claim that he felt no pressure playing for big money on the pro tour. "That's not pressure," he explained. "You don't know what pressure is until you play for five bucks with just two bucks in your pocket."

Playing for just the second time in the U.S. Open in 1967, Trevino finished fifth. He had his first victory at the 1967 Hawaiian Open and joined the Professional Golfers Association (PGA) tour full time. Despite his six years as a pro outside the tour, Trevino was named Rookie of the Year. His first win in a major event came at the 1968 U.S. Open. In an upset win over defending champion **Jack Nicklaus**, Trevino won by four strokes. He became the first golfer ever to shoot under 70 in each of the four rounds of the U.S. Open (a feat later matched by Lee Janzen in 1993). His total score of 275 tied Nicklaus' record-setting performance (though Nicklaus later broke this record with a 272 in 1980).

Trevino was the leading money winner in pro golf in 1970, earning more than $157,000 in prize money. He averaged less than 71 strokes per 18 holes. This gave him the first of a record-setting three straight Vardon Trophies.

Trevino had a remarkable three weeks in 1971. At the U.S. Open, he beat Nicklaus by three strokes in a play-off. He then won a sudden-death play-off at the Canadian Open. Next he held on to win the British Open by a single stroke. This made him just the fourth man ever to win both major Opens in a single year. Yet none of the others (**Bobby Jones**, Gene Sarazen, and **Ben Hogan**) had sandwiched them around a Canadian Open victory. That year,

Trevino was named PGA Player of the Year, the Associated Press Male Athlete of the Year, *The Sporting News* Man of the Year, and *Sports Illustrated*'s Sportsman of the Year.

Trevino beat Nicklaus by a stroke to retain the British Open crown in 1972. Trevino made some incredible shots to win the tournament. On three of the last 21 holes, Trevino chipped in from off the green—once from a sand trap! "God is a Mexican," Trevino joked afterward.

Trevino won his fifth major title, the U.S. PGA Championship, in 1974. He also won his fourth Vardon Trophy in five years. In 1976, however, Trevino was struck by lightning during a tournament outside Chicago. Trevino spent only a short time in an intensive-care unit. But he has suffered from back problems ever since.

In 1980, Trevino averaged just 69.73 strokes per 18 holes—the best since Sam Snead's 69.23 in 1950—to win his fifth Vardon Trophy, tying a record set by Billy Casper. The following year, he was inducted into the World Golf Hall of Fame. By 1984, however, ten years had passed since he had won his last major title, the PGA Championship. Yet incredibly, at age 45, he won it again.

In 1990, his first year on the U.S. Senior Tour, he won seven events including the U.S. Senior Open. He earned a record $1,190,000 for the year. This made Trevino the first senior golfer ever to earn more than the top pro on the PGA Tour. Trevino was named not only Rookie of the Year on the Senior Tour, but Player of the Year as well. Trevino again led all seniors in money earned ($1,027,000) in 1992. In 1994, he won six events, including the PGA Seniors Championship. Trevino will likely finish his career as the most successful senior golfer in history.

Career Capsule

Won U.S. Open (1968 and 1971), British Open (1971–72), and PGA Championship (1974 and 1984). PGA Player of the Year (1971). After winning six majors and nearly $3.5 million on the PGA tour, has earned more than $5 million on the Senior Tour, and won U.S. Senior Open in 1990.

Chris Waddell

born September 12, 1968

Chris Waddell's promise as a championship skier seemed over in 1988. When his binding popped loose and he lost his ski, he crashed into a tree. The accident severed his spinal cord and paralyzed him instantly. The following year, however, he returned to Middlebury College in Vermont, where he had been a member of the ski team. He was the first wheelchair-bound student in the school's history. Yet Middlebury quickly installed ramps and set up first-floor classrooms in order to accommodate him.

By 1992, Waddell was competing as a monoskier—racing down the slopes on one ski mounted with a bucket seat on an adjustable suspension system. In the Winter Paralympics in Albertville, France, Waddell won silver medals in both the slalom and the giant slalom. Yet the international competition for physically challenged athletes was still trying to build a following. And Waddell later complained that with so few people in the stands, "it didn't feel like the Olympics."

Within two years, the Paralympics had grown much more popular. President Bill Clinton offered well wishes via videotape just before Waddell left for

Waddell continues to be a skier in spite of paralysis.

Lillehammer, Norway. One week after the 1994 Winter Olympics ended, the Winter Paralympics began. Waddell won his first gold medal in the downhill mono-ski race—a race that focuses on sheer speed. He then went on to win gold medals in the three precision-turning events: the slalom, the giant slalom, and the Super G. This time, 6,000 spectators cheered Waddell on as he swept all the men's skiing events.

CAREER CAPSULE

Won two silver medals (slalom and giant slalom) in 1992, and four gold medals (downhill, slalom, giant slalom, and Super G) in 1994 Winter Paralympics as a mono-skier.

KENNY WALKER

born April 6, 1967

AN ALL-AMERICAN defensive tackle with the University of Nebraska Cornhuskers, Kenny Walker became only the second profoundly deaf player ever to play in the National Football League (NFL).

Kenny lost almost all ability to hear as a result of spinal meningitis and a high fever at age two. Even with a hearing aid, Kenny could hear little more than his own voice.

As a high school student in Crane, Texas, Kenny made all-state in both basketball and football. Yet as a college football player, Kenny did not become an overnight success. His inability to hear last-second calls on the line made it difficult for him to adjust. He had to ignore opposing players and watch the ball to avoid being drawn offside before the snap. Yet through persistence, alertness, and hard work, he became one of the nation's best defensive players. By his senior year, Walker led the Cornhuskers in quarterback sacks (11), tackles for losses (21), and quarterback hurries (21), and finished second in total tackles (73). United Press International named him the Defensive Player of the Year in the Big Eight Conference. He also became the first deaf player ever chosen for the All-American Football team. An art major, Walker graduated with a 3.1 grade-point average, making the Big Eight all-academic team, too.

Walker was an all-conference linebacker while at Nebraska.

Walker played for two years with the NFL's Denver Broncos. In his final year, the defensive end started in 15 of the team's 16 games. "I feel proud of my deafness," he once said. "It was given to me by God, and I accept it. Maybe I can be an example to deaf children."

CAREER CAPSULE

Earned a spot on the 1990–91 All-American Football team, was Big Eight Defensive Player of the Year and was named to the Big Eight All-Academic team. Drafted by the Denver Broncos where he played defensive end for two years.